Microsoft® Office 2010

FOR DUMMIES®

eLEARNING KIT

Microsoft® Office 2010 FOR DUMMIES® eLEARNING KIT

by Faithe Wempen

WILEY

John Wiley & Sons, Inc.

Microsoft® Office 2010 eLearning Kit For Dummies®

Published by
John Wiley & Sons, Inc.
111 River Street
Hoboken, NJ 07030-5774
www.wiley.com

WILEY

About the Author

Faithe Wempen, MA, is a Microsoft Office Master Instructor and the author of more than 100 books on computer hardware and software, including the *PowerPoint 2007 Bible* and *A+ Certification Workbook For Dummies.* She is an adjunct instructor of Computer Information Technology at Purdue University, and her corporate training courses online have reached more than one-quarter of a million students for clients such as Hewlett-Packard, Sony, and CNET.

Dedication

To Margaret

Author's Acknowledgments

Thanks to the wonderful editorial staff at Wiley for another job well done. You guys are top notch!

Publisher's Acknowledgments

We're proud of this book; please send us your comments at `http://dummies.custhelp.com`. For other comments, please contact our Customer Care Department within the U.S. at 877-762-2974, outside the U.S. at 317-572-3993, or fax 317-572-4002.

Some of the people who helped bring this book to market include the following:

Acquisitions, Editorial, and Vertical Websites

Project Editor: Pat O'Brien

Acquisitions Editor: Katie Mohr

Copy Editor: Virginia Sanders

Technical Editor: Michael Talley

Editorial Manager: Kevin Kirschner

Vertical Websites Project Manager: Laura Moss-Hollister

Vertical Websites Project Manager: Jenny Swisher

Supervising Producer: Rich Graves

Vertical Websites Associate Producers: Josh Frank, Marilyn Hummel, Douglas Kuhn, and Shawn Patrick

Editorial Assistant: Amanda Graham

Sr. Editorial Assistant: Cherie Case

Cover Photo: © iStockphoto.com / Cary Westfall

Cartoons: Rich Tennant (`www.the5thwave.com`)

Composition Services

Project Coordinator: Sheree Montgomery

Layout and Graphics: Andrea Hornberger, Jennifer Mayberry

Proofreaders: Betty Kish, Jessica Kramer, Toni Settle

Indexer: Dakota Indexing

Publishing and Editorial for Technology Dummies

    Richard Swadley, Vice President and Executive Group Publisher

    Andy Cummings, Vice President and Publisher

    Mary Bednarek, Executive Acquisitions Director

    Mary C. Corder, Editorial Director

Publishing for Consumer Dummies

    Kathy Nebenhaus, Vice President and Executive Publisher

Composition Services

    Debbie Stailey, Director of Composition Services

Contents at a Glance

About the Author v

Dedication vii

Author's Acknowledgments ix

Introduction 1

Chapter 1: Getting to Know Office 5
Chapter 2: Creating a Word Document 51
Chapter 3: Paragraph Formatting, Styles, and Tables................................. 89
Chapter 4: Creating Basic Worksheets... 113
Chapter 5: Creating Formulas and Functions.. 143
Chapter 6: Manage E-Mail with Outlook.. 175
Chapter 7: Using Contacts, Notes, and Tasks 219
Chapter 8: Getting Started with PowerPoint 247
Chapter 9: Formatting a Presentation 281
Chapter 10: Adding Graphics and SmartArt.. 303
Chapter 11: Adding Movement and Sound to a Presentation 327
Chapter 12: Presenting a Slide Show... 353

Index 373

Table of Contents

About the Author..*v*

Dedication ....*vii*

Author's Acknowledgments..*ix*

Introduction *1*

    About This Kit...1

    How This Book Works with the Electronic Lessons 2

    Conventions Used in This Book..3

    Foolish Assumptions..3

    Icons Used in This Kit 3

    Class Is In 4

Chapter 1: Getting to Know Office **5**

    Starting an Office Application 7

    Exploring the Office Interface 11

        Exploring the Ribbon and tabs...11

        Understanding the File menu 17

    Creating Your First Document 19

        Starting a new blank document...20

        Typing text...21

        Inserting a picture...24

    Moving Around 27

        Moving using the mouse 28

        Moving using the keyboard 29

    Changing the Onscreen View 31

        Zooming in and out..32

        Changing views 34

    Saving and Opening Documents..37

        Saving your work for the first time...38

        Navigating in the Save and Open dialog boxes 41

        Opening a document 45

        Recovering lost work..47

    Summing Up 48

        Try-it-yourself lab 49

        Know this tech talk..49

Chapter 2: Creating a Word Document 51

Starting a New Word Document 53
Creating a new document using a template 54
Setting page margins 57
Setting page size and orientation..59
Editing Text 62
Filling text placeholders...62
Typing and editing text 64
Selecting Text..65
Formatting Text 67
Choosing text font, size, and color 67
Applying text attributes and effects 70
Working with themes 73
Applying style sets 76
Checking Spelling and Grammar...79
Sharing Your Document with Others..81
E-mailing your document to others..82
Sharing your document in other formats 83
Printing Your Work 85
Summing Up 86
Try-it-yourself lab 87
Know this tech talk 88

Chapter 3: Paragraph Formatting, Styles, and Tables 89

Formatting Paragraphs 91
Applying horizontal alignment..92
Indenting a paragraph 94
Changing vertical spacing..98
Creating Bulleted and Numbered Lists...102
Creating a basic numbered or bulleted list 102
Changing the bullet character..103
Changing the numbering style 106
Summing Up 110
Try-it-yourself Lab 111
Know this tech talk 111

Chapter 4: Creating Basic Worksheets 113

Understanding the Excel Interface 115
Touring the Excel interface 116
Moving the cell cursor 120
Selecting ranges 121
Typing and Editing Cell Content...125
Typing text or numbers into a cell 125
Editing cell content...127

Using AutoFill to fill cell content...129
Copying and moving data between cells 132
Changing the Worksheet Structure..134
Inserting and deleting rows and columns.......................................134
Inserting and deleting cells and ranges 135
Working with Worksheets 137
Summing Up 140
Try-it-yourself lab 141
Know this tech talk..141

Chapter 5: Creating Formulas and Functions 143

Finding Out about Formulas...145
Writing formulas that calculate 145
Writing formulas that reference cells...148
Referencing a cell on another sheet...150
Moving and Copying Formulas 152
Copying formulas with relative referencing...................................152
Copying formulas with absolute referencing 155
Getting to Know Functions 156
Using the SUM function..157
Inserting a function...159
Touring some basic functions..161
Exploring Financial Functions...163
Using the PMT function...164
Using the NPER function 166
Using the PV function 168
Summing Up 170
Try-it-yourself lab 170
Know this tech talk..172

Chapter 6: Manage E-Mail with Outlook 175

Discovering Microsoft Outlook...177
Touring the Outlook interface..178
Setting Up Outlook for E-Mail...183
Changing the mail server type during setup 185
Setting up additional mail accounts...187
Troubleshooting mail setup problems...188
Receiving and Reading Your Mail..191
Sending and receiving e-mail manually...192
Setting the send/receive interval...192
Reading an e-mail message..194
Viewing an e-mail attachment 195
Composing and Sending E-Mail...197
Replying to a message..198
Composing a new message..199
Attaching a file to a message..201

Managing Incoming Mail 203
    Creating folders for managing mail 203
    Moving a message to a folder...206
    Creating a rule that moves messages..207
    Customizing the Favorites list..211
    Deleting e-mail...213
    Flagging an e-mail..214
    Configuring the Junk Mail filter 215
Summing Up 217
    Try-it-yourself lab 217
    Know this tech talk...218

Chapter 7: Using Contacts, Notes, and Tasks 219

Storing Contact Information...221
    Adding and editing a contact 221
    Navigating the Contacts list...224
    Changing how a contact is filed 228
    Deleting and restoring a contact..229
Using Contact Information 231
    Sending an e-mail message to a contact 232
    Attaching contact info to an e-mail..234
Using Tasks and the To-Do List 235
    Displaying the Tasks list 235
    Creating a task..237
    Updating a task...239
    Setting a task reminder 241
    Deleting a task 243
Summing Up 245
    Try-it-yourself lab 246
    Know this tech talk...246

Chapter 8: Getting Started with PowerPoint 247

Exploring the PowerPoint Interface 249
    Move around in a presentation...250
    Understand PowerPoint views..253
Creating a New Presentation..255
    Creating a blank presentation 255
    Create a presentation with a template...257
Creating New Slides...259
    Creating a new slide with the Ribbon 259
    Creating a new slide in the Slides/Outline pane 261
    Duplicating a slide 265
    Deleting a slide 266
Adding Text to a Slide 268
    Typing in a slide placeholder 268
    Manually placing text on a slide 270

Manipulating Slide Content 273
    Moving a slide object 273
    Resizing a slide object...275
    Deleting a slide object..278
Summing Up 279
    Try-it-yourself lab 280
    Know this tech talk...280

Chapter 9: Formatting a Presentation **281**
Understanding and Applying Themes 283
    Changing the presentation theme 283
    Changing the presentation colors 285
    Changing the presentation fonts...288
Formatting Text Boxes and Placeholders 290
    Applying shape styles 290
    Applying a background fill..291
    Applying a border 294
    Applying shape effects 296
    Turning text AutoFit on or off 299
Summing Up 301
    Try-it-yourself lab 301
    Know this tech talk...302

Chapter 10: Adding Graphics and SmartArt **303**
Inserting Graphics 305
    Inserting clip art...306
    Inserting pictures from files 310
Creating SmartArt...313
    Converting text to SmartArt 313
    Inserting a SmartArt diagram 314
    Modifying a SmartArt diagram 318
    Formatting a SmartArt diagram 320
Summing Up 324
    Try-it-yourself lab 324
    Know this tech talk...325

Chapter 11: Adding Movement and Sound to a Presentation **327**
Adding Slide Transition Effects...329
    Applying a transition to a slide 330
    Changing a transition's options 332
    Setting slides to advance manually or automatically..............334
Animating Objects 335
    Creating an entrance animation..335
    Creating an emphasis animation 338

Creating an exit animation..340
Changing an animation's options 342
Inserting Sounds and Videos..344
Inserting a sound clip on a slide 344
Inserting a video clip on a slide 347
Summing Up 350
Try-it-yourself lab 351
Know this tech talk...351

Chapter 12: Presenting a Slide Show 353

Displaying a Slide Show Onscreen 355
Moving between slides..355
Annotating slides with the pen tools...............................359
Creating Handouts..362
Printing handouts 362
Exporting handouts to Word...365
Summing Up 370
Try-it-yourself lab 370
Know this tech talk...371

Index *373*

Introduction

*I*f you've been thinking about taking a class on the Internet (it is all the rage these days), but you're concerned about getting lost in the electronic fray, worry no longer. *Office 2010 eLearning Kit For Dummies* is here to help you, providing you with an integrated learning experience that includes not only the book and CD you hold in your hands but also an extended version of the course online at `https://www.dummieselearning.com/educate/wiley/login/ SelfEnrollment.jsp`. Consider this Introduction your primer.

About This Kit

Each piece of this eLearning kit works in conjunction with the others although you don't need all of them to gain valuable understanding of the key concepts covered here. Whether you pop the CD into your computer to start the lessons electronically, follow along with the book (or not), or go online to see the extended course, *Office 2010 eLearning Kit For Dummies* teaches you

- The basics of Office products
- The techniques of Word documents
- The formulas of Excel spreadsheets
- The messages of Outlook communications
- The impact of Powerpoint presentations

This book is split into 12 lessons:

1: Introducing Office

2: Creating a Word Document

3: Paragraph Formatting, Styles, and Tables

4: Creating Basic Worksheets

5: Creating Formulas and Functions

6: Applying Worksheet Formatting

7: Using Contacts, Notes, and Tasks

8: Getting Started with PowerPoint

9: Formatting a Presentation

10: Adding Graphics and SmartArt

11: Adding Movement and Sound to a Presentation

12: Presenting a Slide Show

There are also bonus chapters on the website: www.dummies.com/go/officeelearning.

The appendix briefly outlines what the CD at the back of this book contains and what you'll find in the extended online course (available at https://www.dummieselearning.com/educate/wiley/login/SelfEnrollment.jsp). The appendix also contains a few technical details about using the CD and troubleshooting tips, should you need them.

How This Book Works with the Electronic Lessons

Windows 7 eLearning Kit For Dummies merges a tutorial-based Dummies book with eLearning instruction contained on the CD and in an online course. Each of the easy-to-access components features foundational instruction, self-assessment questions, skill-building exercises, plentiful illustrations, resources, and examples. The CD contains interactive electronic lessons that correlate to the content of the book, as well as sample files that you can use to practice with. You'll find bonus content in an extended online version of the course. Used in conjunction with the tutorial text, the electronic components give learners the tools needed for a productive and self-guided eLearning experience.

✔ **Lesson opener questions:** To get you warmed up and ready for class, the questions quiz you on particular points of interest. If you don't know the answer, a page number heads you in the right direction to find the answer.

✔ **Summing Up:** This section appears at the end of the lesson. It briefly reiterates the content you just learned.

✔ **Try-It-Yourself Lab:** Test your knowledge of the content just covered by performing an activity "from scratch" — that is, using general steps only and no sample files.

✔ **Know This Tech Talk:** Each lesson contains a brief glossary of related terms.

Conventions Used in This Book

A few style conventions will help you navigate the book piece of this kit efficiently:

✔ Terms or words that I *truly* want to emphasize are *italicized* (and defined).

✔ Web site addresses, or URLs, are shown in a special monofont typeface, `like this`.

✔ Numbered steps that you need to follow and characters you need to type are set in **bold**.

Foolish Assumptions

For starters, I assume you know what eLearning is, need to find out how to use Office (and fast!), and want to get a piece of this academic action the fun and easy way with *Office 2010 eLearning Kit For Dummies*. I assume you have basic Windows and computer skills, like starting the computer and using the mouse.

Icons Used in This Kit

The familiar and helpful Dummies icons point you in the direction of really great information that's sure to help you as you work your way through assignments. Look for these icons throughout *Windows 7 eLearning Kit For Dummies,* in the book and in the electronic lessons, too:

The Tip icon points out helpful information that is likely to make your job easier.

This icon marks a general interesting and useful fact — something that you might want to remember for later use.

The Warning icon highlights lurking danger. When you see this icon, you know to pay attention and proceed with caution.

Sometimes I might change things by directing you to repeat a set of steps but with different parameters. If you're up for the challenge, look for the Practice icon.

Serving as your call to action, this icon sends you online to view Web resources, to complete activities, or to find examples.

In addition to the icons, you also find three friendly study aids that bring your attention to certain pieces of information:

- ✔ **Lingo:** When you see the Lingo box, look for a definition of a key term or concept.

- ✔ **Extra Info:** This box highlights something to pay close attention to in a figure or points out other useful information that is related to the discussion at hand.

- ✔ **Coursework:** Look to this box for homework ideas that help you further hone your skills.

Class Is In

Now that you're primed and ready, it's time to begin. ....

Chapter 1

Getting to Know Office

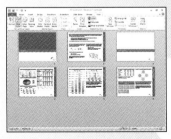

✔ The Office interface *is consistent across all Office programs* and includes the Ribbon, the File menu, Zoom controls, and standard dialog boxes for saving and opening files.

✔ Moving around in a document *enables you to view different parts of the document* that may not be onscreen at the moment. You can use scroll bars, arrow keys, and keyboard shortcuts in any combination.

✔ Changing the onscreen view *helps you focus on the important parts of the document* for the task you want to perform. Each application has its own unique set of views, as well as a Zoom control.

✔ Saving and opening documents *lets you store your work for later use* and then recall it to the screen when you're ready to continue. The Save As and Open dialog boxes share a common look and feel in all applications.

1. How do you start one of the Office applications?

Open up to page 7

2. How can you find out what a certain button on the Ribbon is for?

Buttons take a bow on page 11

3. What is Backstage View?

Peek through the curtain to page 17

4. How can you make the text you're typing appear larger, so it's easier to see onscreen?

Click clack on over to page 32

5. After you've saved a file once, how can you reopen the Save As dialog box so you can save it with a different name?

Boxes bounce back on page 41

6. How can you quickly reopen a recently opened document?

Race over to page 45

*M*icrosoft Office is a suite of applications. A *suite* is a group of applications that are designed to work together and to have similar user interfaces that cut down on the learning curve for each one. Office 2010 includes a word processor (Word), a spreadsheet program (Excel), a presentation graphics program (PowerPoint), and an e-mail program (Outlook). Depending on the version of Office, it may also include other programs too. Sweet, eh? (Er . . . suite.)

Because all the Office apps have similar interfaces, many of the skills you pick up while working with one program also translate to the others. In this chapter, I introduce you to the Office interface and show you some things the programs have in common. For the examples in this chapter, I mostly use Word, the word processor, because it's the most popular of the applications. Keep in mind, though, that the skills you're learning here apply to the other applications, too.

Starting an Office Application

The most straightforward way to start an Office application is to select it from the Start menu in Windows. You can navigate through the folders on the All Programs list of the Start menu, or you can start typing the application's name and then click its name at the top of the Start menu when it appears.

Depending on how your PC is set up, you may also have shortcuts to one or more of the Office apps on your desktop and/or on the taskbar.

TIP

You can double-click a data file that's associated with one of the apps, but because you haven't created any documents yet, you can't do that now.

When you're finished with an application, you can either click its Close (X) button in its upper-right corner, or you can open the File menu and click Exit. If you have any unsaved work, you're prompted to save it.

LINGO

Technically, a **program** can be any type of software, including Windows itself, whereas an **application** is a specific type of program that performs a useful user task, such as word processing.

Most nongeeky computer users don't recognize that distinction, though, and they use the terms interchangeably. So does this book.

In the following exercise, you practice opening and closing Office applications.

Files needed: None

1. In Windows, click the Start button.

The Start menu opens. See Figure 1-1.

Figure 1-1

2. Click All Programs.

A list of all installed applications appears. Some of the applications are organized into folders.

3. Click the Microsoft Office folder.

A list of the Microsoft Office 2010 applications appears. See Figure 1-2.

Figure 1-2

4. **Click Microsoft Excel 2010.**

   The Excel application opens.

5. **Click the Close (X) button in the upper-right corner of the Excel window. (See Figure 1-3.)**

   The Excel application window closes.

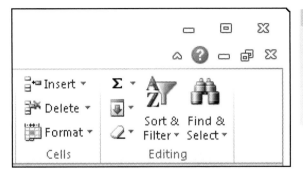

Figure 1-3

EXTRA INFO

In Excel, you can find two Close (X) buttons. The upper one closes the entire application; the lower one closes only the current workbook.

6. **Repeat Steps 1–3 (choose Start⇨All Programs⇨Microsoft Office) to reopen the Microsoft Office folder on the Start menu.**

7. **Click Microsoft PowerPoint 2010.**

   The PowerPoint application opens.

8. **Click the File tab (in the upper-left corner of the PowerPoint window).**

   A menu opens. See Figure 1-4.

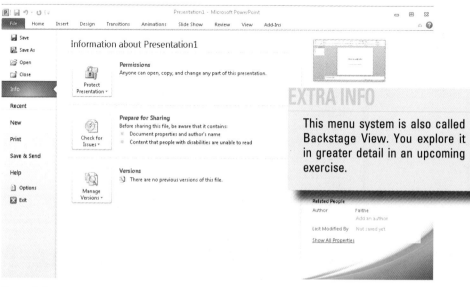

EXTRA INFO

This menu system is also called Backstage View. You explore it in greater detail in an upcoming exercise.

Figure 1-4

9. **Click Exit.**

   The PowerPoint application closes.

10. **Click the Start button.**

11. **Type Word.**

    The Start menu is filtered to show applications that contain those letters in their names. See Figure 1-5.

12. **From the list of applications that appears, click Microsoft Word 2010.**

    The Word application opens.

Leave Word open for the next exercise.

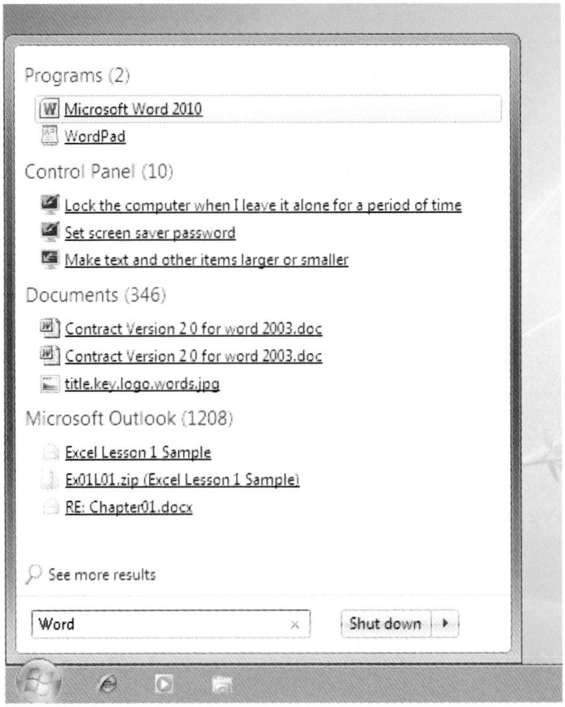

Figure 1-5

Exploring the Office Interface

The Office 2010 interface in each program consists of a tabbed Ribbon, a File menu, a status bar, window controls, and other common features. In the following sections, you become familiar with these common elements.

Exploring the Ribbon and tabs

All Office 2010 applications have a common system of navigation called the *Ribbon,* which is a tabbed bar across the top of the application window. Each tab is like a page of buttons. You click different tabs to access different sets of buttons and features.

In the following exercise, you practice using the commands on the Ribbon in Microsoft Word.

Files needed: None

1. **If Word isn't already open from the previous exercise, open it.**

2. **On the Ribbon, click the Insert tab.**

   The buttons change to show the ones for inserting various types of content.

> **TIP**
>
> Notice that the buttons are organized into groups; the group names appear at the bottom. For example, the Pages group is the leftmost group.

3. **In the Links group, hover the mouse pointer over the Hyperlink button.**

   A ScreenTip appears, telling you the button's name and purpose and showing a keyboard shortcut (Ctrl+K) that you can optionally use to select that command. See Figure 1-6.

Figure 1-6

4. **In the Links group, click the Hyperlink button.**

   An Insert Hyperlink dialog box opens. See Figure 1-7.

Figure 1-7

5. **Click Cancel in the dialog box to close it.**

6. **In the Header & Footer group, click the Header button.**

   A menu opens. See Figure 1-8.

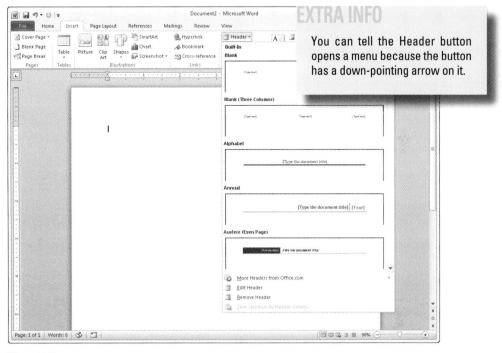

Figure 1-8

7. **Drag the scroll bar on the right side of the menu to view its content.**

8. **Click away from the menu without making a selection to close it.**

9. **Click the Home tab.**

   The buttons change to show the ones on that tab.

10. **In the Font group, click the Bold button.**

    The Bold attribute is toggled on.

11. **Type your first name.**

    Your first name appears in bold. See Figure 1-9.

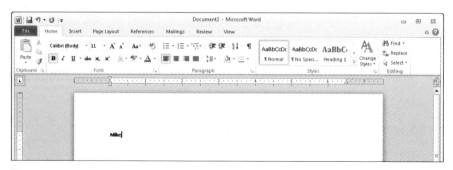

Figure 1-9

12. Click the Bold button again.

The Bold attribute is toggled off.

13. Type your last name.

Your last name does not appear in bold.

In the Paragraph group, notice that the Align Text Left button is selected.

14. Click the Center button in the Paragraph group.

Your name is centered horizontally on the page. See Figure 1-10.

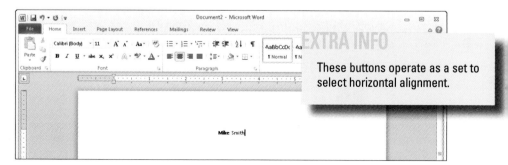

EXTRA INFO

These buttons operate as a set to select horizontal alignment.

Figure 1-10

TIP

The paragraph alignment buttons are a set; when you select one, the previously selected button is deselected.

15. Click the Undo button on the Quick Access Toolbar.

See Figure 1-11. The last action is undone, and the paragraph alignment goes back to left alignment.

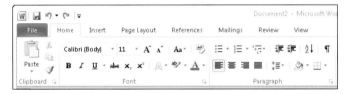

Figure 1-11

16. Click the dialog box launcher button in the bottom-right corner of the Paragraph group.

A Paragraph dialog box opens. See Figure 1-12.

17. Click Cancel to close the Paragraph dialog box.

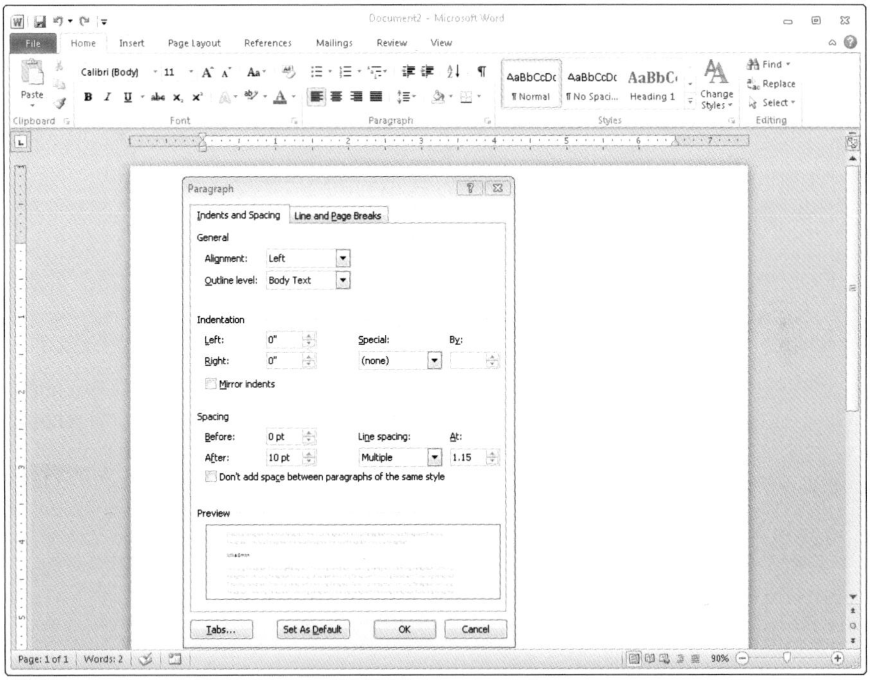

Figure 1-12

18. If the Word window is maximized, click the Restore button in the upper-right corner so that the window is resizable.

See Figure 1-13.

19. Note the buttons available in the Editing group on the Home tab.

Figure 1-13

20. **Drag the right border of the Word window toward the left, decreasing the size of the Word window until the Editing group collapses into a single large button.**

See Figure 1-14.

Figure 1-14

21. **Click the Editing button.**

The menu that opens contains the buttons that were previously available from the Editing group. See Figure 1-15.

Figure 1-15

22. **Drag the right border of the Word window toward the right until the Editing group is expanded again.**

23. **Exit the Word application. When you're prompted to save changes, click No.**

The next exercise uses a different application.

Understanding the File menu

In each Office application, clicking the File tab opens the File menu, also known as *Backstage View*. Backstage View provides access to commands that have to do with the data file you're working with — things like saving, opening, printing, mailing, and checking its properties. The File tab is a different color in each application. In Excel, for example, it's green. To leave Backstage View, click some other tab or press the Esc key.

In the following exercise, you practice using the File menu in Excel.

Files needed: None

1. **Start Microsoft Excel 2010 using any method you like.**

   You can find several methods earlier in this chapter.

2. **Click the File tab on the Ribbon.**

   The File menu opens. Categories of commands are listed at the left.

The category that appears by default depends on the application and on whether any changes have been made to the blank document that opens by default when the application starts.

3. **Click Recent if that category doesn't already appear by default.**

   This category provides shortcuts for reopening recently used files. See Figure 1-16.

4. **Click the Info category and examine the commands available.**

   This category provides commands for permissions, sharing, and versions, as well as basic information about the file itself.

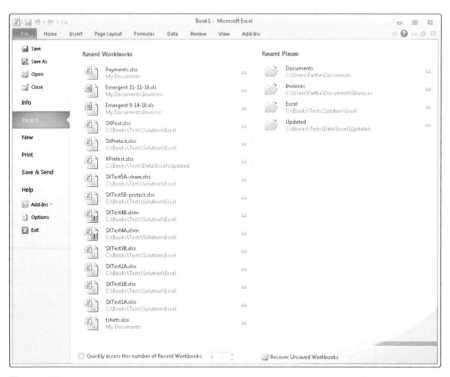

Figure 1-16

5. **Click the Manage Versions button.**

   This button opens a menu of additional commands. See Figure 1-17.

6. **Click away from the menu without selecting a command from it.**

   The menu closes.

7. **Click the New category.**

   Buttons appear for creating a new workbook based on a variety of templates.

8. **Click the Print category.**

   Buttons appear for printing the active workbook.

9. **Click Save & Send.**

   Buttons appear for saving and distributing the active workbook in different formats.

10. **Click Help.**

    Options appear for getting help with the application.

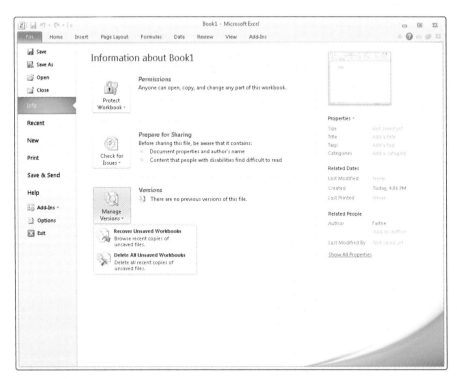

Figure 1-17

11. **Click Close.**

The active workbook closes, and so does Backstage View. Excel itself remains open.

12. **Click the File tab again to reopen Backstage View.**

13. **Click Exit.**

The Excel application window closes.

Creating Your First Document

In all the Office applications discussed in this book (except Outlook, which works somewhat differently), when you start the application, a new, blank document appears automatically. You can begin creating new content in this document and then save your work when you're finished editing. Alternatively, you can open an existing document or start a different type of document.

After starting a new document, you type or insert content into it. Documents can contain text, graphic objects, or a combination of the two. You can use many different types of graphic objects, such as photos, clip art, drawings, diagrams, and charts. You learn about these object types in later chapters.

Starting a new blank document

In the following exercise, you start several new PowerPoint presentations using various methods.

Files needed: None

LINGO

Because this chapter is about Office in general, I use the term **document** generically in this chapter to refer to a data file from Word, Excel, or PowerPoint. *Document* is actually the preferred term for a Word document. An Excel document is more commonly called a **workbook**, and a PowerPoint document is more commonly called a **presentation**.

1. **Start Microsoft PowerPoint 2010 using any method you like.**

   A new, blank presentation opens automatically.

2. **Choose File⇨New.**

   Icons for various template types appear.

3. **Click the Sample Templates icon.**

4. **Click Introducing PowerPoint 2010.**

   See Figure 1-18.

5. **Click the Create button.**

   A new presentation appears with several slides containing sample content.

6. **Choose File⇨Close to close the new presentation.**

   Now no presentations are open. The new, blank one that was created by default when PowerPoint started up was closed automatically because you didn't use it.

7. **Press Ctrl+N to start a new, blank presentation.**

8. **Choose File⇨New, click the Blank Presentation icon, and then click the Create button.**

   A second blank presentation opens.

9. **Choose File⇨Exit to close PowerPoint.**

Neither file is saved. You aren't prompted to save changes because you didn't enter any content into the presentations.

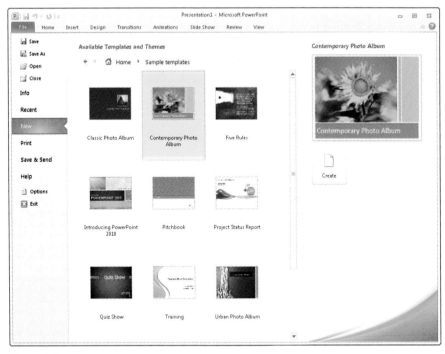

Figure 1-18

Typing text

Because of the layout differences among Excel, Word, and PowerPoint, the process of entering text in each program differs. Excel stores text in *cells,* which are boxes at the intersections of rows and columns. Word stores text directly on the document page. PowerPoint places text in movable, resizable text boxes on slides.

In the following exercise, you place text into documents in Word, Excel, and PowerPoint.

Files needed: None

1. **Start Microsoft Word 2010 by using any method you like.**

   A new, blank document opens.

2. **Type the following text:** ACME Engineering.

3. **Press Enter to start a new paragraph and then type this text:** Making smart engineering decisions since 1962.

   See Figure 1-19.

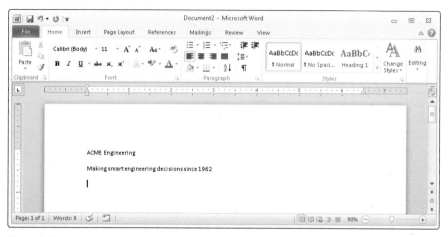

Figure 1-19

4. **Leave Word open and start Microsoft Excel 2010 by using any method you like.**

A new, blank workbook opens.

5. **Type** ACME Engineering **and press Enter.**

The text you just typed appears in cell A1 (that is, the cell at the intersection of column A and row 1).

The text overlaps into column B, too, because column A isn't wide enough to hold it.

An outline appears around cell A2, indicating that it's active. The next text you type will appear there. That outline is called the *cell cursor.*

6. **Type this text:** Making smart engineering decisions since 1962.

7. **Press Enter.**

The text you typed appears in A2. See Figure 1-20.

8. **Leave Excel open and open Microsoft PowerPoint 2010 by using any method you like.**

A new, blank presentation opens.

Figure 1-20

9. **Click in the Click to Add Title box and type** ACME Engineering.

10. **Click in the Click to Add Subtitle box and type the following:** Making smart engineering decisions since 1962.

See Figure 1-21.

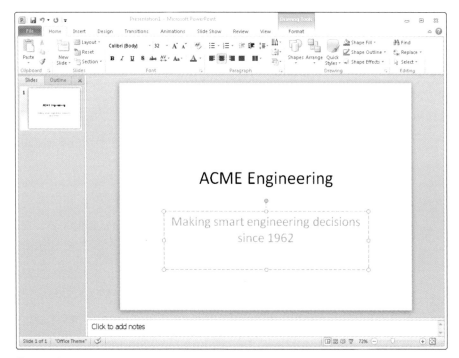

Figure 1-21

Leave PowerPoint open for the next exercise.

Inserting a picture

One of the most common types of graphic is what Office calls a *picture from file* (a picture that's saved as a separate file outside of Office already). You can get pictures from the Internet, from friends, or from your own scanner or digital camera.

In the following exercise, you place the same graphic into documents in Word, Excel, and PowerPoint.

Files needed: `01Graphic01.jpg`

1. **On the Windows task bar, click the Word button to switch to the already-open Word document from the previous exercise.**

LINGO

Office applications support a wide variety of picture formats. Some of the most common formats include JPEG, TIF, GIF, BMP, and PNG. Those are **file extensions**. Most filenames include a period (.) followed by an extension, a code that indicates the file's type. Extensions are customarily three characters long, but do not have to be.

TIP

If you didn't do the previous exercise, go back and perform Steps 1–3 there.

2. **Click at the end of the second paragraph to move the insertion point there; then press Enter to start a new paragraph.**

3. **Click the Insert tab on the Ribbon and then click the Picture button.**

   The Insert Picture dialog box opens.

4. **Navigate to the folder containing the data files for this chapter and select `01Graphic01.jpg`.**

   See Figure 1-22.

5. **Click the Insert button.**

   The picture is inserted in the document at the insertion point position.

6. **Switch to the already-open Excel workbook from the previous exercise.**

LINGO

The **insertion point** is the flashing vertical bar that shows where the next text or graphic will appear. You can move it by clicking where you want it, or by using the arrow keys. Moving the insertion point is covered later in this chapter in more detail.

TIP

If you didn't do the previous exercise, go back and perform Steps 4–7 there.

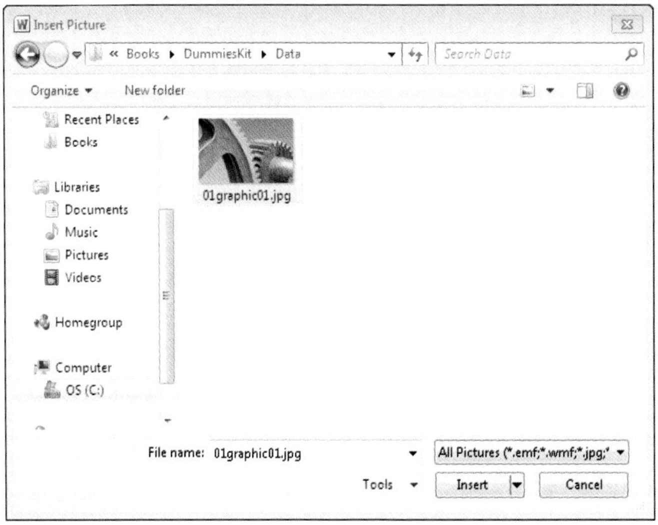

Figure 1-22

7. **Click the Insert tab on the Ribbon and then click the Picture button.**

The Insert Picture dialog box opens. (It's exactly the same dialog box from Step 4.)

8. **Navigate to the folder containing the data files for this chapter and select 01Graphic01.jpg.**

9. **Click the Insert button.**

The picture is inserted in the workbook as a free-floating object. You can drag it around to change its position.

> **TIP**
>
> The picture appears very large — larger than you might want it to be. Chapter 4 covers resizing a picture.

10. **Switch to the already-open PowerPoint presentation from the previous exercise.**

If you didn't do the previous exercise, go back and perform Steps 8–10 there.

11. **Click below the thumbnail image of the slide on the left side of the PowerPoint window.**

A flashing horizontal line appears there. See Figure 1-23.

Figure 1-23

12. **Press Enter to create a new slide.**

13. **In the placeholder box in the center of the slide, click the Insert Picture from File icon.**

    See Figure 1-24. The Insert Picture dialog box opens. (It's exactly the same dialog box from Steps 4 and 7.)

Figure 1-24

14. **Navigate to the folder containing the data files for this chapter and select `01Graphic01.jpg`.**

15. Click the Insert button.

The picture is inserted in the slide placeholder and sized to fit the place-holder box. See Figure 1-25.

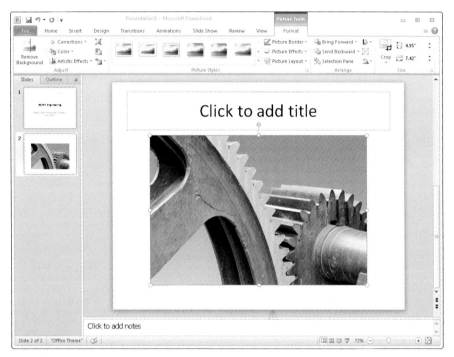

Figure 1-25

16. Close all open Office applications.

Don't save your work.

Moving Around

As you work in one of the applications, you may add so much content that you can't see it all onscreen at once. You might need to scroll through the document to view different parts of it. The simplest way to scroll through a document is by using the *scroll bars* with your mouse.

Scrolling through a document with the scroll bars doesn't move the insertion point, so what you type or insert doesn't necessarily appear in the location that shows onscreen.

You can also get around by moving the insertion point. When you do so, the document view scrolls automatically so you can see the newly selected location. You can move the insertion point either by clicking where you want it or by using keyboard shortcuts.

Moving using the mouse

Here's a summary of the available mouse movements:

> ✔ Click a scroll arrow to scroll a small amount in that direction. In Excel, that's one row or column; in other applications, the exact amount varies per click.

> ✔ Click above or below the scroll box to scroll one full screen in that direction if the document is tall/wide enough that there's undisplayed content in that direction.

> ✔ Drag the scroll box to scroll quickly in the direction you're dragging.

Now practice those skills in the following exercise.

In the following exercise, you move around in an Excel worksheet using the mouse.

Files needed: None

1. Start Microsoft Excel 2010 by using any method you like.

A new, blank workbook opens. See Figure 1-26.

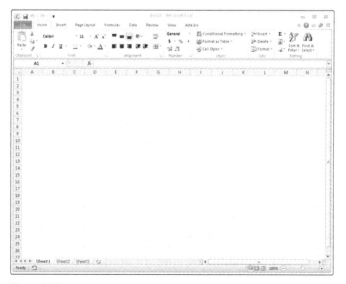

Figure 1-26

2. **Click cell E10 (that is, the cell at the intersection of column E and row 10).**

   The cell cursor moves there

3. **Click the down-pointing arrow at the bottom of the vertical scroll bar.**

   The display scrolls down one row. Notice that row 1 is no longer visible.

4. **Click the up arrow at the top of the vertical scroll bar.**

   Row 1 comes back into view.

5. **Click the space below the scroll box on the scroll bar.**

   The display scrolls down one full screen. Notice that the selected cell, E10, is no longer visible.

6. **Click the space above the scroll box.**

   The display scrolls back up one full screen.

7. **Drag the scroll box downward.**

   The display scrolls down quickly, according to the distance you dragged.

8. **Click the right-pointing arrow on the horizontal scroll bar three times.**

   The display scrolls to the right one column for each click. See Figure 1-27.

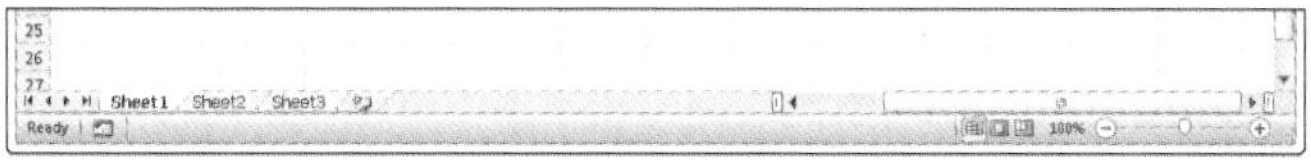

Figure 1-27

9. **Click the space to the left of the scroll box on the scroll bar.**

   The display scrolls to the left one full screen.

Leave Excel open for the next exercise.

Moving using the keyboard

Here's a summary of the ways you can move around in a document using the keyboard:

> EXTRA INFO
>
> The size of the scroll box is an indicator of how much of the document is undisplayed at the moment. In Figure 1-26, the scroll boxes takes up most of the scroll bar, indicating that almost all of the document fits onscreen at once.

✔ Press an arrow key to move the insertion point or cell cursor in the direction of the arrow. The exact amount depends on the application; in Excel, it moves one cell. In Word, up/down arrows move one line, and right/left arrows move one character.

✔ Press Page Up or Page Down to scroll one full screen in that direction.

✔ Press Home to move to the left side of the current row or line.

✔ Press End to move to the right side of the current row or line.

✔ Press Ctrl+Home to move to the upper-left corner of the document.

✔ Press Ctrl+End to move to the lower-right corner of the document.

Now practice those skills in the following exercise.

In the following exercise, you move around in an Excel worksheet using the keyboard.

Files needed: None

1. **If Excel isn't already open from the previous exercise, start Excel.**

   Note that the active cell is A1. See Figure 1-28.

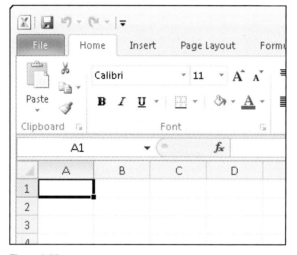

Figure 1-28

2. **Press the right-arrow key on the keyboard twice.**

   The cell cursor moves to cell C1.

3. **Press the down-arrow key twice.**

   The cell cursor moves to cell C3. See Figure 1-29.

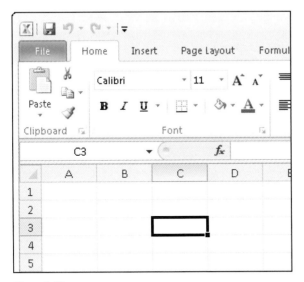

Figure 1-29

4. Hold down the Ctrl key and press the down-arrow key.

The cell cursor moves to the bottom of the worksheet (row 1048576).

5. Hold down the Ctrl key and press the right-arrow key.

The cell cursor moves to the rightmost column of the worksheet (column XFD).

6. Press the Home key.

The cell cursor moves back to column A.

7. Press the Page Up key.

The cell cursor moves up one full screen.

8. Press Ctrl+Home.

The cell cursor moves to cell A1.

Close Excel without saving your changes.

Changing the Onscreen View

Depending on what you're doing to the data in a particular application, you may find that changing the view is useful. Some applications have multiple viewing modes you can switch among; for example, PowerPoint's Normal view is suitable for slide editing, and its Slide Sorter view is suitable for rearranging the slides. In addition, all Office applications have Zoom commands that can make the data appear larger or smaller onscreen as you work.

Zooming in and out

Zooming changes the magnification of the data shown on the screen. It doesn't change the magnification of the application window itself (for example, the Ribbon), and it doesn't change the size of the data on printouts.

Zooming in increases the magnification, and out decreases it.

In this exercise, you explore the Zoom feature in Word.

Files needed: None

1. **In Word, with the document still open from the previous exercise, drag the Zoom slider to the right.**

   See Figure 1-30. The Zoom slider is located in the bottom-right corner of the Word window.

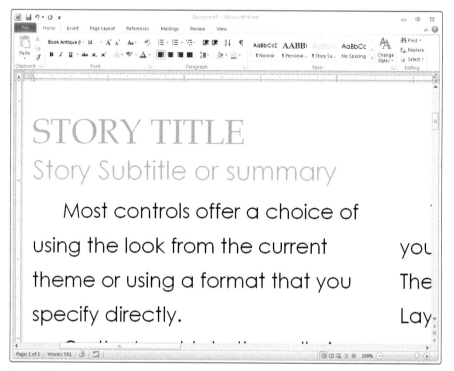

Figure 1-30

2. **Drag the Zoom slider to the left.**

   The Zoom magnification decreases.

3. **Click the plus sign at the right end of the Zoom slider.**

   The zoom increases slightly.

4. **Click the minus sign at the left end of the Zoom slider.**

   The zoom decreases slightly.

5. **Click the current zoom percentage (the number to the left of the Zoom slider).**

   The Zoom dialog box opens. See Figure 1-31.

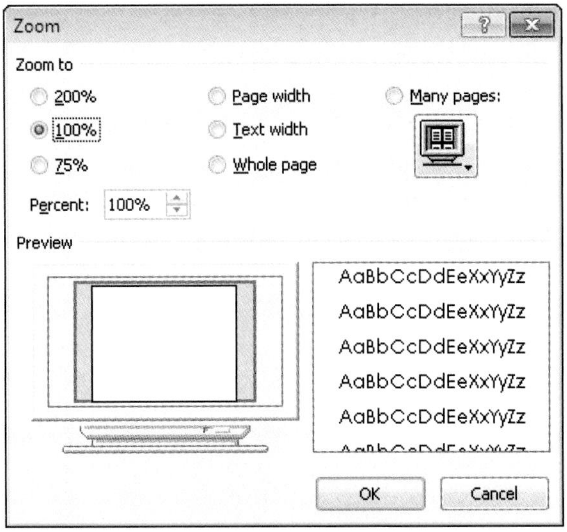

Figure 1-31

 You can also open the Zoom dialog box by clicking the View tab on the Ribbon and clicking the Zoom button.

6. **In the Zoom dialog box, click 100%.**

7. **Click OK.**

   The zoom changes back to 100 percent (the default).

Leave the Word document open for the next exercise.

Changing views

Each application has its own views suited to working with the unique type of content it generates.

In this exercise, you explore the available views in Word and PowerPoint.

Files needed: None

1. **Open PowerPoint.**
2. **Choose File⇨New.**
3. **Click the Sample Templates icon.**
4. **Click the Pitchbook icon and click the Create button.**

   This step gives you a sample presentation to practice with. See Figure 1-32.

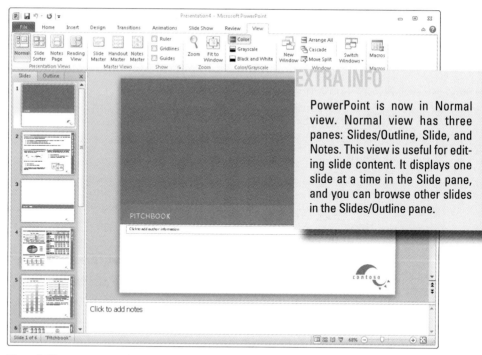

> **EXTRA INFO**
>
> PowerPoint is now in Normal view. Normal view has three panes: Slides/Outline, Slide, and Notes. This view is useful for editing slide content. It displays one slide at a time in the Slide pane, and you can browse other slides in the Slides/Outline pane.

Figure 1-32

5. Click the View tab and then click the Slide Sorter button.

The presentation appears in Slide Sorter view. See Figure 1-33.

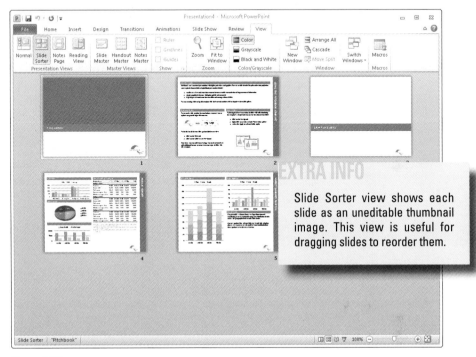

Slide Sorter view shows each slide as an uneditable thumbnail image. This view is useful for dragging slides to reorder them.

Figure 1-33

6. Close PowerPoint without saving your changes.

7. Open Word.

8. Choose File⇨New and click the Sample Templates icon.

9. Click the Apothecary Newsletter icon and click the Create button.

This step gives you a sample document to practice with. Word is now in Print Layout view. See Figure 1-34.

Print Layout view is useful for editing documents in a format that approximates how they'll look when printed.

10. Click the View tab on the Ribbon and then click the Draft button.

The document appears in Draft view. See Figure 1-35.

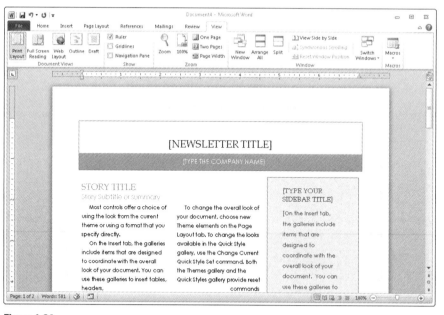

Figure 1-34

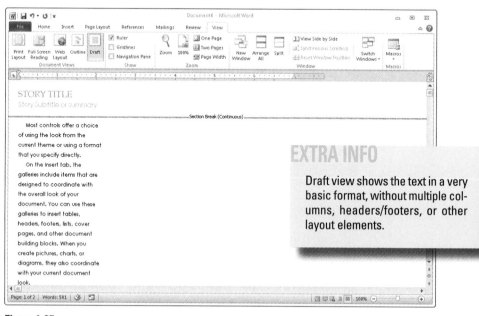

EXTRA INFO

Draft view shows the text in a very basic format, without multiple columns, headers/footers, or other layout elements.

Figure 1-35

11. On the View tab, click the Full Screen Reading button.

The document appears in Full Screen Reading view. See Figure 1-36.

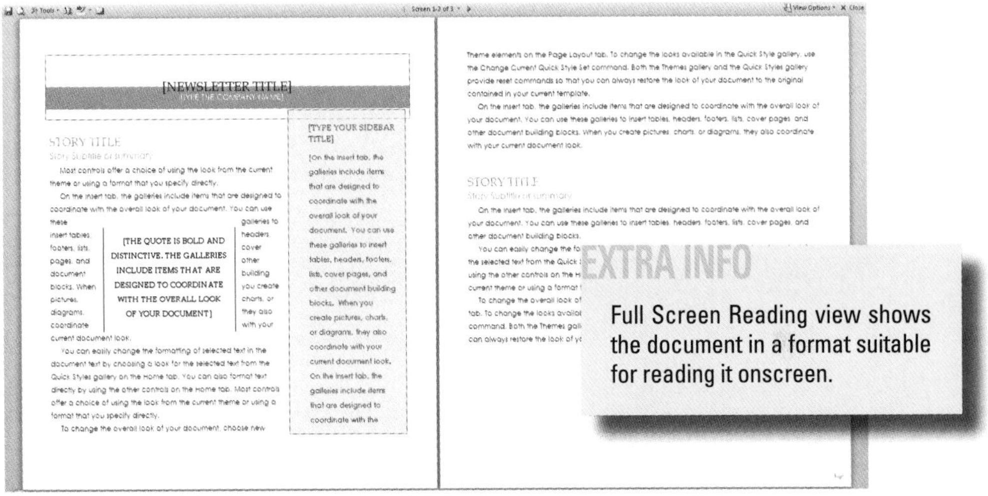

Figure 1-36

> **EXTRA INFO**
> Full Screen Reading view shows the document in a format suitable for reading it onscreen.

12. Click Close in the upper-right corner of the screen.

The document returns to Print Layout view.

Leave Word open for the next exercise.

Saving and Opening Documents

All Office apps can create, open, and save data files. A data file stores your work in a particular application. If you don't save your work, whatever you've entered disappears when you close the application or turn off your computer.

Each Office 2010 application has its own data file format. For example:

- ✓ **Word:** Document files, `.docx`
- ✓ **Excel:** Workbook files, `.xlsx`
- ✓ **PowerPoint:** Presentation files, `.pptx`
- ✓ **Outlook:** Personal folders files, `.pst`

Word, Excel, and PowerPoint use a separate data file for each project you work on. Every time you use one of these programs, you open and save data files. Outlook uses just one data file for all your activities. This file is automatically saved and opened for you, so you usually don't have to think about data file management in Outlook.

The steps for saving and opening data files are almost exactly the same in each application, so mastering it in one program gives you a big head start in the other programs. Throughout the rest of this book, many of the exercises begin with an instruction to open a particular data file and end with an instruction to save it.

Saving your work for the first time

As you work in an application, the content you create is stored in the computer's memory. This memory is only temporary storage. When you exit the application or shut down the computer, whatever is stored in memory is flushed away forever — unless you save it.

The first time you save a file, the application prompts you to enter a name for it in the Save As dialog box. You can also choose a different save location and/or file type.

When you resave an already saved file, the Save As dialog box doesn't reappear; the file saves with the most recent settings. If you want to change the settings (such as the location or file type) or save under a different name, choose File⇨Save As to make the Save As dialog box appear.

Each application has three important file types:

- ✔ **Default:** The default format in each application supports all 2007 and 2010 features except macros. The file extension ends in the letter *X* for each one: Word is .docx; Excel is .xlsx; PowerPoint is .pptx.

- ✔ **Macro-enabled:** This format supports all 2007 and 2010 features, including macros. The file extension ends in the letter *M* for each one: .docm, .xlsm, and .pptm.

Macros are recorded bits of code that can automate certain activities in a program, but they can also carry viruses. The default formats don't support macros for that reason. If you need to create a file that includes macros, you can save in a macro-enabled format.

✔ **97–2003:** The file types for the 2007 and 2010 versions of Office are identical. Each application includes a file format for backward compatibility with earlier versions of the application (versions 97 through 2003). Some minor functionality may be lost when saving in this format. The file extensions are `.doc`, `.xls`, and `.ppt`.

In this exercise, you save a document in Word several times with different names and file types.

Files needed: None

1. **In Word, with the document still open from the previous exercise, choose File⇨Save.**

   The Save As dialog box opens.

2. **In the File Name text box, type** Newsletter Sample.

   See Figure 1-37.

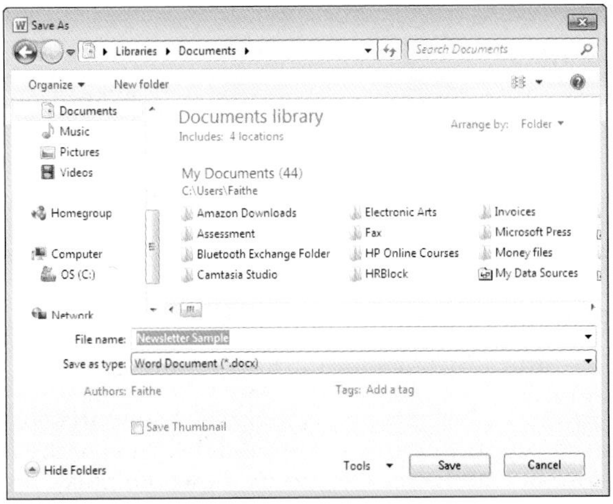

Figure 1-37

3. **Click Save.**

   The file is saved. Newsletter Sample appears in the title bar of the Word application window.

4. **In the document, click the [Newsletter Title] placeholder on the top line and type** My Newsletter **to replace it.**

5. **On the Quick Access Toolbar, click the Save button.**

   See Figure 1-38. The changes to the document are saved.

Figure 1-38

6. **In the document, click in the [Type Your Sidebar Title] placeholder and type** Recent News.

7. **Press Ctrl+S.**

   The changes are saved.

8. **Click in the Story Title placeholder and type** Our Vacation.

9. **Choose File⇨Save As.**

   The Save As dialog box opens.

10. **In the File Name text box, change the filename to** Newsletter Sample 2.

11. **Click drop-down list to the right of Save as Type.**

    A menu of document types opens.

12. **Select the Word 97–2003 Document option.**

    See Figure 1-39.

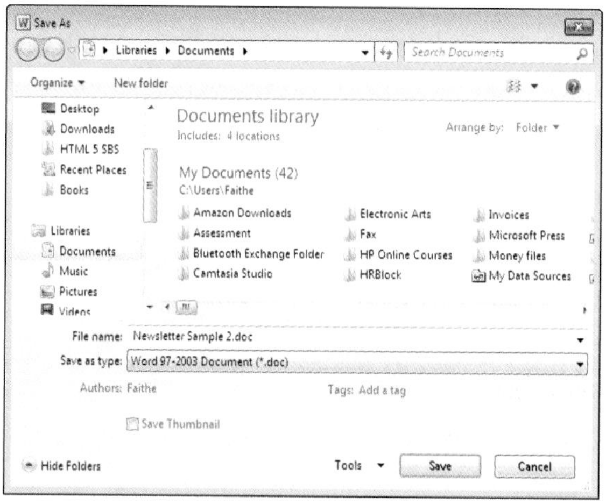

Figure 1-39

13. **Click Save.**

    A Compatibility Checker dialog box opens. See Figure 1-40.

14. Click Continue.

The document is resaved with a different name and a different file type.

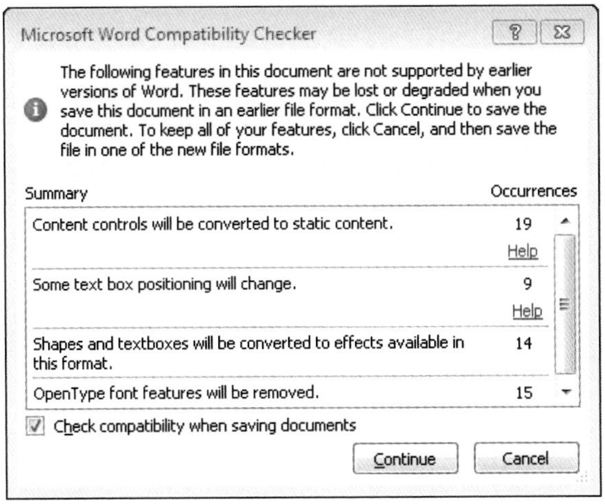

Figure 1-40

EXTRA INFO

The Compatibility Checker points out any Word 2010 features that might appear differently in an earlier-format version of the file. In most cases, the losses are minimal.

Leave the document open in Word for the next exercise.

Navigating in the Save and Open dialog boxes

In Windows Vista and Windows 7, each user has his own Documents folder (based on who is logged into Windows at the moment). That's the default save location. If you want to save somewhere else, you must use the controls in the Save As dialog box to change to a different location before you save.

To understand how to change save locations, you should first understand the concept of a file path. Files are organized into folders, and you can have folders *inside* folders. For example, you might have

- A folder called *Work*
- Within that folder, another folder called *Job Search*
- Within that folder, a Word file called `Resume.docx`

The path for such a file would be

`C:\Work\Job Search\Resume.docx`

When you change the save location, you're changing to a different path for the file. You do that by navigating through the file system via the Save As dialog box. The Save As dialog box provides several different ways of navigating, so you can pick the one you like best.

In this exercise, you experiment with several ways of changing the save location in the Save As dialog box.

Files needed: None

1. **In Word, with the document still open from the previous exercise, choose File⇨Save As.**

   The Save As dialog box opens. See Figure 1-41.

TIP

This exercise assumes you're using Windows 7. In Windows Vista, the Save As dialog box may not show any folders or locations by default. If it doesn't, click the Browse Folders button at the bottom left of the dialog box.

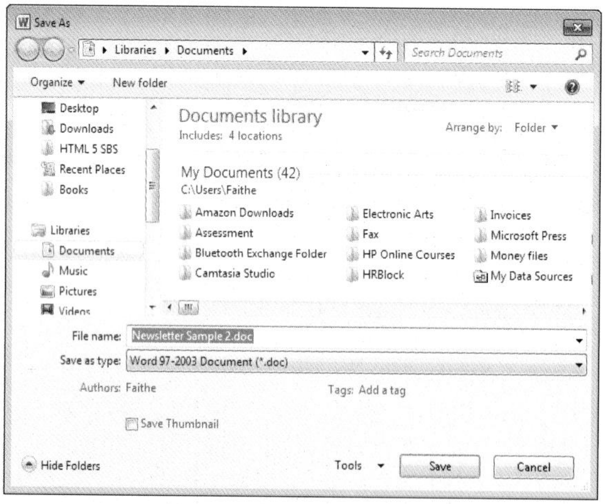

EXTRA INFO

The bar at the left is the Places bar. It provides shortcuts for various places you can save files. The bar across the top is the Address bar. It shows the current location.

Figure 1-41

2. **Scroll through the Places bar to see the available locations for saving files.**

3. **In the Places bar, double-click Computer.**

   A list of drives appears.

4. **Double-click the C: drive.**

   A list of folders on the C: drive appears. See Figure 1-42.

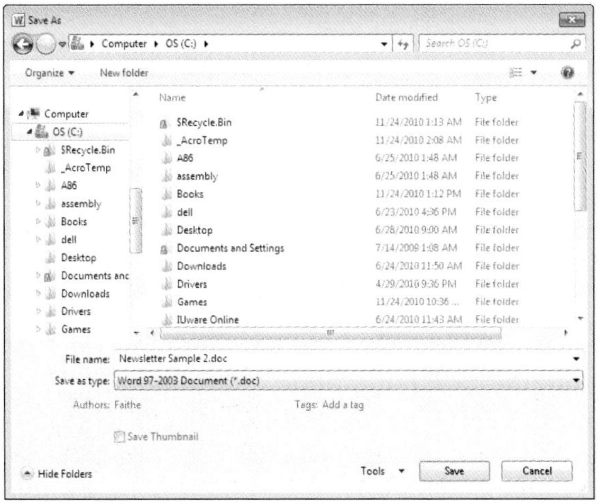

Figure 1-42

5. **Scroll up in the Places bar to locate the Documents shortcut and double-click it.**

   The Documents folder's content appears.

6. **Right-click an empty spot in right pane of the dialog box and click New Folder.**

   A new folder appears, with the name highlighted, ready for you to name it.

7. **Type** Dummies Kit **and press Enter to name the folder.**

   You've just created a folder that you can use to store all the work that you do for this class. See Figure 1-43.

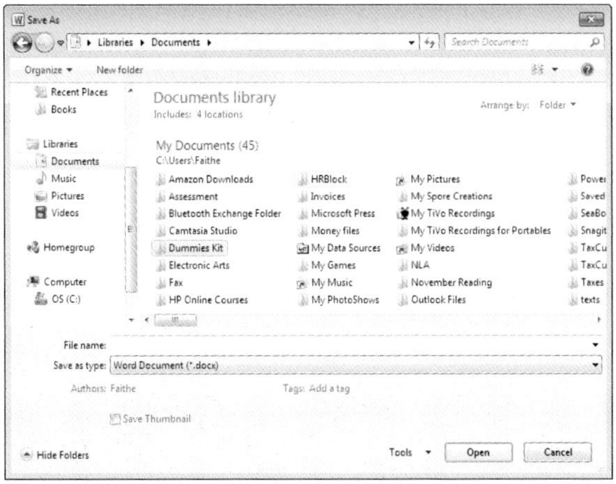

Figure 1-43

8. **Double-click the Dummies Kit folder to open it.**

9. **In the Address bar, click the right-pointing arrow to the left of Dummies Kit.**

   A list of all the other folders in the Documents folder appears.

TIP

In the Address bar, the parts of a path are separated by right-pointing triangles rather than by slashes. You can click any of the triangles to open a drop-down list containing all the *subfolders* (that is, the folders within that folder).

10. **Click any of the folders on that list to switch to that folder.**

11. **In the Address bar, click Documents.**

   The Documents folder reappears.

12. **In the Address bar, click Libraries.**

   A list of the libraries for Windows 7 appears: Documents, Pictures, Music, and Videos. See Figure 1-44.

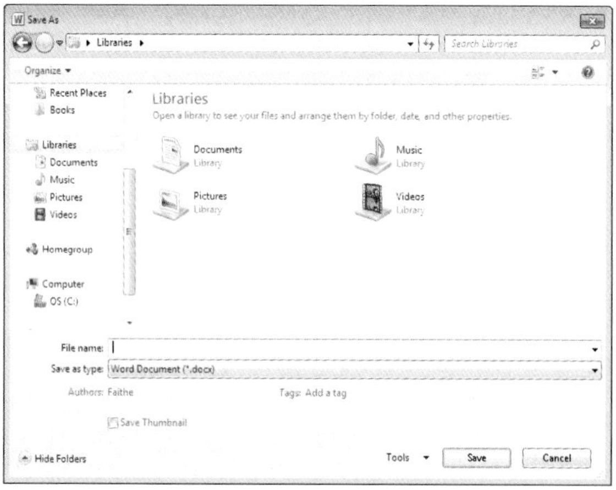

Figure 1-44

13. **Scroll up near the top of the Places bar and click Desktop.**

   You can save directly to your desktop by saving to this location.

14. **In the Places bar, click Documents and then double-click Dummies Kit.**

   The Dummies Kit folder reappears.

15. **In the File Name text box, type Chapter 1 Practice.**

16. **Open the Save as Type drop-down list and select Word Document (.docx).**

See Figure 1-45.

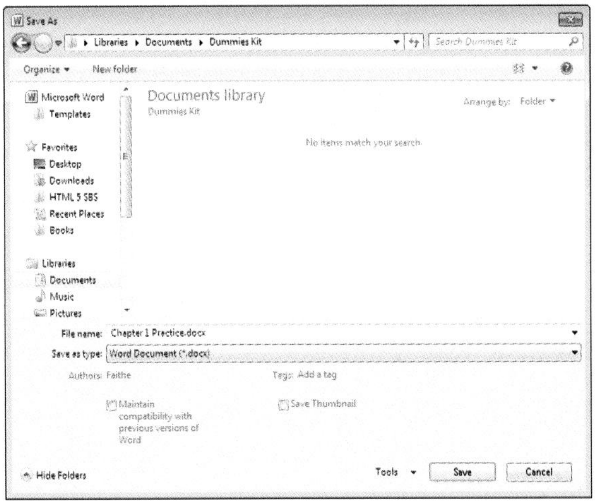

Figure 1-45

17. **Click Save.**

    A message appears to tell you that you're saving the document in the newer file type.

18. **Click OK.**

    The file is saved.

19. **Choose File➪Close to close the document without exiting Word.**

Opening a document

When you open a file, you copy it from your hard drive (or other storage location) into the computer's memory, where Word can access it for viewing and modifying it.

The Open dialog box's navigation controls are almost exactly the same as those in the Save As dialog box, so you can browse to a different storage location if needed.

If you want to reopen a recently used file, there's an even quicker way than using the Open dialog box. Choose File➪Recent and then click the file's name on the Recent Files list.

In this exercise, you open a saved file.

Files needed: Any saved Word document, such as the Chapter 1 Practice file you save in the previous exercise

1. **In Word, choose File⇨Open.**

   The Open dialog box appears.

2. **On the Places bar, click Documents.**

   The Documents folder appears if it didn't already appear.

3. **Double-click the Dummies Kit folder to navigate to the location where you stored the file earlier.**

4. **Click Chapter 1 Practice.**

   See Figure 1-46.

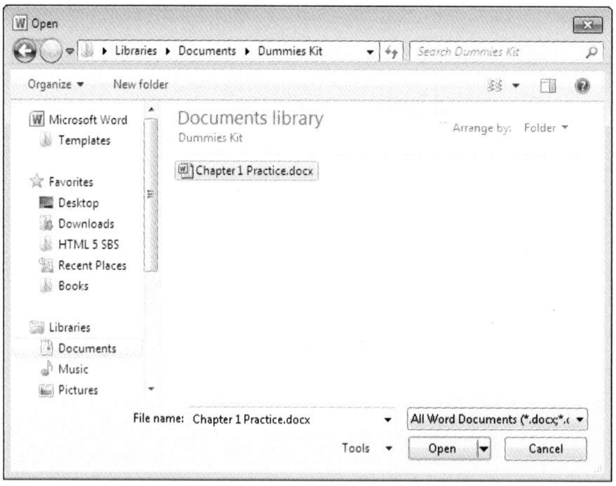

Figure 1-46

5. **Click Open.**

   The file opens in Word.

6. **Choose File⇨Close to close the document without exiting Word.**

7. **Choose File⇨Recent.**

   A list of recently opened files appears.

8. **Click Chapter 1 Practice.**

   That file reopens.

9. **Choose File⇨Close to close the document again.**

Recovering lost work

Computers lock up occasionally, and applications crash in the middle of important projects. When that happens, any work that you haven't saved is gone.

To minimize the pain of those situations, Word, Excel, and PowerPoint all have an AutoRecover feature that silently saves your drafts as you work, once every ten minutes or at some other interval you specify. These drafts are saved in temporary hidden files that are deleted when you close the application successfully (that is, not abruptly due to a lockup, crash, or power outage). If the application crashes, those temporary saved files appear for your perusal when the program starts back up. You can choose to do either of the following:

✔ Save them if their versions are newer than the ones you have on your hard drive.

✔ Discard them if they contain nothing you need.

In this exercise, you change the interval at which Word saves backup drafts for AutoRecover.

Files needed: None

1. **In Word, choose File⇨Options.**

   The Word Options dialog box opens.

2. **Click the Save category on the left.**

3. **Make sure that the save AutoRecover Information Every xx Minutes check box is selected.**

4. **If desired, change the value in the Minutes box to another number.**

   For example, to save every 5 minutes, type **5** there.

   See Figure 1-47.

5. **Click OK.**

Exit Word without saving your changes to any open files.

Figure 1-47

 Summing Up

Excel, Word, and PowerPoint are all very similar in their basic functionality and appearance. In this chapter, you explored several different applications and learned how to start and exit the programs, create and save your work, and insert text and graphics.

- ✔ The Ribbon and Start menu provide a consistent interface for managing files and issuing commands in each application.

- ✔ Word, Excel, and PowerPoint all start a new, blank document when they open. You can use this document, or you can open an existing one. Excel documents are called workbooks; PowerPoint documents are called presentations.

- ✔ To enter text in a document, click where you want to place it; that moves the insertion point there. Then type.

- ✔ To insert a picture, click the Insert tab on the Ribbon and then click the Picture button. It works the same in Word, Excel, and PowerPoint.

- ✔ Scroll bars enable you to scroll to different parts of a document. You can also move around by clicking where you want to go or by using the arrow keys to move the insertion point.

- ✔ Each application has a different set of views for working with data in different ways. You can switch among them on the View tab.

✔ The Zoom feature increases or decreases the magnification of the data displayed onscreen. Use the Zoom slider and controls in the lower-right corner of the application window.

✔ To save your work, use the Save command on the File menu, or press Ctrl+S, or click the Save button on the Quick Access Toolbar.

✔ To open a file, use the Open command on the File menu. You can also select a recently used file from the Recent section of the File menu.

Try-it-yourself lab

For more practice with the features covered in this chapter, try the following exercise on your own.

1. **Start Excel and, in the new workbook that appears, in cell A1, type** Grocery List.

2. **Starting in cell A3, type a grocery shopping list of at least six items, with each item appearing in a different cell in column A.**

3. **Save the file as** Chapter 1 Grocery List **in the Dummies Kit folder you created earlier.**

4. **Close Excel.**

Know this tech talk

application: A program that performs a useful user task, such as creating a word processing document or calculating a number.

Backstage View: The section of an Office application that appears when the File menu is open. It contains commands for working with files, options, importing, exporting, and printing.

cell cursor: In Excel, the dark outline around the active cell.

data file: A file in which the information you enter in an application is stored for later reuse.

document: A data file in a word processing program. Can also refer generically to any data file.

file extension: The code following the period at the end of a file name, indicating the file's type. Some file extensions are hidden by default in Windows.

folder: An organizing container on a hard drive in which to store files.

insertion point: In a text editing application, a flashing vertical line indicating where text will be inserted when typed.

presentation: A data file in a presentation program such as PowerPoint.

scroll bar: A bar along the right and/or bottom side of a window that can be used to change the viewing area.

scroll box: The movable box inside the scroll bar.

suite: A collection of programs with complementary functions and common user interface elements.

workbook: A data file in a spreadsheet program such as Excel.

Creating a Word Document

✔ Starting new documents based on templates can *save time and provide guidance as to what content to insert and where to place it.* Many templates are available for free via Office.com.

✔ Selecting text before issuing a command *enables you to act on large blocks of text at a time.* You can select text either with the keyboard or the mouse.

✔ Formatting text *makes your documents more attractive and readable.* You can apply different fonts, sizes, and colors, as well as use style sets and themes to automate the process of formatting an entire document.

✔ Check your spelling and grammar in order to *avoid embarrassing errors* in documents you distribute to others. Word can help you check both individual words and the entire document easily.

✔ You can *share your documents with other people* via e-mail or by printing them. You can begin sending a document via e-mail from within Word, and your default e-mail program opens to send the message.

1. How do you start a document based on an online template?

Guide yourself to page 53

2. How can you change a document's margins?

There's space on page.. 57

3. How do you set the paper size and page orientation?

Find your bearings on page 59

4. What are two ways to change the font size?

The font is found on page 67

5. What kinds of formatting does a theme affect?

That motif on page.. 70

6. What does it mean when text has a wavy red underline?

There are all kinds of squiggles on page.............................. 79

7. How do you send Word documents via e-mail?

Electronic greetings seek page.. 81

*M*icrosoft Word is the most popular of the Office applications because nearly everyone needs to create text documents of one type or another. With Word, you can create everything from fax cover sheets to school research papers to family holiday letters.

In this chapter, I explain how to create, edit, format, and share simple documents. By the end of this chapter, you'll have a good grasp of the entire process of document creation, from start to finish, including how to share your work with others via print or e-mail. Later chapters will then build on this knowledge, adding in the fancier aspects such as using styles, graphics, and multiple sections.

Starting a New Word Document

As you learn in Chapter 1, you can create a blank new document, or you can base a new document on a template. Each Office application has some templates that are stored locally on your hard drive and many more that are available via the Internet. After starting a new document, you can adjust the paper size and orientation if needed.

Even when you start a blank document, you're still (technically) using a template. It's a template called Normal, and it specifies certain default settings for a new blank document, such as the default fonts (Calibri for body text and Cambria for headings), default font sizes (11 point for body text), and margins (1 inch on all sides).

LINGO

A **template** is a special type of document that's designed to be a model for new documents. Templates have a different file extension than regular documents (.dotx or .dotm). When you start a new document based on a template, the template file itself is unaffected, so it's always the same each time you use it.

Creating a new document using a template

In the following exercise, you start two new Word documents. One uses a local template, and one uses a template from Office.com.

Files needed: None

1. **In Word, choose File⇨New.**

   Icons for creating new documents appear, as shown in Figure 2-1.

2. **In the Office.com Templates section, click Brochures and Booklets.**

   A set of three folders appears: Brochures, Catalogs, and Programs.

3. **Double-click the Brochures folder.**

   Word uses your Internet connection to retrieve a list of available brochure templates.

4. **Scroll down to and click the Hawaii Brochure template.**

   A preview of it appears. See Figure 2-2.

5. **Click the Download button below the preview.**

   A license agreement appears.

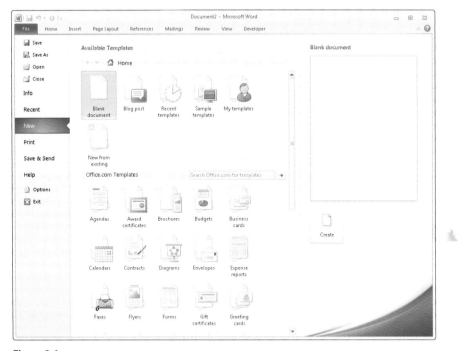

Figure 2-1

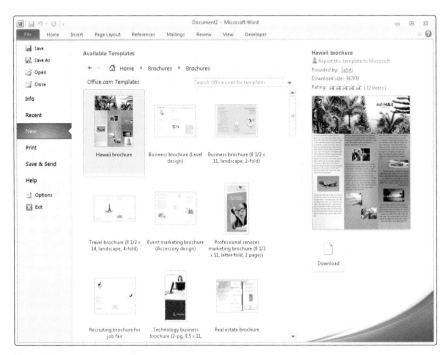

Figure 2-2

6. **Click I Accept.**

   The template is downloaded, and a new document appears based on it.

   See Figure 2-3.

Figure 2-3

7. **Examine the document to see what types of content the template provided.**

8. **Choose File⇨Close to close the document.**

   If prompted to save your changes, click Don't Save.

9. **Choose File⇨New.**

   The icons reappear for new document types.

10. **Click Sample Templates.**

    A list of the templates stored on your local hard drive appears.

11. **Scroll down to the bottom of the listing and click Urban Report.**

    A sample of it appears. See Figure 2-4.

12. **Click the Create button.**

    A new document opens based on the selected template.

13. **Scroll through the new document and notice the placeholders ready for you to fill in to create your own version of the report.**

14. **Save the document as** Chapter 2 Practice.

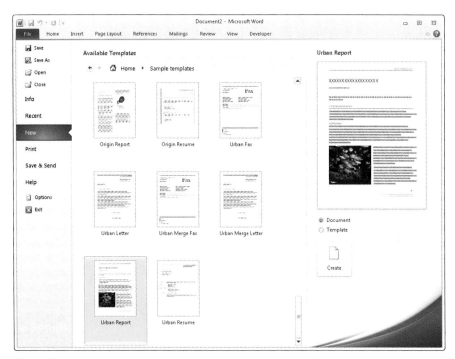

Figure 2-4

Leave Word and the document file open for the next exercise.

For more practice, create several more new documents by using different templates. Don't save any of them.

Setting page margins

Word provides several easy-to-use presets. You can also individually specify the margins for each side of the page if you prefer.

In the following exercise, you change the page margins in two different ways: using a preset and using an exact value.

Files needed: Chapter 2 Practice, created in the previous exercise

LINGO

The **margins** are the amounts of blank space that Word reserves on each side of the paper. In most cases, you want them to be roughly the same on all sides, or at least the same at both the right/left, so the document looks symmetrical. In special cases, though, such as when you're going to bind the document on the left or at the top, you want to leave more blank space on one particular side.

1. **In Word, with the Chapter 2 Practice document still open from the previous exercise, click the Page Layout tab.**

2. **Click the Margins button.**

   A Margins drop-down list opens, as shown in Figure 2-5.

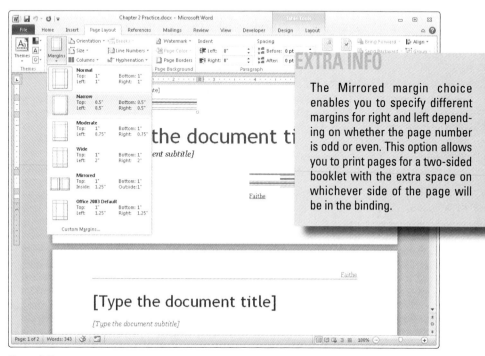

Figure 2-5

3. **Click the Narrow option.**

   Presets for narrow margins are applied to the top, bottom, right, and left margins for the document.

4. **Click the Margins button again and then click Custom Margins.**

   The Page Setup dialog box opens.

5. **In the Top, Bottom, Right, and Left boxes, type** 1.3, **as in Figure 2-6.**

6. **Click OK.**

   The margins change.

You can tell because the sample text is positioned differently on the pages.

7. Save your work.

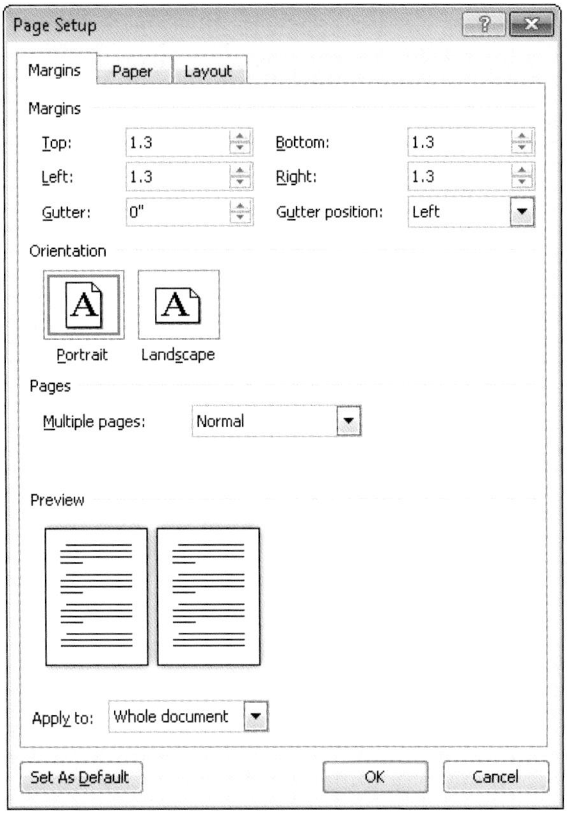

Figure 2-6

Leave Word and the document file open for the next exercise.

Setting page size and orientation

A template might not always use the right paper size or page orientation for the work you want to create. In some cases, either or both may require adjustment.

The standard paper size in the U.S. is 8.5 x 11 inches, also known as Letter. Most of the

LINGO

A document's **orientation** can be either portrait or landscape.

Portrait is a standard page in which the tall part of the paper runs along the sides.

Landscape is a rotated page in which the tall part of the paper runs along the top and bottom.

templates available through Word use this paper size, although some exceptions exist. For example, an envelope template might use a page size that matches a standard business envelope, or a legal brief template might use legal-size paper (8.5 x 14 inches).

In the following exercise, you set the page orientation of a document to Landscape and change its paper size.

Files needed: Chapter 2 Practice, created in the previous exercise

1. **In Word, with the Chapter 2 Practice document still open from the previous exercise, click the Page Layout tab if it isn't displayed.**

2. **Click the Orientation button.**

   A drop-down list opens and gives you two options: Portrait and Landscape.

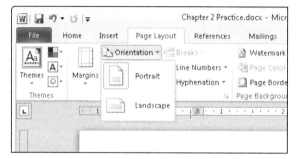

Figure 2-7

3. **Click the Landscape option.**

   The page changes to Landscape mode.

4. **Change the orientation back to Portrait.**

5. **Click the Size button.**

   A list of common paper sizes appears. See Figure 2-8.

Look online for websites that explain the paper sizes common in various countries. Here's one such site to start you out:

`http://www.cl.cam.ac.uk/~mgk25/iso-paper.html`

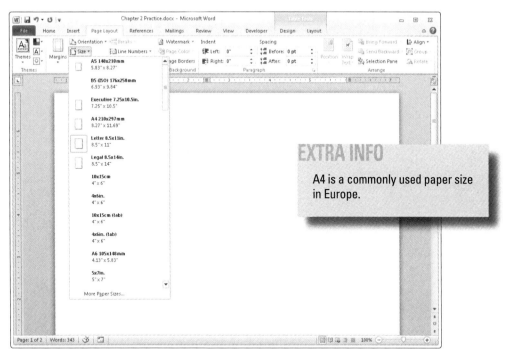

Figure 2-8

> ### 6. Click the option A4 210x297 mm. You may need to scroll down the list to find it.
>
> The paper size changes.

Changing the paper size in Word doesn't change the paper size in your printer, of course, so if you print on a different size paper than you tell Word you're using, the printing may not be centered on the paper.

For more practice, click More Paper Sizes at the bottom of the Size menu and set up a custom paper size by entering a width and height on the Paper tab of the Page Setup dialog box.

> ### 7. Save your work.

Leave Word and the document file open for the next exercise.

Editing Text

After creating a document and setting its basic properties like margins, orientation, and page size, you're ready to start editing its content. Editing can include adding text, deleting text, modifying text, and moving and copying blocks of text from one location to another.

If you used a template to get started, you may already have some sample content in the document (text and/or graphics). You can edit this content, or you can delete it and start from scratch.

Filling text placeholders

Some templates include placeholders to guide you in creating content in a specific format. You aren't required to use the placeholders; you can delete them if you like. However, if you aren't sure how to get started with a particular type of document, the template's placeholders can be helpful guides.

In the following exercise, you edit a document's text by filling in placeholders.

Files needed: Chapter 2 Practice, created earlier in this chapter

1. **In Word, with the Chapter 2 Practice document still open from the previous exercise, click in the [Type the document title] placeholder on the first page.**

   The placeholder becomes highlighted. See Figure 2-9.

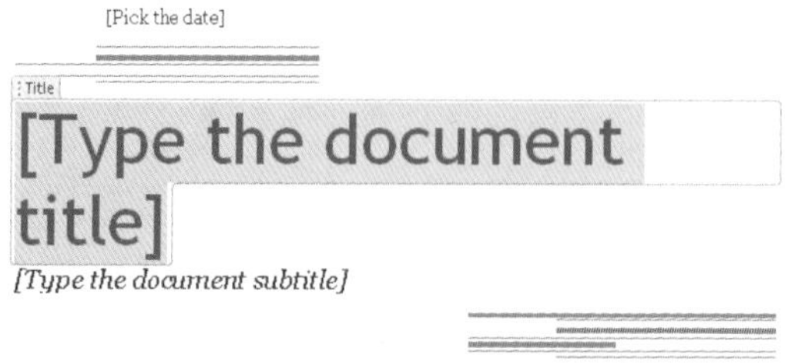

[Pick the date]

: Title

[Type the document title]

[Type the document subtitle]

Figure 2-9

2. **Type** Mountain Vista Vacations.

   The text appears in the placeholder box.

3. **Click in the [Type the document subtitle] placeholder and type** Affordable Family Fun.

4. **Click in the [Pick the date] placeholder.**

   The text becomes highlighted, and a drop-down arrow appears to its right.

5. **Click the arrow to open a date picker.**

   See Figure 2-10.

Vista Vacations

Figure 2-10

6. **Click the Today button to select today's date.**

7. **Click the name below the green horizontal lines.**

   By default, it's the name of the registered user of this copy of Word.

8. **Type your own name to replace the default name.**

   The cover page information is now complete, as shown in Figure 2-11.

12/8/2010

Mountain Vista Vacations
Affordable Family Fun

Joe Smith

Figure 2-11

9. **Save your work and close the document.**

Leave Word open for the next exercise.

Typing and editing text

Most documents don't contain text placeholders, so you're on your own in deciding what to type. Fortunately, it's easy to type and edit text in Word.

To delete text, press Delete (to delete the character to the right of the insertion point) or Backspace (to delete the character to the left of the insertion point). To delete more than one character at once, select the block of text to delete and then press Delete or Backspace.

You can also select some text and then type over it. When you type after selecting text, the selected text is replaced by what you type.

In the following exercise, you type some text in a new document and then edit it using several different editing techniques.

Files needed: None

1. **In Word, press Ctrl+N to start a new blank document.**

2. **Type the following text in the document:**

   Dear Karen:

   Florida is certainly a long way from home, and although we are enjoying our trip, we are looking forward to being home again with our good friends.

   We are having a wonderful time on our vacation. The weather has been perfect. Elroy and George have been collecting shells, and Judy and I have been enjoying the pool.

3. **Triple-click the last paragraph to select it.**

4. **Drag the paragraph up and drop it between the other two paragraphs (between the salutation and the first body paragraph).**

   See Figure 2-12.

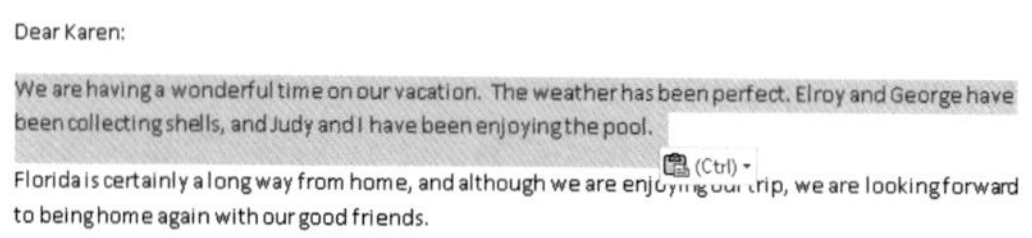

Dear Karen:

We are having a wonderful time on our vacation. The weather has been perfect. Elroy and George have been collecting shells, and Judy and I have been enjoying the pool.

(Ctrl) ▾

Florida is certainly a long way from home, and although we are enjoying our trip, we are looking forward to being home again with our good friends.

Figure 2-12

5. **Double-click the name** *Karen* **in the first paragraph and type** Rosie.

6. **Click to move the insertion point after the word Florida in the last paragraph. Press Backspace until the entire word is deleted.**

7. **Type** California.

8. **Use the arrow keys to move the insertion point before** *shells* **in the second paragraph and then type** sea.

The document resembles Figure 2-13.

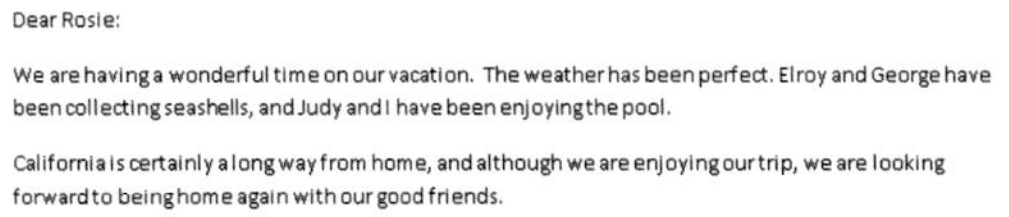

Dear Rosie:

We are having a wonderful time on our vacation. The weather has been perfect. Elroy and George have been collecting seashells, and Judy and I have been enjoying the pool.

California is certainly a long way from home, and although we are enjoying our trip, we are looking forward to being home again with our good friends.

Figure 2-13

9. **Save the document as** Chapter 2 Vacation.

Leave the document open for the next exercise.

Selecting Text

Selecting blocks of text before you issue an editing or formatting command allows you to act on the entire block at once. For example, you can select multiple paragraphs before applying new line spacing or indentation settings, and those settings will apply to every paragraph in the selection.

You have many ways to select text:

- ✔ You can drag across the text with the mouse (with the left mouse button pressed) to select any amount of text.

- ✔ You can move the insertion point to the beginning of the text and then hold down the Shift key while you press the arrow keys to extend the selection.

- ✔ You can press the F8 key to turn on Extend mode, and then you can use the arrow keys to extend the selection.

- ✔ You can double-click a word to select it or triple-click a paragraph to select it.

- ✔ You can press Ctrl+A to select the entire document.

- ✔ You can click to the left of a line to select that line.

In the following exercise, you practice selecting parts of a document.

Files needed: Chapter 2 Vacation, created in the previous exercise

1. **In Word, in the** Chapter 2 Vacation **file, triple-click the second paragraph to select it.**

2. **Hold down the Shift key and press the down-arrow key twice to extend the selection to the next paragraph.**

   See Figure 2-14.

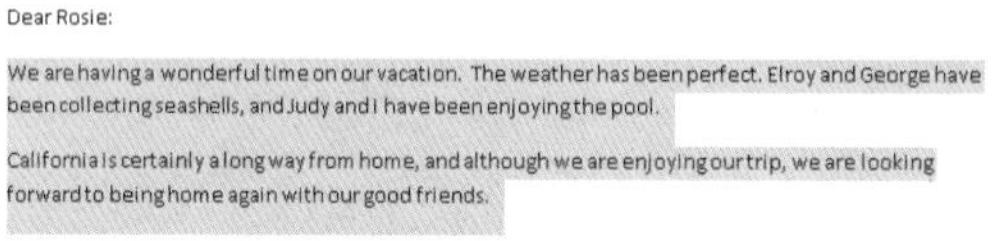

   Dear Rosie:

   We are having a wonderful time on our vacation. The weather has been perfect. Elroy and George have been collecting seashells, and Judy and I have been enjoying the pool.

   California is certainly a long way from home, and although we are enjoying our trip, we are looking forward to being home again with our good friends.

Figure 2-14

For more practice, click away from the selected paragraphs to deselect them and then double-click several words to select them. Then try double-clicking one word and holding down the Shift key while you double-click a different word. Try it again with the Ctrl key instead of Shift.

3. **Press Ctrl+A to select the entire document.**

4. **Click away from the selected text to deselect it.**

5. **Drag the mouse across the word** *wonderful* **in the second paragraph to select it.**

6. **Position the mouse pointer to the left of the first line in the second paragraph.**

   The mouse pointer turns into a white arrow that points diagonally up and to the right.

   If you don't see the arrow, make sure you are in Print Layout view. On the View tab, click Print Layout.

7. **Click to select the line.**

   See Figure 2-15.

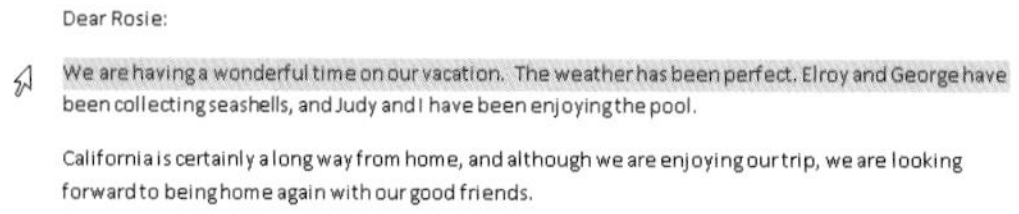

   Dear Rosie:

   We are having a wonderful time on our vacation. The weather has been perfect. Elroy and George have been collecting seashells, and Judy and I have been enjoying the pool.

   California is certainly a long way from home, and although we are enjoying our trip, we are looking forward to being home again with our good friends.

Figure 2-15

Leave the document open for the next exercise. You don't have to save your work because you didn't make any changes.

Formatting Text

Text formatting can make a big difference in the readability of a document. By making certain text larger, boldface, or a different font, you can call attention to it and add interest for your readers.

You can apply each type of character formatting individually, or you can use style sets or themes to apply multiple types of formatting at once.

Choosing text font, size, and color

Each font is available in a wide variety of sizes. The sizes are measured in **points**, with each point being 1/72 of an inch on a printout. (The size it appears onscreen depends on the display zoom. You learn about zoom in Chapter 1.) Text sizes vary from very small (6 points) to very large (100 points or more). An average document uses body text that's between 10 and 12 points, and headings between 12 and 18 points.

You can also color each font by using either a **standard color**, which doesn't change when you change document themes, or a **theme color**, which does change. Later in the chapter, you learn how to change themes, and you see what happens to the text colors you've applied when the theme colors change.

You can apply fonts, sizes, and colors either from the Home tab of the Ribbon or from the Mini toolbar.

In the following exercise, you format some text by applying different fonts, sizes, and colors to it.

Files needed: Chapter 2 Vacation, from the previous exercise

1. **In Word, in the Chapter 2 Vacation file, move the insertion point to the beginning of the document and press Enter to create a new line.**

2. **Press the up-arrow key once to move the insertion point into the new line and then type Our Vacation.**

3. **Triple-click Our Vacation to select the entire paragraph.**

4. **Point the mouse pointer at the selected paragraph so that the Mini toolbar appears. At first it appears dim; move the mouse over the Mini toolbar to make it brighter.**

   See Figure 2-16.

Calibri (E ▼ 11 ▼ A⌃ A⌄ 津 津
B *I* U̲ ≣ ab̲c̲ ▼ **A** ▼ 𝒥

Our Vacation

Dear Rosie:

We are having a wonderful time on our vacation. The weather has been perfect. Elroy and George have been collecting seashells, and Judy and I have been enjoying the pool.

California is certainly a long way from home, and although we are enjoying our trip, we are looking forward to being home again with our good friends.

Figure 2-16

5. **Open the Font drop-down list on the Mini toolbar and click Arial Black.**

6. **Open the Font Size drop-down list on the Mini toolbar and click 14.**

   If the Mini toolbar is no longer visible, right-click the text to make the Mini toolbar reappear.

   For more practice, change the font and font size by using the controls in the Font group on the Ribbon.

7. **On the Ribbon, click the Grow Font button to increase the font size of the selected text to 16 points.**

   See Figure 2-17.

8. **Click the face of the Font Color button.**

   Whatever color was already displayed on the button is applied to the text. (The color that appears depends on the most recently used font color.)

9. **Click the down arrow to the right of the Font Color button.**

   A palette of colors appears. See Figure 2-18.

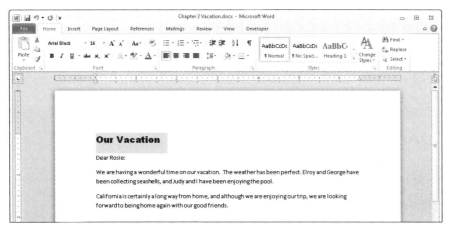

Figure 2-17

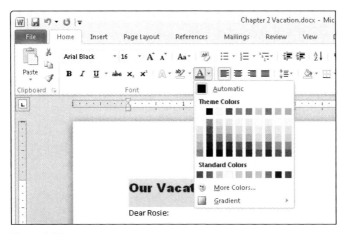

Figure 2-18

10. **Click the red square under Standard Colors.**

    The text becomes red.

11. **Click the down arrow on the Font Color button again to reopen the color palette.**

12. **Click the Red, Accent 2 square on the top row of the Theme Colors section.**

TIP

Pointing at a square makes its name appear in a ScreenTip.

PRACTICE

For more practice, try some of the tints and shades below the theme colors. A tint is a lighter version of a color, and a shade is a darker version of it.

Leave the document open for the next exercise.

Applying text attributes and effects

Figure 2-19 shows samples of some of these attributes. Table 2-1 summarizes the keyboard shortcuts for them.

LINGO

You can modify text with a variety of **attributes**, such as bold, italics, underlining, and so on. Some of these can be applied from the Mini toolbar and/or the Font group on the Home tab. Others are available in the Font dialog box. Some of them also have keyboard shortcuts.

Bold	*Italics*	Underline
Super^{script}	Sub$_{script}$	~~Strikethrough~~
SMALL CAPS	ALL CAPS	~~Double Strikethrough~~

Figure 2-19

Table 2-1	Keyboard Shortcuts for Applying Text Attributes
Attribute	*Keyboard Shortcut*
Bold	Ctrl+B
Italic	Ctrl+I
Underline	Ctrl+U
Subscript	Ctrl+=
Superscript	Ctrl+Shift++ (plus sign)
Underline words but not space	Ctrl+Shift+W
Double underline text	Ctrl+Shift+D
Small caps	Ctrl+Shift+K
All caps	Ctrl+Shift+A

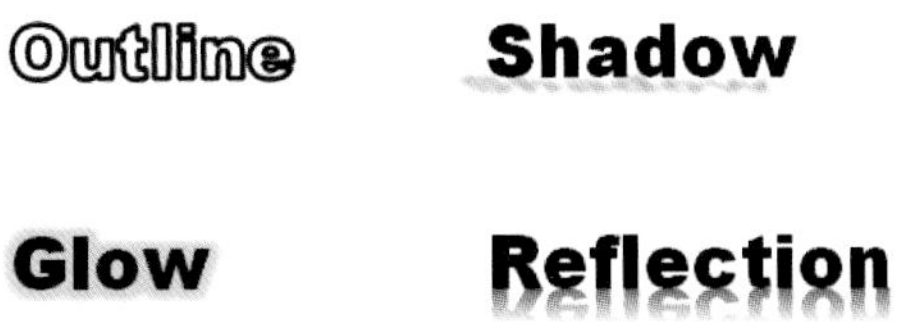

Outline   **Shadow**

Glow   **Reflection**

Figure 2-20

In the following exercise, you format some text by applying some attributes and effects to it.

Files needed: Chapter 2 Vacation, from the previous exercise

1. **In Word, in the** Chapter 2 Vacation **file, triple-click the title** *(Our Vacation)* **to select it.**

2. **On the Home tab, click the Text Effects button and click the second sample in the bottom row.**

   The text is formatted with an orange gradient fill and an inner shadow.

   See Figure 2-21.

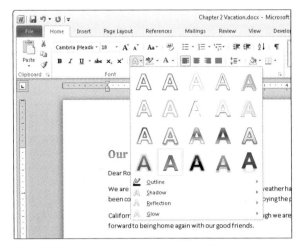

Figure 2-21

3. **Click the Text Effects button again, point to Reflection, and click the first effect in the Reflection Variations section.**

   See Figure 2-22.

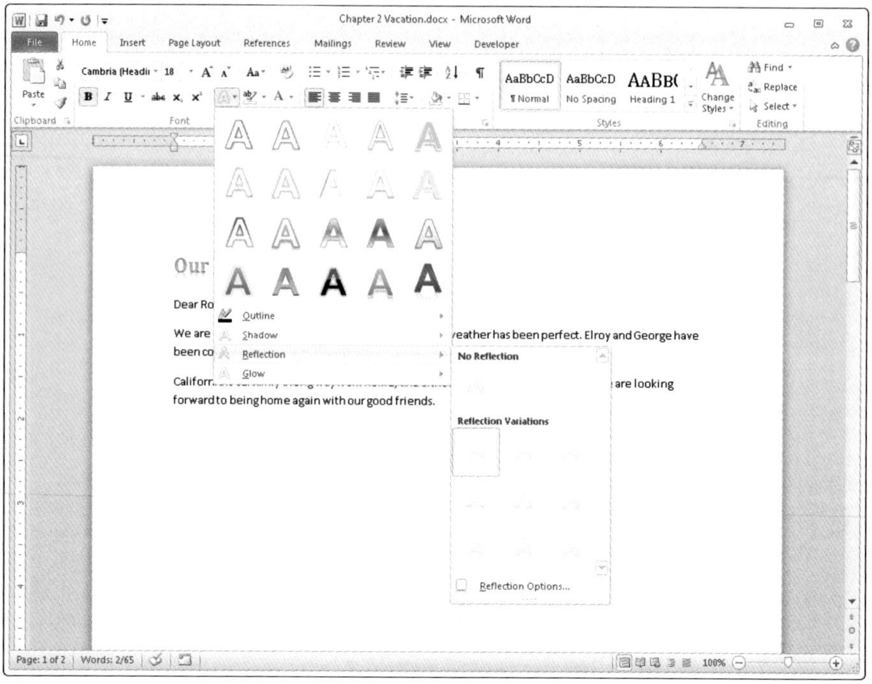

Chapter 2

Figure 2-22

4. **Click the Italic button on the Home tab.**

   The text is italicized.

5. **Click the dialog box launcher in the lower-right corner of the Font group on the Home tab.**

   See Figure 2-23. The Font dialog box opens.

Figure 2-23

6. **Select the Small Caps check box. See Figure 2-24. Then click OK.**

7. **Save your work.**

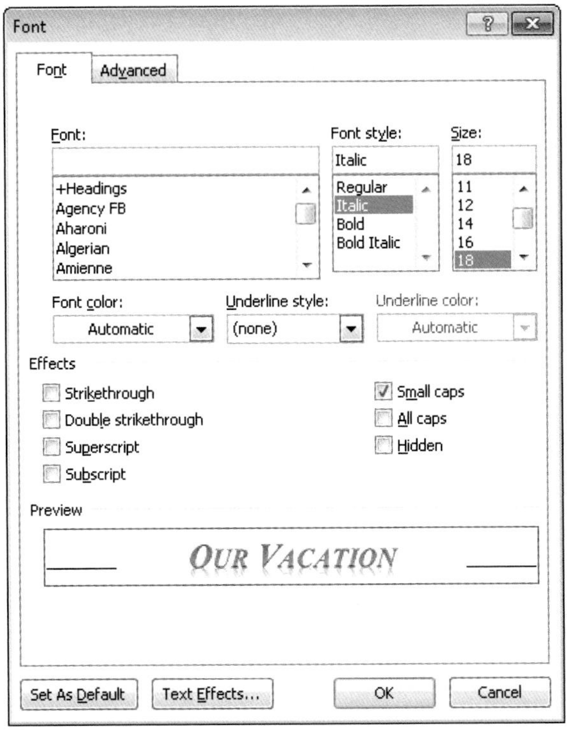

Font dialog box:

Font | Advanced

Font: | Font style: | Size:
| Italic | 18

+Headings | Regular | 11
Agency FB | Italic | 12
Aharoni | Bold | 14
Algerian | Bold Italic | 16
Amienne | | 18

Font color: | Underline style: | Underline color:
Automatic | (none) | Automatic

Effects

☐ Strikethrough | ☑ Small caps
☐ Double strikethrough | ☐ All caps
☐ Superscript | ☐ Hidden
☐ Subscript

Preview

OUR VACATION

Set As Default | Text Effects... | OK | Cancel

Figure 2-24

Leave the document open for the next exercise.

Working with themes

All the Office applications use the same set of themes, so themes can help you standardize the look of your work across multiple applications. For example, you could make the fonts and colors on a brochure you create in Word similar to a presentation you create in PowerPoint.

TIP In a Word document that contains only text, you won't notice the effect changes when you switch to a different theme, but the font and color changes will be apparent.

LINGO

A **theme** is a file that contains settings for fonts (heading and body), colors, and object formatting effects (such as 3D effects for drawn shapes and SmartArt diagrams, both of which you learn about in later chapters). Themes enable you to dramatically change the look of a document quickly.

You can also apply color themes, font themes, and/or effect themes separately. This ability is useful when none of the available themes exactly match what you want. After you make the selections you want to create the right combination of colors, fonts, and effects, you can save your choices as a new theme to use in other documents (including in Excel and PowerPoint as well as in Word).

Themes affect only text that hasn't had manual formatting applied that overrides the defaults. For example, if you've specified a certain font or font color for some text, that text doesn't change when you change the theme. You can strip off manual formatting with the Clear Formatting button on the Home tab.

In the following exercise, you format some text by applying some attributes and effects to it.

Files needed: Chapter 2 Vacation, from the previous exercise

1. **In Word, in the** Chapter 2 Vacation **file, click Page Layout, Themes.**

   A list of themes appears. See Figure 2-25.

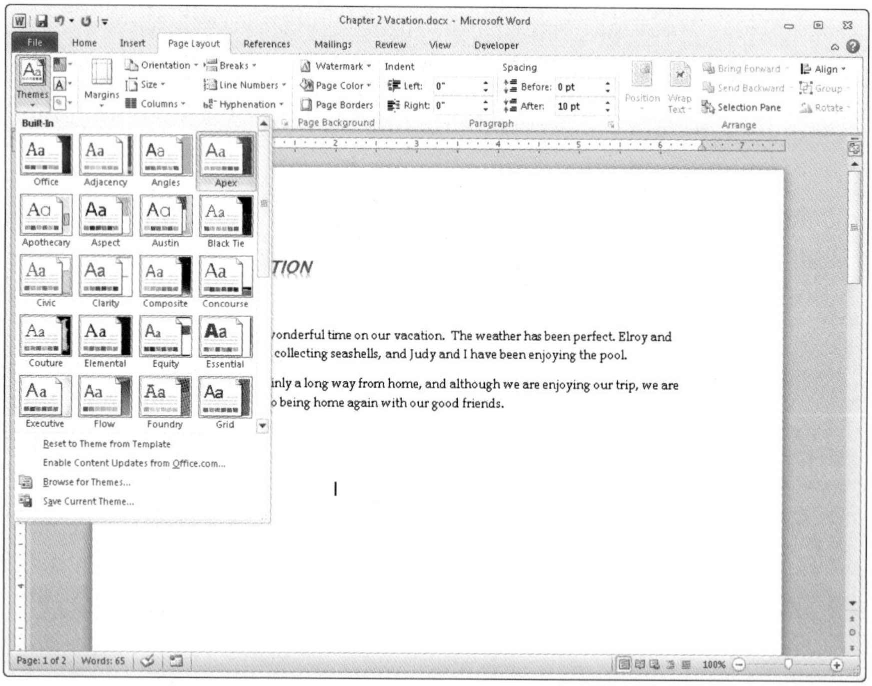

Figure 2-25

Before selecting a theme, point the mouse cursor at several other themes and see their effects in the text behind the open menu.

2. Click the Apex theme.

The colors and fonts in the document change to match the theme.

3. Click the Theme Fonts button.

A list of available theme font sets appears. See Figure 2-26.

Before selecting a font theme, point the mouse at several other font themes and see their effects in the text behind the open menu.

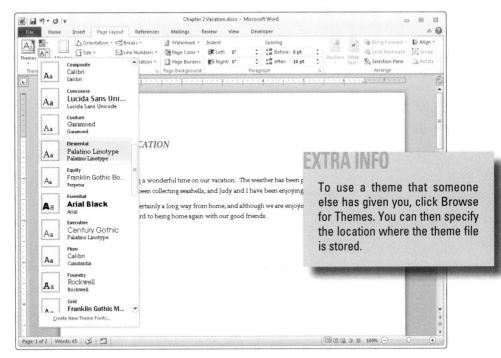

EXTRA INFO

To use a theme that someone else has given you, click Browse for Themes. You can then specify the location where the theme file is stored.

Figure 2-26

4. Click the Elemental font theme.

The fonts in the document change.

5. **Click the Theme Colors button.**

   A list of available theme color sets appears. See Figure 2-27.

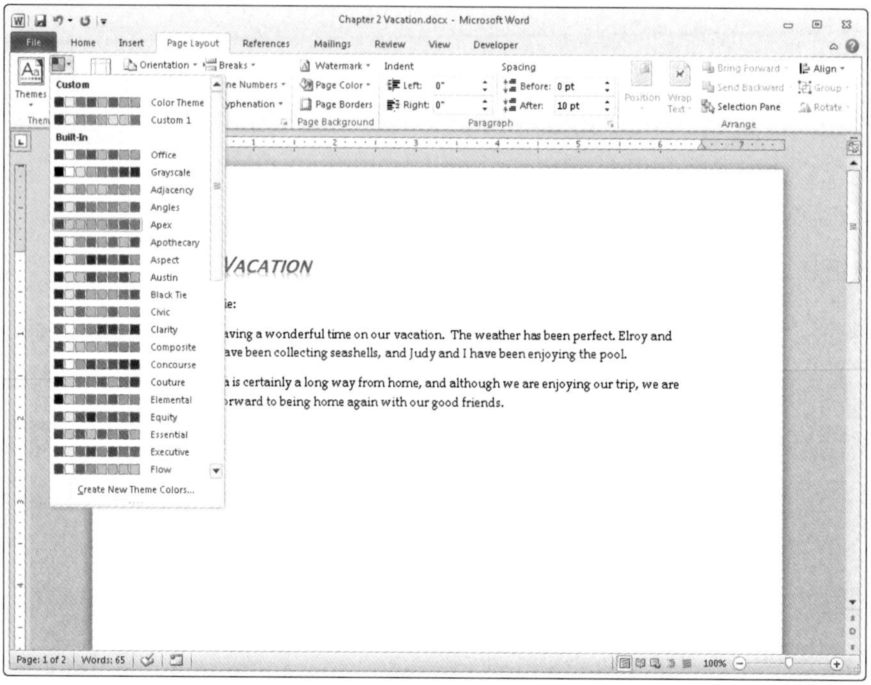

Figure 2-27

6. **Click the Module color theme.**

   The color of the heading changes from orange to red.

7. **Save your work and close the document.**

Leave Word open for the next exercise.

Applying style sets

LINGO

At the top of the Font list are two entries: one designated for Headings and one for Body. If you use these settings rather than specifying individual fonts, you can reformat the document by choosing a different **style set.** A style set is a preset combination of fonts, paragraph line spacing, character spacing, and indentation. Style sets enable you to quickly change the look of the document without manually reformatting each paragraph.

If you've manually applied specific fonts, as in the preceding exercise, you won't see a change when you apply a different style set. If you don't get the results you expect with a style set, select the entire document (Ctrl+A) and then clear the formatting by clicking the Clear Formatting button on the Home tab or by pressing Ctrl+spacebar.

In the following exercise, you format some text by applying different fonts, sizes, and colors to it.

Files needed: Chapter 2 Vacation, from the previous exercise

1. **In Word, in the** Chapter 2 Vacation **file, triple-click the title** *(Our Vacation)* **to select it, if it is not already selected.**

2. **Click the Clear Formatting button on the Home tab to remove all the formatting you've applied to the selected text.**

   See Figure 2-28.

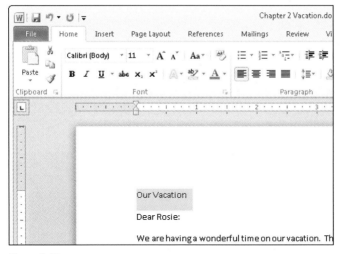

Figure 2-28

3. **Open the Font drop-down list and click Cambria (Headings) at the top of the list.**

4. **Select the rest of the document (everything except the *Our Vacation* paragraph). Then open the Font drop-down list and click Calibri (Body) at the top of the list.**

5. **On the Home tab, click the Change Styles button and point to Style Set.**

   A list of available style sets appears. See Figure 2-29.

Pointing to an item previews it. Point to each of the styles sets on the Style Set menu, one by one, and watch the document's formatting change.

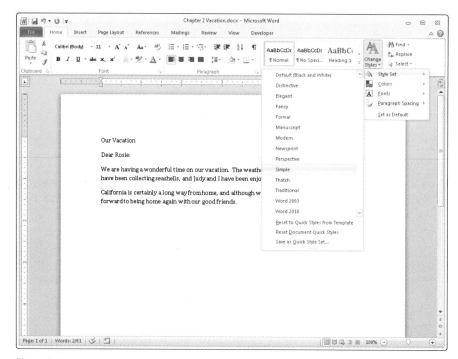

Figure 2-29

6. **Click Simple.**

   The Simple style set is applied. The paragraph formatted as a heading changes to the new font designated for headings, and the paragraphs formatted as body change to the new font designated for body text.

7. **Triple-click the *Our Vacation* paragraph and change the font size to 18 point. Then click away from the text to deselect it.**

   The document should look like Figure 2-30.

Our Vacation

Dear Rosie:

We are having a wonderful time on our vacation. The weather has been perfect. Elroy and George have been collecting seashells, and Judy and I have been enjoying the pool.

California is certainly a long way from home, and although we are enjoying our trip, we are looking forward to being home again with our good friends.

Figure 2-30

8. Save your work.

Leave the document open for the next exercise.

Checking Spelling and Grammar

Spelling and grammar errors in your documents can leave a bad impression with your audience, and can be the cause of lost customers, jobs, and opportunities. Fortunately, Word can help save you from the consequences of such errors, whether they're errors due to carelessness or errors due to lack of knowledge of spelling and grammar.

Word automatically checks your spelling and grammar as you type. Wavy red underlines indicate possible spelling errors, and wavy blue underlines indicate possible grammar errors. To correct one of these errors on the fly, right-click the underlined text and choose a quick correction from the shortcut menu.

You can also run the full-blown Spelling and Grammar utility within Word to check the entire document at once. One by one, each potential error appears in a dialog box, and you click buttons to decide how to deal with each one.

One of the choices when dealing with a potentially misspelled word is to add the word to the dictionary so that it isn't flagged as misspelled in any future spell check in any document. The dictionary file is common to all the Office applications, so any word you add to the dictionary in Word will also no longer be flagged as misspelled in Excel, PowerPoint, or Outlook.

Word has a more robust and powerful Spelling and Grammar checker than the other Office applications do, but they all have similar functionality. After you learn how to check spelling in Word, you can also do it in the other Office apps.

In the following exercise, you correct spelling and grammar errors in a document.

Files needed: `Chapter 2 Spelling.docx`

1. **In Word, open the Chapter 2 Spelling file and save it as Chapter 2 Spelling Corrected.**

2. **Right-click the misspelled word *eerors* and, on the shortcut menu, click the correct spelling, *errors*.**

   See Figure 2-31.

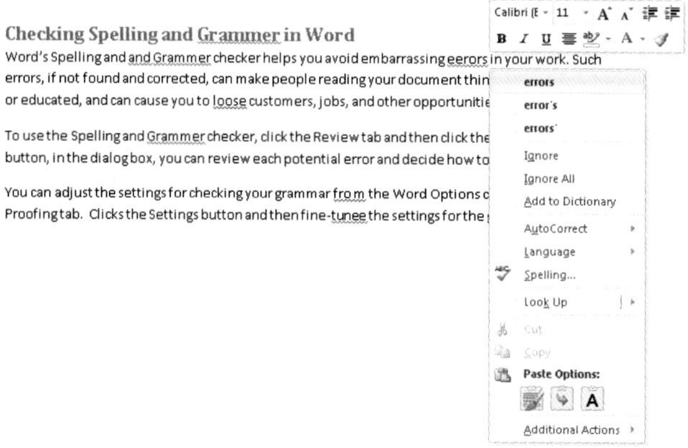

Figure 2-31

3. **Click at the beginning of the document to move the insertion point there.**

4. **On the Review tab, click Spelling & Grammar.**

   The Spelling and Grammar dialog box opens, with the first mistake high-lighted (Grammer). See Figure 2-32.

5. **Click Change All to change all instances of *grammer* to *grammar*.**

   The next mistake found is a duplicate word: *and and.*

6. **Click Delete to delete one of the instances.**

   The next mistake found is a possible grammar area: the capitalization of *Spelling.* In this case, the capitalization is correct.

7. **Click Ignore Once to skip the correctly capitalized word.**

   The next mistake found is the misuse of *loose* to mean *lose.*

Checking Spelling and Grammer in Word

Word's Spelling and and Grammer checker helps you avoid embarrassing errors in your work. Such
errors, if not found and corrected, can make people reading your document think you're less intelligent
or educated, and can c...

To use the Spelling and...
button, in the dialog b...

You can adjust the sett...
Proofing tab. Clicks th...

Figure 2-32

8. **Click Change to change to the correct word.**

   The next mistake found is an extra space in the word *from*.

9. **Click Change to remove the extra space.**

   The next mistake is the misspelling of *tune* as *tunee*.

10. **Click Change to make the change.**

    A dialog box appears to tell you that the spell check is complete.

11. **Click OK to accept it.**

12. **Save your work.**

Leave the document open for the next exercise.

Sharing Your Document with Others

If the people with whom you want to share your work are also Office 2010 users, sharing with them is easy. Just give them your data file. You can transfer a data file to someone else via a USB drive, a portable disc such as writeable CD or DVD, or e-mail. Users of Office 2007 can also work freely with your Office 2010 data files because the file formats are identical.

To share with people who don't have Office 2007 or 2010, you can save in other formats. Word (and the other Office apps) support a variety of saving formats, so you're sure to find a format that bridges the distance between Office and the program that your recipient has to work with.

E-mailing your document to others

Some versions of Office include Microsoft Outlook, an e-mail, calendar, and contact management program. If you don't have Outlook, you might have some other e-mail program, such as Windows Mail (which comes with Windows Vista and is available for free download for other Windows versions), Outlook Express (which comes with Windows XP), or some non-Microsoft program like Eudora. When you send a document via e-mail from within Word, Word calls up your default e-mail application, whatever that may be. The steps in this book assume Outlook 2010 is your default e-mail application; your steps might be different if you have something else.

LINGO

One way to distribute your work to others is to send it to them via e-mail. Your document piggy-backs on an e-mail as an **attachment**. An attachment is a file that's separate from the body of the e-mail, travelling along with the e-mail to its destination.

 WARNING!

If you use a Web-based e-mail application, such as Hotmail, Gmail, or Yahoo mail, you can't follow along with the steps in this section. You can still send Word files as e-mail attachments, but you can't initiate the process from within Word. You start a new e-mail message from within the Web interface and then attach the file from there.

In the following exercise, you send a document to yourself as an e-mail attachment. These steps assume that Outlook is your default e-mail program and that your e-mail account is already set up in it.

Files needed: Chapter 2 Spelling.docx, *from the previous exercise*

1. **In Word, with** Chapter 2 Spelling **open, choose File⇨Save & Send.**

2. **Click Send As Attachment.**

   A new message opens in Outlook (or your default e-mail application) with the Chapter 2 Spelling.docx file already attached. The filename also appears in the Subject line. See Figure 2-33.

3. **Click in the To box and type your own e-mail address there.**

4. **Click Send.**

   The file is sent to you.

5. **In Outlook, on the Home tab, click Send/Receive All Folders.**

   You receive the sent file as a new message in your Inbox.

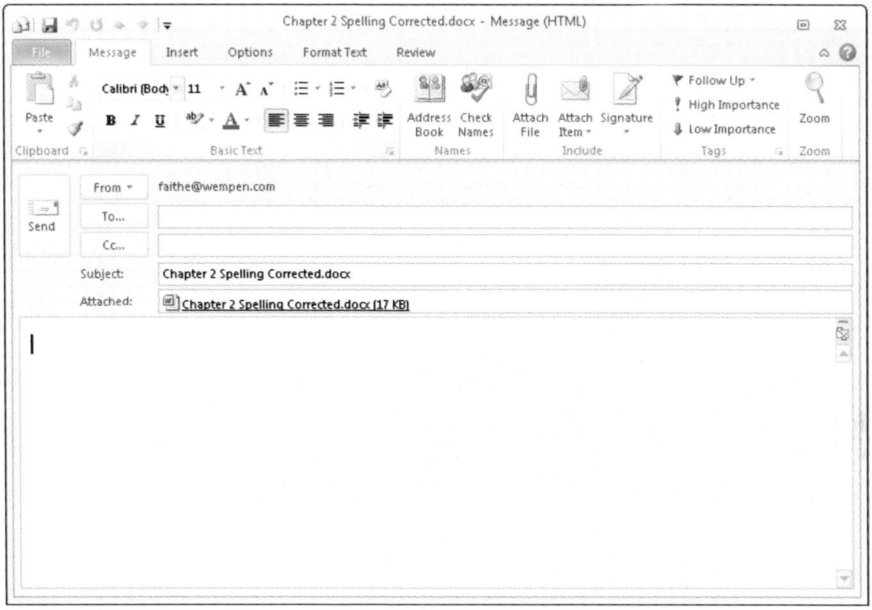

Figure 2-33

TIP If it doesn't come immediately, repeat the Send/Receive All Folders command.

6. **Close Outlook and return to Word.**

7. **Close the document (but not Word), saving your changes if prompted.**

Leave Word open for the next exercise.

Sharing your document in other formats

If your intended recipients use earlier versions of Office or don't have Office at all, you must save your work in another format before transferring the file to them. All the Office programs allow you to export your work in other formats, so you can transfer just about any data to just about any other application.

WARNING!

The farther away you get from the original version of the file, the more formatting features you lose. For example, saving in Word 2010 format preserves the most features, and saving in Word 97–2003 format loses some features. RTF loses still more, and plain text loses all formatting.

In the following exercise, you save a file in two different formats.

Files needed: `Chapter 2 Distribution.docx`

1. **In Word, open Chapter 2 Distribution.**

2. **Choose File⇨Save As.**

   The Save As dialog box opens.

3. **Open the Save As Type drop-down list and click Word 97–2003 Document.**

   See Figure 2-34.

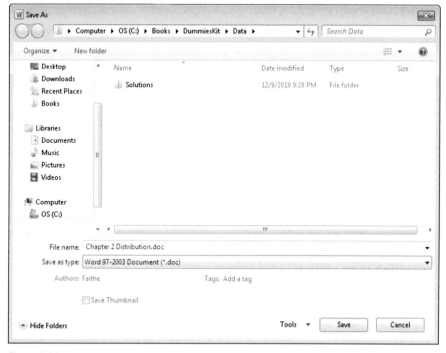

Figure 2-34

4. **Click Save.**

   Your document is saved in a format that's compatible with earlier Word versions (Word 97 through Word 2003). It's also usable in Word 2007 and Word 2010.

5. **Choose File⇨Save As.**

6. **Open the Save As Type drop-down list and click Rich Text Format.**

7. **Click Save.**

   Your document is saved in Rich Text Format. This format is useful for exchanging data with someone who has a different brand of Word processor, such as WordPerfect.

Leave the document open for the next exercise.

Printing Your Work

Another way to distribute your work is by printing it, provided you have access to a printer. You can do a quick print with the default settings, or you can specify a certain printer, number of copies, page range, and other settings.

In the following exercise, you print a document.

Files needed: `Chapter 2 Distribution.docx`, *or any other document file*

1. **In Word, with `Chapter 2 Distribution.docx` open, choose File⇨Print.**

2. **In the Copies box, click the up arrow once to change the number to 2. Then click the down arrow to change it back to 1.**

3. **Open the Printer drop-down list and select the printer you want to use.**

   See Figure 2-35.

For more practice, check out the additional print options. For example, you can change the page range, orientation, the paper size, the margins, and the duplex setting (that is, print one-sided or two-sided). The settings for duplex and collation, as well as for printing only specific pages, don't apply to the document used in this exercise because it has only one page.

4. **Click Print.**

   The document prints.

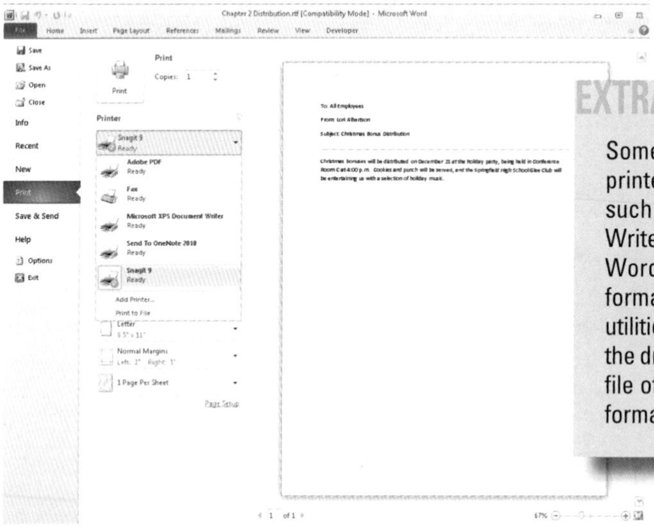

Figure 2-35

Want more help learning the basics of Word document creation and editing? Go to this address and click any of the Word tutorials listed there:

http://office.microsoft.com/en-us/word-help/CH010369478.aspx

EXTRA INFO

Some of the items on the list of printers are not actually printers, such as Microsoft XPS Document Writer, or Send to OneNote 2010. Word outputs to some external formats by treating the converter utilities as printers. You "print" to the driver, which then generates a file of the document in a different format.

 Summing Up

Word makes it easy to create a basic document. You can either start typing in the blank document that opens automatically at startup, or choose one of the templates provided. Here are the key points this chapter covered:

✔ To start a new blank document, press Ctrl+N, or choose File⇨New and then click Blank Document.

✔ To start a document based on a template, choose File⇨New, pick the template you want, and then click Create.

✔ To set page margins, click Page Layout, Margins.

✔ To change the paper size, click Page Layout, Size.

✔ Portrait and Landscape are the two page orientations. Portrait is the default. To switch, click Page Layout, Orientation.

✔ Fonts, or typefaces, are lettering styles. Choose a font from the Home tab or from the Mini toolbar.

✔ Font sizes are measured in points. A point is 1/72 of an inch. Choose font sizes from the Home tab or from the Mini toolbar.

✔ A style set applies a different appearance to a document including fonts, paragraph spacing, character spacing, and indentation. To change the style set, click Home, Change Styles, Style Set.

✔ Some text attributes and effects can be applied from the Mini toolbar or the Font group on the Home tab. Others must be applied from the Font dialog box. To open the Font dialog box, click the dialog box launcher icon in the Font group.

✔ A theme is a file that contains settings for fonts, colors, and object formatting effects. Apply a theme by clicking Page Layout, Themes.

✔ Word checks spelling and grammar automatically, and underlines errors with either red wavy underline (for spelling) or blue wavy underline (for grammar).

✔ You can also launch a full spelling and grammar check by clicking Review, Spelling & Grammar.

✔ To e-mail your document to others, choose File⇨Save & Send and then click Send As Attachment.

✔ To print your document, choose File⇨Print.

Try-it-yourself lab

For more practice with the features covered in this chapter, try the following exercise on your own.

1. **Start Word and write a description of a funny or embarrassing incident that happened recently to you or someone you know.**

2. **Add a new paragraph at the beginning of the document and type a title there (such as** My Most Embarrassing Day Ever**).**

3. **Format the title with an eye-catching font, font size, and color. Use one of the theme colors.**

4. **Apply a different style set to the document.**

5. **Apply a different theme to the document.**

6. **Check your spelling and grammar and make any corrections needed.**

7. **E-mail the document to yourself or to a friend you want to share it with.**

8. **Print one copy of the document.**
9. **Close Word.**

Know this tech talk

attachment: A file attached to an e-mail so that the file is sent along with the message.

attributes: Formatting options such as bold, italics, and underline.

character formatting: Formatting that affects individual characters, such as font choices. Contrast this to paragraph formatting, such as indentation and line spacing, that affects only entire paragraphs.

effects: Special WordArt-style effects applied to text such as glow, reflection, and shadowing.

font: Also called a *typeface.* A style of lettering, such as Arial, Times New Roman, or Calibri.

insertion point: In a text editing application, a flashing vertical line indicating where text will be inserted when typed.

landscape: A page orientation in which the wide part of the paper forms the top and bottom.

margins: The space between the edge of the paper and the text.

orientation: The direction the text runs on a piece of paper where one dimension is greater than the other. See also *portrait* and *landscape.*

point: A unit of measure that's $\frac{1}{72}$ of an inch. Font size is measured in points.

portrait: A page orientation in which the narrow part of the paper forms the top and bottom.

standard color: A fixed color that doesn't change when you change to a different theme.

style set: A set of font, indentation, and line spacing options.

template: An example file on which new documents may be based.

theme: A set of font, color, and graphic effect settings stored in a separate file, accessible to all Office applications.

theme color: A set of color choices that are applied to color placeholders in a document.

typeface: See *font.*

Paragraph Formatting, Styles, and Tables

- ✔ Paragraph formatting enables you to *control the indentation, line spacing, and horizontal alignment* of a paragraph.

- ✔ *Indenting a paragraph can set it off visually* from the rest of the document for greater emphasis.

- ✔ *To make a text-heavy document easier to read,* increase its line spacing so that more space appears between each line.

- ✔ Create a numbered list to *organize a list in which the order of the items is significant;* use a bulleted list when the order is not significant.

- ✔ Apply styles to paragraphs that have similar functions, such as headings or quotations, to *ensure formatting consistency throughout the document.*

- ✔ Using tables allows you to *organize complex sets of data in an orderly fashion.*

1. **What is justified alignment?**

It's lined up for you on page.. 92

2. **How do you create a hanging indent?**

The answer is hanging out on page... 94

3. **How do you double-space a document?**

March double-time to page... 98

4. **How do you create a numbered list that uses Roman numerals?**

Do as they do on page.. 106

Paragraphs are essential building blocks in a Word document. Each time you press Enter, you start a new paragraph. If you've ever seen a document where the author didn't use paragraph breaks, you know how important paragraphs can be. They break up the content into more easily understandable chunks, which helps the reader both visually and logically.

In this chapter, you learn how to apply various types of formatting to paragraphs, and how to simplify and automate paragraph formatting by using text formatting presets called styles. This chapter also takes a look at tables, which are row-and-column grid structures that you can place in a document to help organize bits of text in an orderly way.

Formatting Paragraphs

If you apply paragraph formatting when no text is selected, the formatting applies to the paragraph in which the insertion point is currently located.

If you apply paragraph formatting when text is selected, the formatting applies to whatever paragraphs are included in that selection, even if only one character of the paragraph is included. Being able to format paragraphs this way is useful because you can select multiple paragraphs at once and then format them as a group.

LINGO

Paragraph formatting is formatting that affects whole paragraphs and cannot be applied to individual characters. For example, line spacing is a type of paragraph formatting, along with indentation and alignment.

TIP

To set the paragraph formatting for the entire document at once, press Ctrl+A to select the entire document and then issue the paragraph formatting commands.

Applying horizontal alignment

The horizontal alignment choices are Align Text Left, Align Text Right, Center, and Justify. Figure 3-1 shows an example of each of the alignment types.

LINGO

Horizontal alignment refers to the positioning of the paragraph between the right and left margins.

Each of those is pretty self-evident except the last one. *Justify* aligns both the left and right sides of the paragraph with the margins, stretching out or compressing the text in each line as needed to make it fit. The final line in the paragraph is exempt and appears left-aligned.

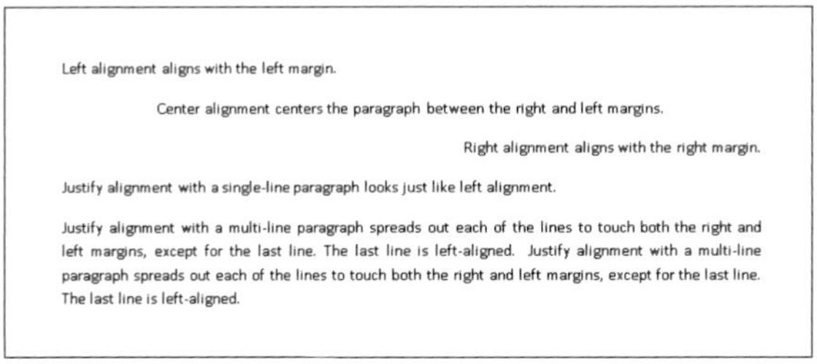

Left alignment aligns with the left margin.

Center alignment centers the paragraph between the right and left margins.

Right alignment aligns with the right margin.

Justify alignment with a single-line paragraph looks just like left alignment.

Justify alignment with a multi-line paragraph spreads out each of the lines to touch both the right and left margins, except for the last line. The last line is left-aligned. Justify alignment with a multi-line paragraph spreads out each of the lines to touch both the right and left margins, except for the last line. The last line is left-aligned.

Figure 3-1

REMEMBER

If you apply Justify alignment to a paragraph that contains only one line, it looks like it is left-aligned. However, if you then type more text into the paragraph, so it wraps to additional lines, the Justify alignment becomes apparent.

In the following exercise, you apply horizontal alignment changes to a business letter.

Files needed: Chapter 3 Time Out.docx

1. In Word, open `Chapter 3 Time Out.docx` from the data files for this chapter and save it as Chapter 3 Time Out Letter.

2. Select the first three lines (the facility's name and address) and click the Center button on the Home tab or press Ctrl+E.

   See Figure 3-2.

3. Click in the first body paragraph (the paragraph that starts with "Thank you . . .") and click the Justify button on the Home tab.

   The paragraph changes to Justify alignment.

Figure 3-2

4. Select the last four body paragraphs of the document (starting with "Our sales and support staff . . .") and click the Justify button again.

   Those paragraphs change to Justify alignment. Figure 3-3 shows the results.

Figure 3-3

5. Save the changes to the document.

Leave Word and the document file open for the next exercise.

Indenting a paragraph

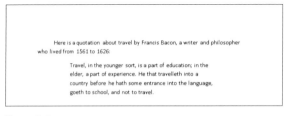

Figure 3-4

LINGO

When a paragraph has no indentation, it's allowed to take up the full range of space between the left and right margins. When you set **indentation** for a paragraph, its left and/or right sides are inset by the amount you specify. Many people like to indent quotations to set them apart from the rest of the text for emphasis, for example, as in Figure 3-4.

First-line indents are sometimes used in reports and books to help the reader's eye catch the beginning of a paragraph. In layouts where there is vertical space between paragraphs, first-line indents are less useful because it's easy to see where a new paragraph begins without that help. Hanging indents are typically used to create listings. In a bulleted or numbered list, the bullet or number hangs off the left edge of the paragraph, in a hanging indent. However, in Word, when you create bulleted or numbered lists (covered later in this chapter), Word adjusts the paragraph's hanging indent automatically, so you don't have to think about it.

In the following exercise, you apply indents to paragraphs in a letter.

Files needed: `Chapter 3 Time Out Letter. docx`

LINGO

In addition to a left and right indent value, each paragraph can optionally have a special indent for the first line. If the first line is indented more than the rest of the paragraph, it's known as a **first-line indent**. (Clever name.) If the first line is indented less than the rest of the paragraph, it's called a **hanging indent**.

1. **In Word, with the `Chapter 3 Time Out Letter.docx` document still open from the previous exercise, triple-click the paragraph containing the quotation to select it (the paragraph that begins with "I really enjoy . . .").**

2. **Click the Increase Indent button on the Home tab.**

   The left indent increases by 0.5 inch. See Figure 3-5.

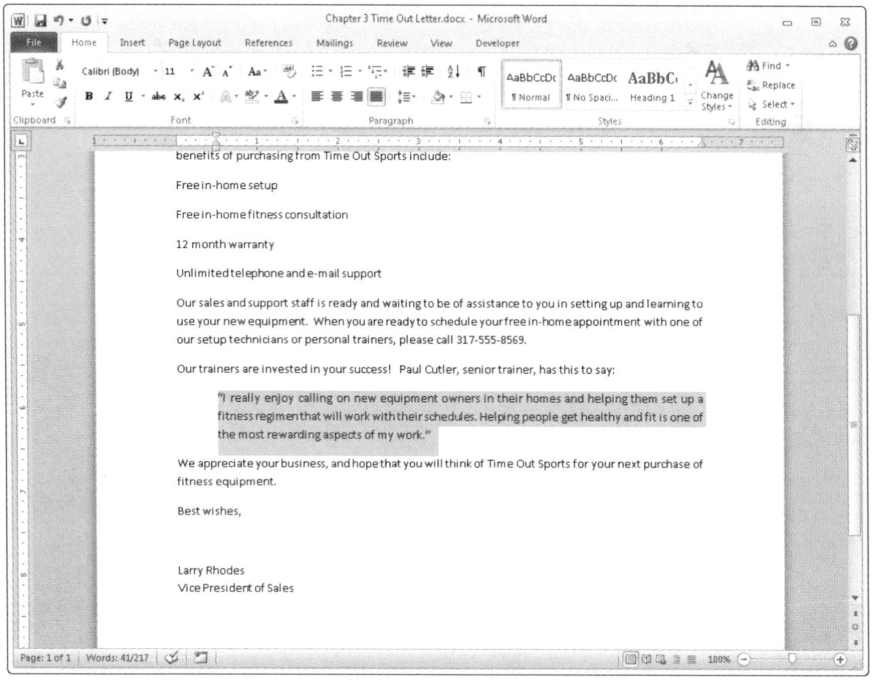

Figure 3-5

3. **Click the dialog box launcher in the Paragraph group to open the Paragraph dialog box.**

4. **Click the up increment arrow on the Right text box to increase the right indent to 0.5 inch.**

   See Figure 3-6.

5. **Click OK.**

   Now the paragraph is indented 0.5 inch on each side.

6. **Click in the paragraph that begins "Our sales . . ." and click the dialog box launcher again to reopen the Paragraph dialog box.**

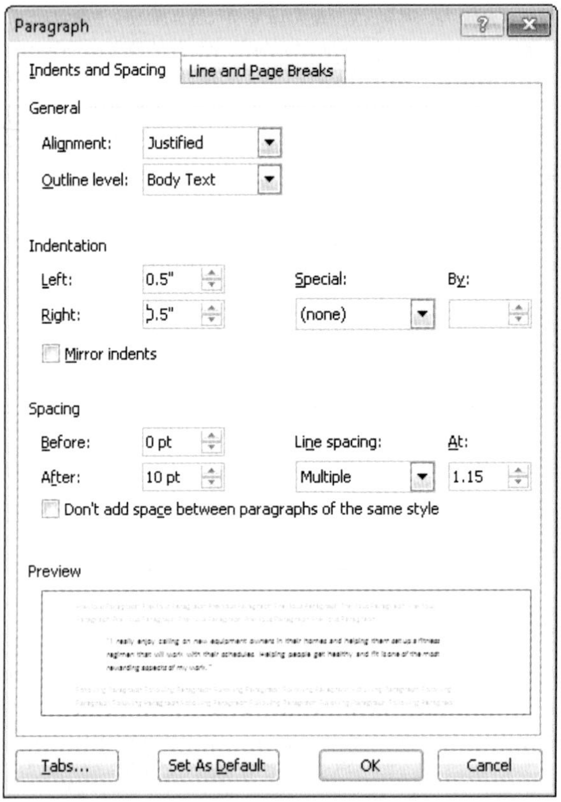

Figure 3-6

7. **Open the Special drop-down list and select First Line.**

   A first line indent default value of 0.5 inch appears. See Figure 3-7.

8. Click OK.

That paragraph is now first-line indented by 0.5 inch.

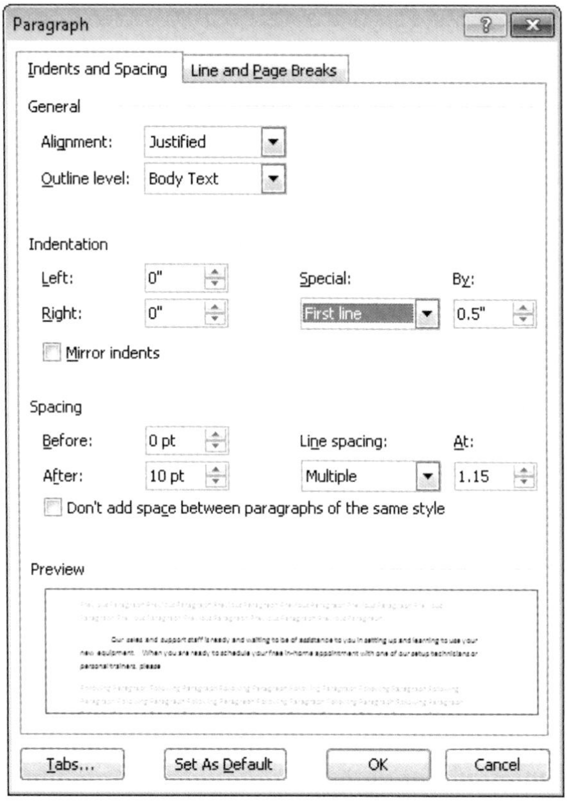

Paragraph
Indents and Spacing
Line and Page Breaks
General
Alignment:
Justified
Outline level:
Body Text
Indentation
Left:
0"
Right:
0"
Special:
By:
First line
0.5"
Mirror indents
Spacing
Before:
0 pt
After:
10 pt
Line spacing:
At:
Multiple
1.15
Don't add space between paragraphs of the same style
Preview
Tabs...
Set As Default
OK
Cancel

Figure 3-7

EXTRA INFO

You can also create a first-line indent by positioning the insertion point at the beginning of a paragraph and pressing the Tab key. Normally this would place a 0.5-inch tab at the beginning of the paragraph, but Word's AutoCorrect feature immediately converts it to a real first-line indent for you.

PRACTICE

For more practice, try setting a hanging indent for one of the remaining paragraphs. Choose Hanging from the Special drop-down list in the Paragraph dialog box. When you're finished, press Ctrl+Z to undo.

9. Save the changes to the document.

Leave Word and the document file open for the next exercise.

Changing vertical spacing

You can set line spacing to any of several presets, such as Single, Double, and 1.5 Lines, or to an exact value, measured in points. You may remember from Chapter 2 that a *point* is ¹⁄₇₂ of an inch. Space before and after a paragraph is specified in points, too.

WARNING!

If you specify an exact amount of space per line and you change the font size, the text may not look right anymore. For example, if you change the font size to a larger size than the exact spacing is set for, the lines might overlap vertically. If you aren't sure what font sizes you need, don't use exact spacing.

LINGO

Vertical spacing refers to the amount of space (also known as the **leading**) between each line. A paragraph has three values you can set for its spacing.

Line spacing: The space between the lines within a multi-line paragraph.

Before: Extra spacing added above the first line of the paragraph.

After: Extra spacing added below the last line of the paragraph.

In the following exercise, you change the line spacing for paragraphs in a letter.

Files needed: `Chapter 3 Time Out Letter.docx`

1. **In Word, with the `Chapter 3 Time Out Letter.docx` document still open from the previous exercise, press Ctrl+A to select the entire document.**

2. **Click the Line Spacing button on the Home tab, opening its menu, and choose 1.0.**

   The line spacing in every paragraph changes to single-spacing. See Figure 3-8.

3. **Select the paragraph beginning with "Free in-home setup . . ." and the next two paragraphs following it.**

4. **Click the Line Spacing button again and then choose Remove Space After Paragraph.**

   See Figure 3-9.

5. **Select the Time Out Sports heading at the top of the document.**

6. **Click the Line Spacing button again and then choose Line Spacing Options.**

   The Paragraph dialog box opens.

Figure 3-8

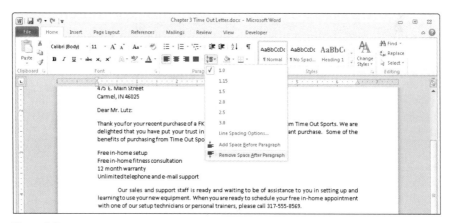

Figure 3-9

TIP

You can also click the dialog box launcher for the Paragraph group to open the Paragraph dialog box if you prefer that method.

7. Decrease the value in the After text box to 6 pt.

See Figure 3-10.

8. Click OK to accept the new setting.

9. Triple-click the quotation paragraph to select it.

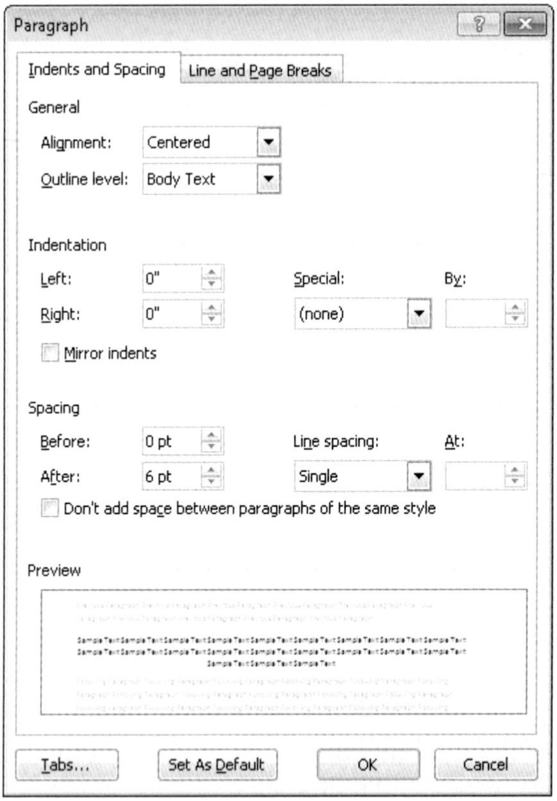

Figure 3-10

10. Click the Line Spacing button again and choose Line Spacing Options.

The Paragraph dialog box opens again.

11. Open the Line Spacing drop-down list and choose Exactly, and type 15 **into the text box to its right.**

See Figure 3-11.

Paragraph	? ✕

Indents and Spacing   Line and Page Breaks

General

Alignment: Justified ▼

Outline level: Body Text ▼

Indentation

Left: 0.5" ⬍   Special: By:

Right: 0.5" ⬍   (none) ▼   ⬍

☐ Mirror indents

Spacing

Before: 0 pt ⬍   Line spacing: At:

After: 10 pt ⬍   Exactly ▼   15 pt ⬍

☐ Don't add space between paragraphs of the same style

Preview

Tabs...	Set As Default	OK	Cancel

Figure 3-11

12. Click OK to accept the new setting.

For more practice, set the font size for the paragraph you just formatted to 24 points and watch what happens to the line spacing. It stays at 15 points, and the lines overlap. Press Ctrl+Z to undo when you're finished experimenting.

13. Save the changes to the document.

Leave Word and the document file open for the next exercise.

Creating Bulleted and Numbered Lists

You can create a list from existing paragraphs, or you can turn on the list feature and type the list as you go. Either way, you're working with the Bullets button or the Numbering button on the Home tab.

Creating a basic numbered or bulleted list

In the following exercise, you convert some paragraphs into a numbered list and then change it to a bulleted list.

Files needed: Chapter 3 Time Out Letter. docx

1. **In Word, with the Chapter 3 Time Out Letter.docx document still open from the previous exercise, select the list of four benefits, starting with "Free in-home setup . . .".**

2. **Click the Numbering button on the Home tab.**

   The list becomes numbered.

3. **Click the Bullets button.**

   The list switches to a bulleted list. See Figure 3-12.

Leave Word and the document file open for the next exercise.

LINGO

Word makes it easy to create bulleted and numbered lists in your documents. Use a **bulleted list** for lists where the order of items isn't significant, and the same "bullet" character (such as • or ⇨) is used in front of each item. You might use a bulleted list for a packing list for a trip, for example, or a go-forward list. In contrast, use a **numbered list** for lists where the order of items *is* significant and a where sequential step number is used to indicate order. A numbered list might contain the steps for a recipe or a meeting agenda.

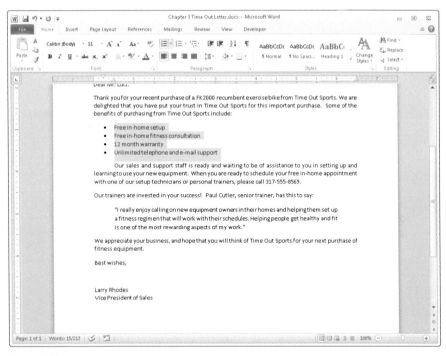

Figure 3-12

Changing the bullet character

You can use any character you like for the bullets in a bulleted list; you're not limited to the standard black circle. Word offers a choice of several common characters on the Bullets button's palette, and you can also select any picture or character from any font to use.

In the following exercise, you change the bullet character to several different text-based and graphical.

Files needed: `Chapter 3 Time Out Letter.docx`

1. **In Word, with the `Chapter 3 Time Out Letter.docx` document still open from the previous exercise, select the four bulleted paragraphs.**

2. **Click the down arrow on the Bullets button, opening its palette.**

   See Figure 3-13.

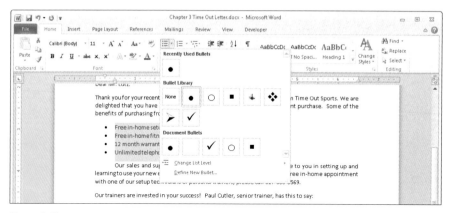

Figure 3-13

3. **Click the check mark bullet.**

   The list changes to use that character.

4. **Click the down arrow on the Bullets button again, reopening its palette.**

5. **Choose Define New Bullet.**

   The Define New Bullet dialog box opens.

6. **Click the Symbol button.**

   The Symbol dialog box opens.

7. **Open the Font drop-down list and select Wingdings.**

   See Figure 3-14.

8. **Click the six-pointed black star in the top row.**

9. **Click OK to close the Symbol dialog box.**

10. **Click OK to close the Define New Bullet dialog box.**

    The bulleted list appears with the new star bullets.

11. **Click the down arrow on the Bullets button again, reopening its palette.**

12. **Choose Define New Bullet.**

    The Define New Bullet dialog box opens.

13. **Click the Picture button.**

    The Picture Bullet dialog box opens. See Figure 3-15.

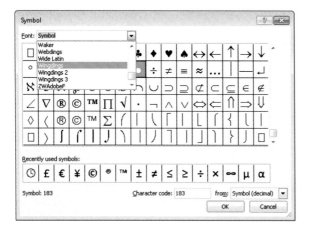

Figure 3-14

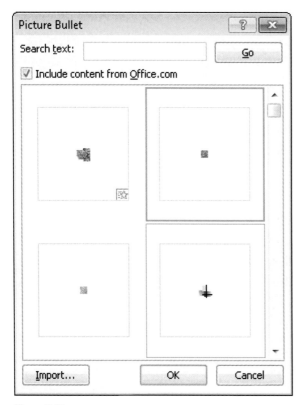

Figure 3-15

14. **Click any of the picture bullets that appeals to you and then click OK.**

15. **Click OK to close the Define New Bullet dialog box.**

    The picture bullets appear on the list.

16. **Save the changes to the document.**

Leave Word and the document file open for the next exercise.

Changing the numbering style

Changing the numbering style is much like changing the bullet character, except you have a few extra options, like choosing a starting number. You can select from various styles of numbering that include uppercase or lowercase letters, Roman numerals, or Arabic (regular) numerals.

In the following exercise, you change the numbering format for a numbered list.

Files needed: `Chapter 3 Time Out Letter.docx`

1. **In Word, with the `Chapter 3 Time Out Letter.docx` document still open from the previous exercise, select the four bulleted paragraphs if they aren't already selected.**

2. **Click the down arrow on the Numbering button on the Home tab, opening its palette.**

3. **In the Numbering Library section of the palette, click the numbering style that uses uppercase letters.**

    See Figure 3-16.

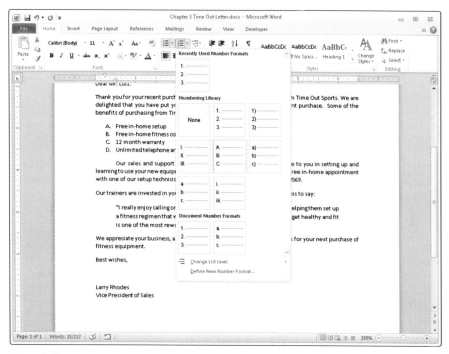

Figure 3-16

4. **Click the down arrow on the Numbering button on the Home tab and then click Define New Number Format.**

5. **In the Number Format text box, delete the period following the shaded A and type a colon (:).**

See Figure 3-17.

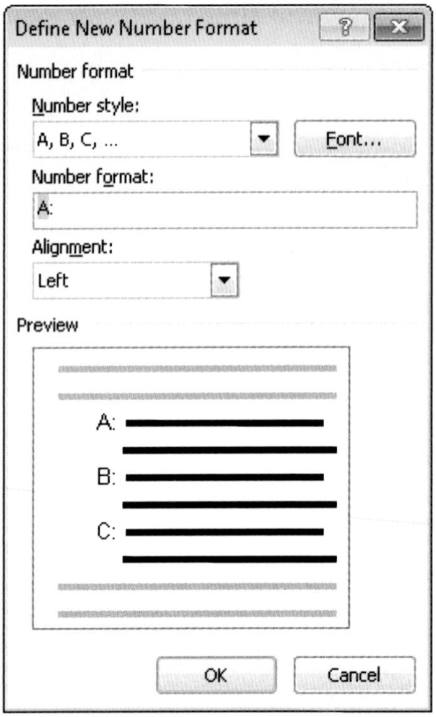

Figure 3-17

6. **Click the Font button.**

   The Font dialog box opens.

7. **Set the Font Size to 14 points.**

   See Figure 3-18.

8. **Click OK to return to the Define New Number Format dialog box and then click OK to accept the new format.**

   The list now appears with extra-large letters, followed by colons. See Figure 3-19.

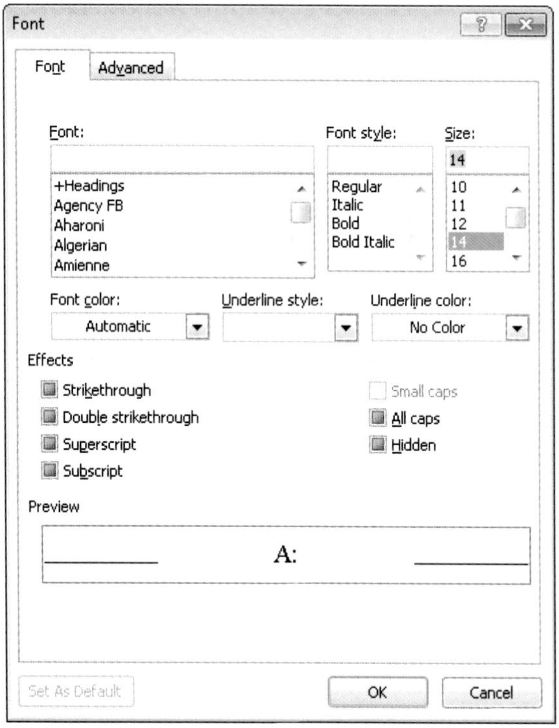

Figure 3-18

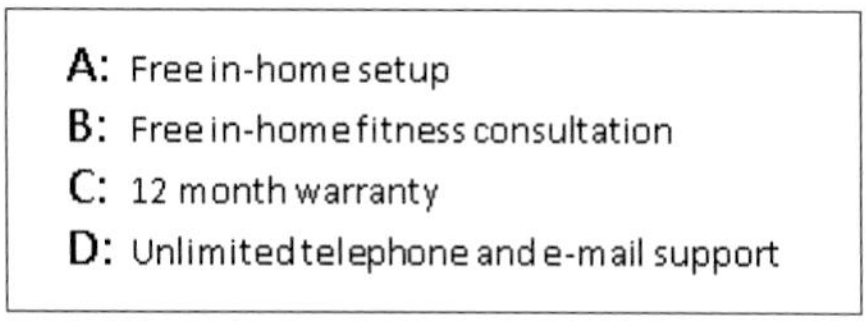
A: Free in-home setup
B: Free in-home fitness consultation
C: 12 month warranty
D: Unlimited telephone and e-mail support

Figure 3-19

9. Save the changes to the document and close it.

Leave Word open for the next exercise in Chapter 4.

Summing Up

Word provides several ways to format paragraphs and tables and to help automate formatting. Here are the key points from this chapter:

- To apply horizontal alignment, use the buttons in the Paragraph group on the Home tab. Your choices are Align Text Left, Align Text Right, Center, and Justify.

- A paragraph can be indented at the left or right (all lines) and can have a first-line or hanging indent applied.

- To indent the entire paragraph at the left, you can use the Increase Indent button in the Paragraph group on the Home tab.

- To set other indentation, open the Paragraph dialog box by clicking the dialog box launcher in the Paragraph group.

- You can set vertical spacing from the Line and Paragraph Spacing button on the Home tab or from the Paragraph dialog box.

- To create a default numbered or bulleted list, use their respective buttons on the Home tab. Each button has a drop-down list from which you can select other bullet or numbering styles.

- Styles are named formatting combinations that are stored in the template. You can apply them to paragraphs to quickly format the paragraphs with standardized settings.

- Some styles are available on the Quick Style gallery on the Home tab; others must be applied from the Styles task pane.

- You can redefine a style by example, or you can manually edit a style's definition.

- You can create a new table from the Insert tab either by specifying a number of rows and columns or by drawing the table. You can also convert existing delimited text into a table.

- You can drag the borders of a table to resize rows and columns.

- Tables have gridlines (nonprinting lines that show where the rows and columns are) and, optionally, borders (formatting applied to the gridlines).

- You can format a table's borders from the Table Tools Design tab.

Try-it-yourself Lab

For more practice with the features covered in this chapter, try the following exercise on your own.

1. **Use the Internet to research a new technology or medical advance that interests you.**

2. **Using Word, write a report that summarizes what you learned. Use Word's built-in styles to format the report (Title, Heading 1, Heading 2, and so on).**

3. **Create a new style and name it Body. Format it using a different font than Normal style uses. Apply the Body style to all the body paragraphs in your document.**

4. **Center the document title at the top of the document.**

5. **Write your name above the title. Format it with the Subtitle style and right-align it.**

6. **Add a table to your document that presents information related to your topic. Format the table so it's attractive and easy to read.**

7. **Save your document with a name of your choice and close Word.**

Know this tech talk

border: A line placed on top of a table gridline (or on the outside of some other object) to make its outline appear with certain formatting and to make the outline appear on printouts.

bulleted list: A list in which each paragraph is preceded by the same symbol.

delimited: Multi-column data where the columns are separated using a consistent character, such as tab.

first-line indent: A positive indent that affects the first line of the paragraph only. When negative, it's called a *hanging indent.*

gridlines: The nonprinting lines that (optionally) show onscreen where the edges of a table's rows and columns are.

hanging indent: A negative indent that affects the first line of the paragraph only. When positive, it's called a *first-line indent.*

horizontal alignment: The positioning of a paragraph between the right and left margins.

indentation: The amount that a paragraph is offset from the left or right margin

justified: A horizontal alignment that stretches the text out so that it touches both the right and left margins.

leading: Vertical spacing between the lines of text.

numbered list: A list in which each paragraph is preceded by a consecutive number.

paragraph formatting: Formatting that affects whole paragraphs and cannot be applied to individual characters.

point: A measure of $\frac{1}{72}$ of an inch.

Quick Style gallery: A short list of commonly used styles appearing on the Home tab.

style: A named set of formatting specifications stored with a template or document.

table: A grid of rows and columns for storing and displaying information in a multi-column layout.

vertical spacing: The amount of space (leading) between each line

Chapter 4

Creating Basic Worksheets

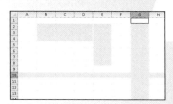

✔ Selecting ranges enables you to apply a *single command to multiple cells at once.*

✔ You can *edit the content of a cell* either in the cell itself or in the formula bar.

✔ Moving and copying data between cells *saves data entry time and effort.*

✔ Dragging the fill handle copies cell content quickly into many cells at once.

✔ Inserting and deleting rows and columns in a worksheet *changes its structure without having to move content.*

✔ Renaming a worksheet tab enables you to *assign a more meaningful title to a sheet.*

✔ By inserting new worksheets in a workbook, you *expand a workbook's capacity.*

1. How do you move the cell cursor quickly back to cell A1?

Jump over to page 120

2. How do you select a noncontiguous range?

Explore the great expanse on page 121

3. How do you clear a cell's content?

Don't delete the info on page 125

4. How do you move and copy cell content with the Clipboard?

Mosey on over to page 127

5. How can you quickly fill a set of increasing values into a large range?

Increase your chances on page 129

6. How can you insert new rows and columns?

Line it up on page 134

7. How can you change the color of a worksheet tab?

Bookmark this info on page 137

*M*icrosoft Word works great for typing text, but sometimes you want something a little more structured for data. When you have more complex needs for column-based organizing than what Word's tables can provide, Excel is a great step up to the next level. Excel is much more than just a column organizer, though; it enables you to write formulas that perform calculations on your data. This feature makes Excel an ideal tool for storing financial information, such as checkbook register and investment portfolio data.

In this chapter, I introduce you to the Excel interface and teach you some of the concepts you need to know. You learn how to move around in Excel, how to type and edit data, and how to manipulate rows, columns, cells, and sheets.

Understanding the Excel Interface

Excel is very much like Word and other Office applications. It has a File tab that opens a Backstage View, and it has a Ribbon with multiple tabs that contain commands you can click to execute. It has a Quick Access Toolbar, a status bar, scroll bars, and a Zoom slider. Those features should be familiar to you from Chapter 1 or from working with Word in Chapters 1 through 4. Figure 4-1 provides a quick review.

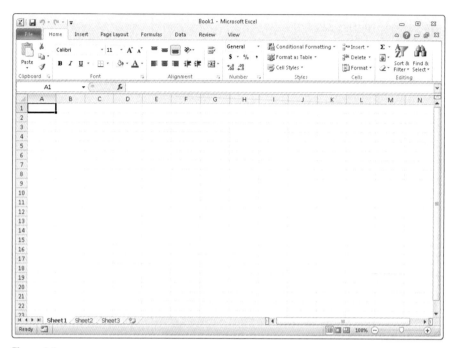

Figure 4-1

The next several sections walk you through the Excel interface, including both the commands and the work area, and show you how to move around. After you get your bearings in Excel, you find out how to create worksheets.

Touring the Excel interface

The best way to learn about a new application is to jump in and start exploring. Work through this exercise to see how Excel is set up.

In the following exercise, you start Excel and explore its interface.

Files needed: None

1. **To open Excel, choose Start⇨All Programs⇨Microsoft Office⇨Microsoft Excel 2010.**

   See Figure 4-2. Excel opens with a new, blank workbook ready to go.

LINGO

Here's some basic terminology for working with Excel: A **spreadsheet** is a grid comprised of rows and columns. At the intersection of each row and column is a **cell**. You can type text, numbers, and formulas into cells to build your spreadsheet. In Excel, spreadsheets are called **worksheets**. Worksheets are stored in data files called **workbooks**. Each workbook can contain multiple worksheets. **Worksheet tabs** at the bottom of workbook window enable you to quickly switch between worksheets.

Figure 4-2

If Excel has been recently used on your computer, it may appear on the top level of the Start menu; you can click it there if you see it. You can also click Start, start typing **Excel,** and then click Microsoft Excel 2010 when it appears at the top of the Start menu. For more practice, close Excel and then reopen it by using one of those methods.

2. **Click the File tab.**

   Backstage View opens, as in Word and other Office applications.

3. **Click Info.**

   Information about the active document appears. See Figure 4-3.

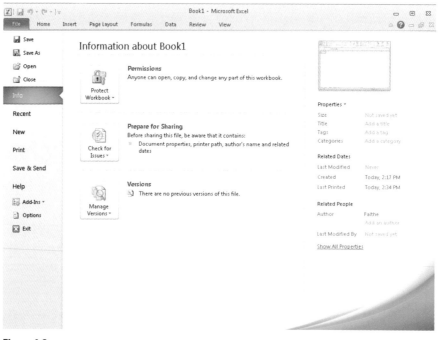

Figure 4-3

4. Click the Home tab or press Esc to return to normal viewing.

See Figure 4-4.

LINGO

Figure 4-4 shows a basic worksheet in Excel. Notice that each row has a unique number, and each column a unique letter. The combination of those forms a **cell address**. For example, the cell in the upper left corner is A1. When you type something in Excel, your typing is entered into the **active cell**. The active cell is the one where the **cell cursor** is, a thick black outline. The active cell's name appears in the **Name box**.

Figure 4-4

5. Click the View tab.

The commands on the Ribbon change to show that tab. The tabbed Ribbon works the same in Excel as it does in Word and other Office applications.

6. Click the Zoom button.

The Zoom dialog box opens. See Figure 4-5.

Figure 4-5

7. Select 200% and click OK.

The magnification changes to show each cell in a more close-up view.

8. At the bottom-right corner of the Excel window, drag the Zoom slider to 100%, changing the Zoom back to its original setting.

See Figure 4-6.

Figure 4-6

Leave the workbook open for the next exercise.

Moving the cell cursor

To type in a cell, you must first make the cell active by moving the cell cursor there. As shown in Figure 4-4, the cell cursor is a thick, black outline. You can move the cell cursor by pressing the arrow keys, by clicking the desired cell, or by using one of Excel's keyboard shortcuts. Table 4-1 lists some of the most common keyboard shortcuts for moving the cell cursor.

Table 4-1	Excel Movement Shortcuts
Press This . . .	**To Move . . .**
Arrow keys	One cell in the direction of the arrow
Tab	One cell to the right
Shift+Tab	One cell to the left
Ctrl+any arrow key	To the edge of the current data region in a worksheet (the first or last cell that isn't empty)
End	To the cell in the lower-right corner of the window
	This works only when the Scroll Lock key has been pressed on your keyboard to turn on the Scroll Lock function.
Ctrl+End	To the last cell in the worksheet, in the lowest used row of the rightmost used column
Home	To the beginning of the row containing the active cell
Ctrl+Home	To the beginning of the worksheet (cell A1)
Page Down	One screen down
Alt+Page Down	One screen to the right
Ctrl+Page Down	To the next sheet in the workbook
Page Up	One screen up
Alt+Page Up	One screen to the left
Ctrl+Page Up	To the previous sheet in the workbook

In the following exercise, you move the cell cursor in a worksheet.

Files needed: None

1. **In Excel, on any worksheet (the blank one you worked with in the previous exercise is fine), click cell C3.**

   The cell cursor moves there.

2. **Press the right-arrow key once.**

   The cell cursor moves to cell D3.

3. **Press the down-arrow key once.**

   The cell cursor moves to D4.

4. **Press the Home key.**

   The cell cursor moves to cell A4. (Refer to Table 4-1; pressing Home moves to the beginning of the current row.)

5. **Press the Page Down key.**

REMEMBER

The cell cursor moves to a cell that's one full screen down from the previous position. Depending on the window size and screen resolution, the exact cell will vary, but it will still be in column A.

6. **Use the vertical scroll bar to scroll the display up so cell A1 is visible.**

   Notice that the cell cursor didn't move. The Name box still displays the name of the cell you moved to previously.

7. **Press Ctrl+Home.**

   The cell cursor moves to cell A1.

Leave the workbook open for the next exercise.

Selecting ranges

LINGO

REMEMBER

Technically, a range can consist of a single cell. However, a range most commonly consists of multiple cells.

You might sometimes want to select a multicell **range** before you issue a command. For example, if you want to format all the text in a range a certain way, select that range and then issue the formatting command.

Range names are written with the upper-left cell followed by a colon and then the lower-right cell, like this: A1:F3. When a range contains noncontiguous cells, the pieces are separated by commas, like this: B8:C14,D8:G14.

You can select a range by using either the keyboard or the mouse. Table 4-2 provides some of the most common range selection shortcuts.

LINGO

A range is usually **contiguous**, meaning all the cells are in a single rectangular block, but they don't have to be. You can also select noncontiguous cells in a range, by holding down the Ctrl key as you select additional cells.

Table 4-2	Range Selection Shortcuts
Press This . . .	*To Extend the Selection To . . .*
Ctrl+Shift+any arrow key	The last nonblank cell in the same column or row as the active cell; or if the next cell is blank, to the next nonblank cell
Ctrl+Shift+End	The last used cell on the worksheet (the lower-right corner of the range containing data)
Ctrl+Shift+Home	The beginning of the worksheet (A1)
Ctrl+Shift+Page Down	The current and next sheet in the workbook
Ctrl+Shift+Page Up	The current and previous sheet in the workbook
Ctrl+spacebar	The entire column where the active cell is located
Shift+spacebar	The entire row where the active cell is located
Ctrl+Shift+spacebar or Ctrl+A	The entire worksheet

In the following exercise, you practice selecting ranges.

Files needed: None

1. **In Excel, on any worksheet (the blank one you worked with in the previous exercise is fine), click cell B2 to move the cell cursor there.**

2. **Hold down the Shift key and press the right-arrow key twice and the down-arrow key twice, extending the selection to the range B2:D4.**

   See Figure 4-7.

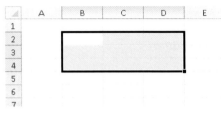

Figure 4-7

3. Hold down the Ctrl key and click cell E2.

It becomes included in the selected range.

4. Holding down the left mouse button, drag from E2 to E6.

Now the range is B2:D4,E2:E6, as shown in Figure 4-8.

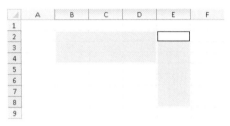

Figure 4-8

5. Hold down Ctrl and click the header for row 10 (the number 10 at the left edge of the row).

That row is added to the selected range.

6. Hold down Ctrl and click the header for column G (the letter G at the top of the column).

That column is added to the selected range. The selection should look like Figure 4-9 at this point.

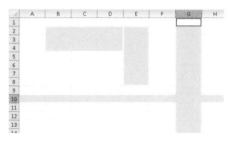

Figure 4-9

7. **Click any cell.**

   The range selection is cancelled, and only that cell becomes selected.

8. **Press Ctrl+spacebar.**

   The entire column becomes selected.

9. **Click any cell.**

   The range selection is cancelled.

10. **Press Shift+spacebar.**

    The entire row becomes selected.

11. **Click the Select All button.**

    It's the button in the upper-left corner of the spreadsheet grid, where the row numbers and the column letters intersect. The entire worksheet becomes selected. See Figure 4-10.

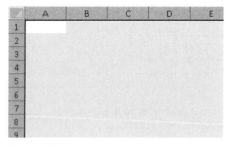

Figure 4-10

 Instead of clicking the Select All button, you can press Ctrl+Shift+spacebar.

12. Click any cell.

The range selection is cancelled.

Leave the workbook open for the next exercise.

Typing and Editing Cell Content

Up to this point in the chapter, I've introduced you to some spreadsheet basics. Now, it's time to actually do something: You enter text and numbers into cells.

Typing text or numbers into a cell

To type in a cell, you simply select the cell and begin typing. When you finish typing, you can leave the cell in any of these ways:

- ✔ Press Enter to move to the next cell down.
- ✔ Press Tab to move to the next cell to the right.
- ✔ Press Shift+Tab to move to the next cell to the left.
- ✔ Press an arrow key to move in the direction of the arrow.
- ✔ Click in another cell to move to that cell.

If you make a mistake when editing, you can press Esc to cancel the edit before you leave the cell. If you need to undo an edit after having left the cell, press Ctrl+Z or click the Undo button on the Quick Access Toolbar.

In the following exercise, you enter text into a worksheet.

Files needed: None

1. In Excel, on any worksheet (the blank one you worked with in the previous exercise is fine), click cell A1.

2. Type Mortgage Calculator **and press Enter.**

3. Click cell A1 again to reselect it.

Notice that the cell's content appears in the formula bar. See Figure 4-11.

LINGO

The **formula bar** is the text area immediately above the worksheet grid, to the right of the Name box. It shows the active cell's contents. When the content is text or a number, what appears in the cell and what appears in the formula bar are identical. When the content is a formula or function, the formula bar shows the actual formula/function, and the cell shows the result of it.

Figure 4-11

4. **Click cell A3, type** Loan Amount **and press Tab.**

   The cell cursor moves to cell B3.

5. **Type** 250000 **and press Enter.**

   The cell cursor moves to A4.

6. **In cell A4, type** Interest **and press Tab.**

   The cell cursor moves to cell B4.

7. **Type** .05 **and press Enter.**

   The cell cursor moves to cell A5.

8. **Type** Periods **and press Tab.**

   The cell cursor moves to cell B5.

9. **Type** 360 **and press Enter.**

   The cell cursor moves to cell A6.

10. **Type** Payment **and press Enter.**

    The cell cursor moves to cell A7. The worksheet should look like Figure 4-12 at this point.

	A	B	C
1	Mortgage Calculator		
2			
3	Loan Amo	250000	
4	Interest	0.05	
5	Periods	360	
6	Payment		
7			
8			

Figure 4-12

11. Save the file as Chapter 4 Mortgage.xlsx.

As a reminder, to save a file take these steps: Choose File⇨Save to open the Save As dialog box. Navigate to the location where you want to save the file. In the File Name text box, type **Chapter 4 Mortgage**. Click the Save button.

Leave the workbook open for the next exercise.

Editing cell content

If you need to edit what's in the cell, you have these choices:

- ✔ Click the cell to select it and then click the cell again to move the insertion point into it. Edit like you would in Word or any text program.
- ✔ Click the cell to select it and then type a new entry to replace the old one.

If you decide you don't want the text you typed in a particular cell, you can get rid of it in several ways:

- ✔ Select the cell; then right-click the cell and choose Clear Contents from the menu that appears.
- ✔ Select the cell; then click the Home tab, click the Clear button, and choose Clear Contents.
- ✔ Select the cell, press spacebar, and then press Enter. This action technically doesn't clear the cell's content but instead replaces it with a single, invisible character — a space.
- ✔ Select the cell and press the Delete key.

Don't confuse Clear (Delete key on the keyboard) with the Delete command on the Ribbon. A Delete command is available on the Home tab, but using it doesn't clear the cell content; instead, it removes the entire cell. You find out more about deleting cells in the upcoming section, "Changing the Worksheet Structure."

And while I'm on the subject, don't confuse Clear with Cut, either. The Cut command works in conjunction with the Clipboard. It moves content to the Clipboard, from which you can then paste it somewhere else. In Excel, though (unlike in other applications), using the Cut command doesn't immediately remove the content. Instead, it puts a flashing dotted box around the content and waits for you to reposition the cell cursor and issue the Paste command. If you do something else in the interim, the cut-and-paste operation is cancelled, and the content that you cut remains in its original location. You learn more about cutting and pasting in the section "Copying and moving data between cells," later in this chapter.

In the following exercise, you edit text in a worksheet.

Files needed: `Chapter 4 Mortgage.xlsx`

1. **In the Chapter 4 Mortgage file from the preceding exercise, click cell A3.**

2. **Click in the formula bar to move the insertion point there and then double-click the word *Loan* to select it. Press Delete on the keyboard. Press Delete one more time to also delete the space before the remaining word *Amount*.**

3. **Press Enter to finalize the edit.**

   The cell cursor moves to cell A4.

4. **Click in B3, type** 300000 **and press Enter.**

   The new value replaces the old one.

5. **Right-click cell B4 and choose Clear Contents. Then type** 0.0635 **and press Enter.**

6. **Click cell B5 to select it and then double-click in B5 to move the insertion point there. Position the insertion point to the right of the 6, press Backspace twice, and type** 18, **changing the value in the cell to** 180. **Press Enter when you're finished.**

   The worksheet should now look like Figure 4-13.

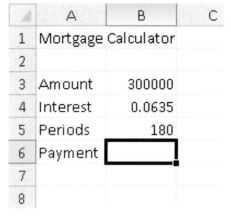

Figure 4-13

7. **Save the changes to the workbook.**

Leave the workbook open for the next exercise.

Using AutoFill to fill cell content

When you have a lot of data to enter and that data consists of some type of repeatable pattern or sequence, you can save time by using AutoFill. To use AutoFill, select the cell(s) that already contain an example of what you want to fill and then drag the *fill handle.* The fill handle is the little black square in the lower-right corner of the selected cell or range.

Depending on how you use it, AutoFill can fill the same value into every cell in the target area, or it can fill in a sequence (like days of the month, days of the week, or a numeric sequence like 2, 4, 6, 8). Here are the general rules for how it works:

- ✔ When AutoFill recognizes the selected text as a member of one of its preset lists, such as days of the week or months of the year, it automatically increments those. For example, if the selected cell contains August, Auto Fill would place September in the next adjacent cell.

- ✔ When AutoFill doesn't recognize the selected text, it fills with a duplicate of the selected text.

- ✔ When AutoFill is used on a single cell containing a number, it fills with a duplicate of the number.

- ✔ When Auto Fill is used on a range of two or more cells containing numbers, AutoFill attempts to determine the interval between them, and it continues filling using that same pattern. For example, if the two selected cells contain 2 and 4, the next adjacent cell would be filled with 6.

In the following exercise, you move and copy cell content using two different methods.

Files needed: `Chapter 4 Mortgage.xlsx`

1. **In the Chapter 4 Mortgage file from the preceding exercise, select A8 and type** Amortization Table**.**

2. **Type the following:**

   In cell A10, type **Date**.

   In cell B10, type **Pmt#**.

   In cell A11, type **January 2012.** (Note that Excel automatically changes it to *Jan-12*.)

   In B11, type **1**.

3. **Click A11 and move the mouse pointer over the fill handle.**

   The mouse pointer becomes a black crosshair. See Figure 4-14.

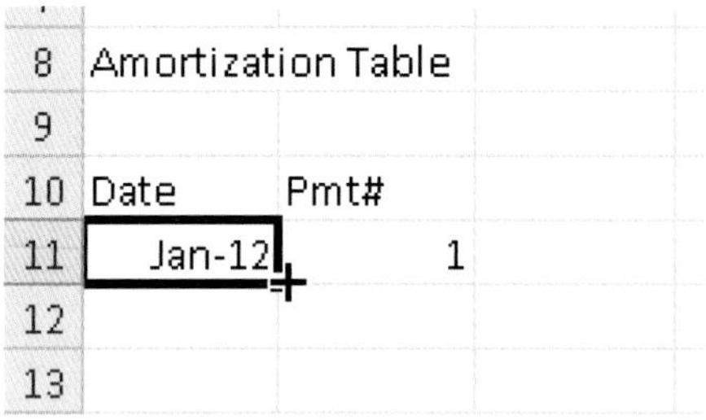

8	Amortization Table	
9		
10	Date	Pmt#
11	Jan-12	1
12		
13		

Figure 4-14

4. Drag the fill handle down to cell A22.

The first year of dates fill into the cells. See Figure 4-15.

8	Amortization Table	
9		
10	Date	Pmt#
11	Jan-12	1
12	Feb-12	
13	Mar-12	
14	Apr-12	
15	May-12	
16	Jun-12	
17	Jul-12	
18	Aug-12	
19	Sep-12	
20	Oct-12	
21	Nov-12	
22	Dec-12	
23		
24		

Figure 4-15

5. Click B11 and drag the fill handle down to C22.

TIP

Note that the same number is filled into all cells. That's not what you want.

6. Press Ctrl+Z to undo the fill.

7. Click B12 and type 2.

8. Select B11:B12 and drag the fill handle down to B22.

This time the series is filled in correctly. Figure 4-16 shows the completed series.

7		
8	Amortization Table	
9		
10	Date	Pmt#
11	Jan-12	1
12	Feb-12	2
13	Mar-12	3
14	Apr-12	4
15	May-12	5
16	Jun-12	6
17	Jul-12	7
18	Aug-12	8
19	Sep-12	9
20	Oct-12	10
21	Nov-12	11
22	Dec-12	12
23		
24		

Figure 4-16

9. Select A22:B22 and drag the fill handle down to B190.

Both series are filled in, down to row 190, where the date is December 2026 and the payment number is 180.

Step 9 is performed because the number of periods for this loan is 180 (see cell C5), so the number of payments should be 180 in the amortization table.

10. **Press Ctrl+Home to return to the top of the worksheet.**

11. **Save the changes to the workbook.**

Leave the workbook open for the next exercise.

Copying and moving data between cells

When you're creating a spreadsheet, it's common to not get everything in exactly the right cells to begin with. Fortunately, moving content between cells is easy.

Here are the two methods you can use to move content.

- ✔ **Mouse method:** Point at the dark outline around the selected range, and then drag to the new location. If you want to copy rather than move, hold down the Ctrl key while you drag.

- ✔ **Clipboard method:** Click the Home tab and click the Cut button or press Ctrl+X. Then click the destination cell and click the Paste button on the Home tab or press Ctrl+V. If you want to copy rather than move, choose Copy (Ctrl+C) rather than Cut.

If you're moving or copying a multicell range with the Clipboard method, you can select the same size and shape of block for the destination, or you can select a single cell, in which case the paste occurs with the selected cell in the upper-left corner.

In the following exercise, you move and copy cell content using two different methods.

Files needed: `Chapter 4 Mortgage.xlsx`

1. **In the Chapter 4 Mortgage file from the preceding exercise, select the range A1:B6.**

2. **Point at the border of the selection so that the mouse pointer shows a four-headed arrow along with the arrow pointer.**

3. Drag the selection to C1:D6.

An outline shows the selection as you drag it, and a ScreenTip shows the cell address of the destination. See Figure 4-17.

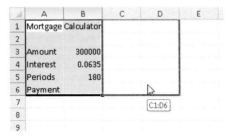

Figure 4-17

4. Click cell C1 and press Ctrl+X to cut.

A dotted outline appears around C1.

5. Click cell B1 and press Ctrl+V to paste.

The text moves from C1 to B1.

6. Select C3:D6, click the Home tab, and click the Cut button.

7. Click B3 and then click the Paste button on the Home tab.

The completed worksheet is shown in Figure 4-18.

▲	A	B	C	D
1		Mortgage Calculator		
2				
3		Amount	300000	
4		Interest	0.0635	
5		Periods	180	
6		Payment		
7				

Figure 4-18

8. Save the changes to the workbook.

Leave the workbook open for the next exercise.

Changing the Worksheet Structure

Even if you're a careful planner, you'll likely decide that you want to change your worksheet's structure. Maybe you want data in a different column, or certain rows turn out to be unnecessary. Excel makes it easy to insert and delete rows and columns to deal with these kinds of changes.

Inserting and deleting rows and columns

When you insert a new row or column, the existing ones move to make room for it. You can insert multiple rows or columns at once by selecting multiple ones before issuing the Insert command. (There's no limit on the number you can insert at once!) Similarly, you can delete multiple rows or columns by selecting them before using the Delete command.

In the following exercise, you insert and delete rows and columns.

Files needed: `Chapter 4 Mortgage.xlsx`

1. **In the Chapter 4 Mortgage file from the preceding exercise, click anywhere in column A.**

2. **On the Home tab, click the down arrow below the Insert button.**

   A menu appears.

3. **Click Insert Sheet Columns.**

   See Figure 4-19. A new column is placed to the left of the selected column.

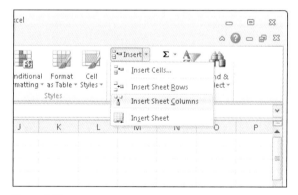

Figure 4-19

4. **Click the column header for column A to select the entire column.**

5. **Click the Home tab and then the Delete button.**

   The entire column is deleted.

6. **Select rows 7 and 8 by dragging across their row headers.**

7. **On the Home tab, click the Insert button.**

   Two new rows are inserted.

8. **Right-click any cell in row 7.**

9. **On the Home tab, click the down arrow below the Delete button.**

   A menu appears.

10. **Choose Delete Sheet Rows.**

   Figure 4-20 shows the worksheet after the insertions and deletions.

	A	B	C	D	E
1		Mortgage Calculator			
2					
3		Amount	300000		
4		Interest	0.0635		
5		Periods	180		
6		Payment			
7					
8					
9	Amortization Table				
10					
11	Date	Pmt#			
12	Jan-12		1		
13	Feb-12		2		
14	Mar-12		3		
15	Apr-12		4		
16	May-12		5		

Figure 4-20

Leave the workbook open for the next exercise.

Inserting and deleting cells and ranges

You can insert and delete individual cells or ranges that don't neatly correspond to entire rows or columns. When you do so, the surrounding cells shift. In the case of an insertion, cells move down or to the right of the area where the new cells are being inserted. In the case of a deletion, cells move up or to the left to fill in the voided space.

Deleting a cell is different from clearing a cell's content, and this fact becomes apparent when you start working with individual cells and ranges. When you clear the content, the cell itself remains. When you delete the cell itself, the adjacent cells shift.

When shifting cells, Excel is smart enough that it tries to guess which direction you want existing content to move when you insert or delete cells. If you have content immediately to the right of a deleted cell, for example, it shifts it left. If you have content immediately below the deleted cell, it shifts it up. You can override that, though, when needed.

In the following exercise, you insert and delete rows and columns.

Files needed: Chapter 4 Mortgage.xlsx

1. **In the Chapter 4 Mortgage file from the preceding exercise, select A1:A6.**

2. **Click the Home tab and then click the Delete button.**

   Excel guesses that you want to move the existing content to the left, and it does so.

3. **Click A1, and click the Insert button on the Home tab.**

   This time Excel guesses that you want to move the existing content down, which was incorrect. Now the content in column B is all off by one row, as shown in Figure 4-21.

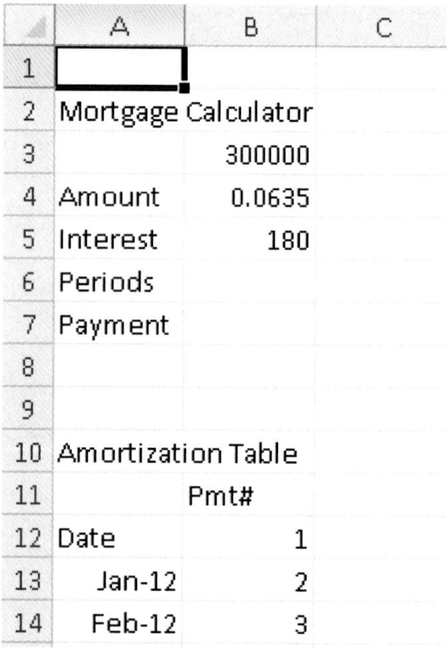

	A	B	C
1			
2	Mortgage Calculator		
3		300000	
4	Amount	0.0635	
5	Interest	180	
6	Periods		
7	Payment		
8			
9			
10	Amortization Table		
11		Pmt#	
12	Date	1	
13	Jan-12	2	
14	Feb-12	3	

Figure 4-21

4. **Press Ctrl+Z to undo the insertion.**

5. **On the Home tab, click the down arrow on the Insert button and then choose Insert Cells.**

   The Insert dialog box opens. See Figure 4-22.

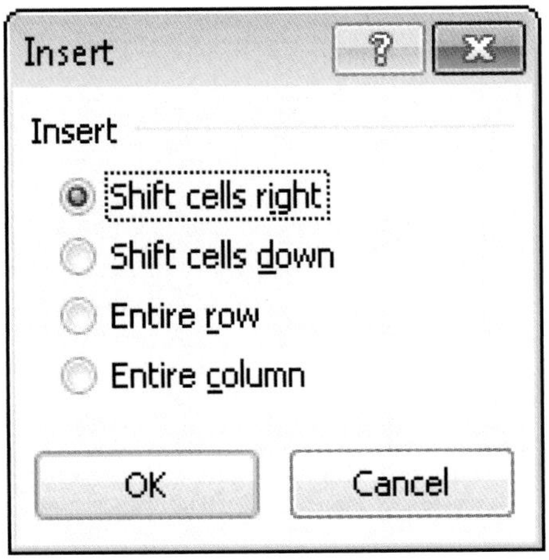

Figure 4-22

6. **Click Shift Cells Right and then click OK.**

   A new cell A1 is inserted, and the previous A1 content moves into B1.

7. **Save the changes to the workbook.**

Leave the workbook open for the next exercise.

Working with Worksheets

Each new workbook starts with three sheets, named Sheet1, Sheet2, and Sheet3. (Not the most interesting names, but you can change them.) You can also add or delete worksheets, rearrange the worksheet tabs, and apply different colors to the tabs to help differentiate them from one another or to create logical groups of tabs.

In the following exercise, you insert, rename, and delete worksheets, and change a tab color.

Files needed: `Chapter 4 Mortgage.xlsx`

1. **In the Chapter 4 Mortgage file from the preceding exercise, double-click the Sheet1 worksheet tab to move the insertion point into it.**

2. **Type** Calculator **and press Enter.**

   The new worksheet name replaces the old one.

3. **Right-click the worksheet tab, point to Tab Color, and select the Red standard color.**

   See Figure 4-23.

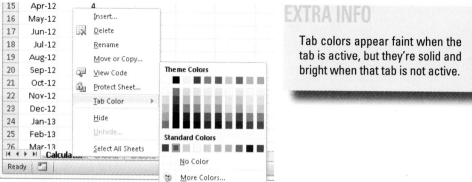

Figure 4-23

4. **Right-click the Sheet2 tab and click Delete.**

5. **Double-click the Sheet3 tab, type** Amortization, **and press Enter.**

6. **Right-click the Amortization tab and choose Insert.**

   The Insert dialog box opens. See Figure 4-24.

7. **Click the Worksheet icon and click OK.**

   A new worksheet is inserted.

Figure 4-24

8. **Double-click the new Sheet4 tab that you just inserted, type** Chart, **and press Enter.**

   The three tabs in the workbook should be named and arranged as shown in Figure 4-25.

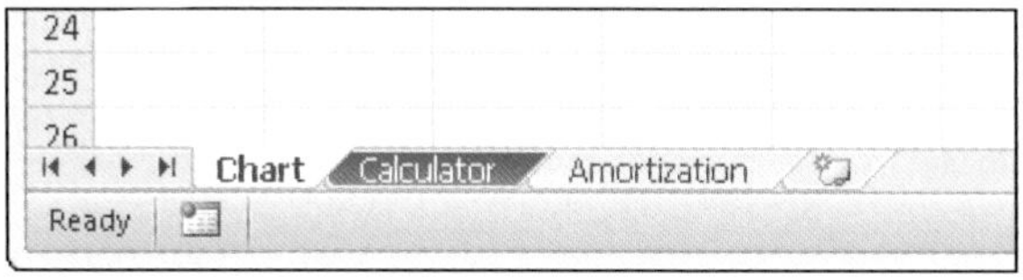

Figure 4-25

9. **Save the changes to the workbook.**

Close the workbook and exit Excel.

 *Summing Up*

Excel is an excellent choice for storing data in rows and columns. In this chapter, you learned how to navigate the Excel interface, including entering and editing content in cells, inserting and deleting cells, and selecting ranges. Here's a quick review:

- ✔ Excel data files are called workbooks. Each workbook can hold multiple worksheets. Each worksheet has a tab at the bottom of the Excel window for quick access to it.

- ✔ Each cell has a cell address consisting of the column letter and row number, such as A1.

- ✔ The active cell is indicated by the cell cursor, a thick black outline. You can move the cell cursor with the mouse or the arrow keys. When you type text, it's entered into the active cell.

- ✔ A range is a selection that consists of one or more cells. (It's usually more than one.) A contiguous range consists of a single rectangular block of cells.

- ✔ To clear cell contents, select the cell and press Delete or click Home, Clear, Cell Contents.

- ✔ To move data between cells, point to the black outline and drag the data or use the Cut and Paste commands. To copy data, hold down Ctrl and drag it, or use the Copy and Paste commands.

- ✔ To fill data from the selected range to adjacent cells, drag the fill handle, which is the black rectangle in the lower-right corner of the selected range.

- ✔ To insert a row or column, on the Home tab open the Insert button's menu and select either Insert Sheet Rows or Insert Sheet Columns.

- ✔ When you insert individual cells, the existing content moves over to make room. You can choose which direction it should move.

- ✔ To insert a new sheet, right-click an existing sheet's tab and choose Insert. To delete a sheet, right-click its tab and click Delete.

- ✔ To rename a sheet, double-click its tab name and type a new name.

Try-it-yourself lab

For more practice with the features covered in this chapter, try the following exercise on your own.

1. **Start Excel and, in cell A1, type** Membership List.

2. **In row 3, enter the column headings you would need to store information about the members of an organization you're part of.**

   For example, you might have First, Last, and Phone.

3. **Starting in row 4, enter the information about the members of the organization.**

   If there are many members, choose 10 to enter as examples.

4. **Insert a new column between two of the existing columns.**

   For example, you could enter an MI column (for Middle Initial) between First and Last.

5. **Change the name of the worksheet tab to Membership.**

6. **Save your document as** `Chapter 4 Lab.xlsx` **and close it.**

7. **Close Excel.**

Know this tech talk

active cell: The cell in which new content that you type will be placed.

cell address: The column letter and row number of a cell, such as A1.

cell cursor: The thick black border surrounding the active cell.

cell: The intersection of a row and column in a spreadsheet.

contiguous: Adjacent to one another. A range in which all the selected cells are adjacent to one another, in a rectangular block, is contiguous.

Name box: The box to the left of the formula bar that lists the active cell's cell address.

range: One or more selected cells.

spreadsheet: A grid of rows and columns in which you can store data.

workbook: An Excel data file.

worksheet: The Excel term for a spreadsheet.

worksheet tabs: Tabs at the bottom of a workbook for each worksheet that it contains.

Creating Formulas and Functions

	A	B	C
1	**Fixed Expense**		
2	Rent	$850	
3	Car Payment	$325	
4	Student Loan	$250	
5	**Total Fixed**	$1,425	
6			
7	**Variable Expense**		
8	Utilities	$175	
9	Food	$450	
10	Entertainment	$150	
11	Clothes	$100	
12	Miscellaneous	$100	
13	**Total Variable**	$975	
14			
15	**Total Expenses**	$2,400	
16			
17			

- ✔ Formulas *perform math calculations* on fixed numbers or on the contents of cells.

- ✔ The order of precedence *settles any uncertainties* about which math operations execute first.

- ✔ You can use cell references that include sheet names to *reference cells on other sheets*.

- ✔ If you use relative cell referencing, *cell references automatically update when copied*.

- ✔ Absolute cell referencing *keeps a cell reference fixed* when copied to other locations.

- ✔ You can use functions to *perform complex math operations* on cell content.

- ✔ You can use Insert Function to *choose and construct a function*.

- ✔ The SUM function *sums a range of cells*.

- ✔ The PV, FV, PMT, RATE, and NPER functions *calculate parts of a loan or investment*.

Insert Function

Search for a function:

average   [Go]

Or select a category: Recommended

Select a function:

- AVERAGE
- DAVERAGE
- AVERAGEIFS
- AVERAGEIF
- AVERAGEA
- SUMIFS
- AVEDEV

AVERAGE(number1,number2,...)
Returns the average (arithmetic mean) of its arguments, which can be numbers or names, arrays, or references that contain numbers.

Help on this function   [OK] [Cancel]

	A	B	C	D	E
1		Calculate Periods			
2					
3	Price	$30,000			
4	# of Payments	=nper(			
5	Payment	NPER(rate, pmt, pv, [fv], [type])			
6	Yearly Rate	5%	Monthly Rate	0.004167	
7					
8					

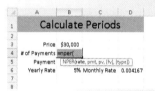

1. Which comes first in a formula: exponentiation or division?

The order is formed on page.. 146

2. What character must all formulas and functions start with?

The personality begins on page... 148

3. How do you reference a cell on a different worksheet?

Don't do differently than page 150

4. What does a dollar sign mean in a cell address?

The buck stops on page.. 155

5. How do you refer to a range in a function?

Find your functions on page.. 157

6. How can you use a function if you don't know its exact name?

Title this on page 159

7. What function inserts today's date?

Today the content is found on page.. 161

8. What function calculates the payments on a loan?

Compute the answer on page... 163

*M*ath. Excel is really good at it, and it's what makes Excel more than just data storage. Even if you hated math in school, you might still like Excel because it does the math for you.

In Excel, you can write math formulas that perform calculations on the values in various cells, and then if those values change later, the formula results update automatically. You can also use built-in functions to handle more complex math activities than you might be able to set up with formulas. That capability makes it possible to build complex worksheets that calculate loan rates and payments, keep track of your bank accounts, and much more.

In this chapter, I show you how to construct formulas and functions in Excel, as well as how to move and copy formulas and functions (there's a trick to it) and how to use functions to create handy financial spreadsheets.

Finding Out about Formulas

In Excel, formulas are different from regular text in two ways:

- They begin with an equal sign, like this:
  =2+2

- They don't contain text (except for function names and cell references). They contain only symbols that are allowed in math formulas, such as parentheses, commas, and decimal points.

LINGO

A **formula** is a math calculation, such as 2 + 2 or 3(4 + 1).

Writing formulas that calculate

Excel's formulas can do everything that a basic calculator can do, so if you're in a hurry and don't want to pull up the Windows Calculator application, you can enter a formula in Excel to get a quick result. Experimenting with this type of formula is a great way to get accustomed to formulas in general.

Excel also has an advantage over some basic calculators (including the one in Windows): It easily does exponentiation. For example, if you want to calculate 5 to the 8th power, you write it in Excel as =5^8.

Just like in basic math, formulas are calculated by using an order of precedence—that is, an order in which operations will be processed. Table 5-1 lists the order.

Table 5-1	Order of Precedence in a Formula	
Order	**Item**	**Example**
1	Anything in parentheses	=2*(2+1)
2	Exponentiation	=2^3
3	Multiplication and division	=1+2*2
4	Addition and subtraction	=10×4

In the following exercise, you enter some formulas that perform simple math calculations.

Files needed: None

1. **Start Excel, if needed, so that a new, blank workbook appears.**

   If you already have another workbook open, press Ctrl+N to create a new one.

2. **Click cell A1, type =2+2, and press Enter.**

   The result of the formula appears in cell A1.

3. **Click cell A1 again to move the cell cursor back to it. Then look in the formula bar.**

   Notice that the formula you entered appears there. See Figure 5-1.

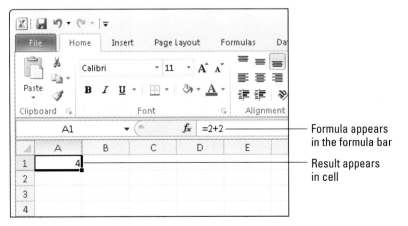

Figure 5-1

4. **Click cell A2, type** =2+4*3, **and press Enter.**

   The result of the formula appears in cell A2.

   In this case, because of the order of precedence (see Table 5-1), the multiplication was done first (4 times 3 equals 12) and then the 2 was added, for a result of 14. See Figure 5-2.

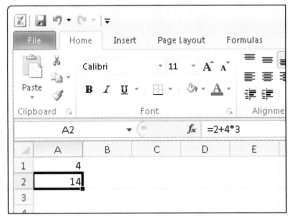

Figure 5-2

5. In cell A3, type =(2+4)*3 **and press Enter.**

In this case, the parentheses forced the addition to occur first (2 plus 4 equals 6), and then the multiplication was performed, for a result of 18. See Figure 5-3.

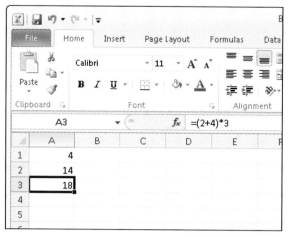

Figure 5-3

6. Close the workbook without saving changes to it.

Leave Excel open for the next exercise.

Writing formulas that reference cells

One of Excel's best features is its ability to reference cells in formulas. When a cell is referenced in a formula, whatever value it contains is used in the formula. When the value changes, the result of the formula changes, too.

In the following exercise, you enter some formulas that contain cell references.

Files needed: Chapter 5 Budget.xlsx

1. **Open** Chapter 5 Budget.xlsx **from the data files for this lesson and save it as** Chapter 5 Budget Calculations.xlsx.

2. **In cell E6, type** =E4.

The value shown in E4 is repeated there.

In cell E6, you could have just as easily retyped the value from E4, but this way if the value in E4 changes, the value in E6 also changes.

3. **In cell B7, type** =B4+B5+B6.

   B7 now shows $1,425.

4. **In cell B15, type** =B10+B11+B12+B13+B14.

   B15 now shows $975.

That's a lot of typing, to type each of those cell references. Later in this chapter, you find out how to use the SUM function to dramatically cut down on the typing required to sum the values in many cells at once.

5. **In cell B17, type** =B7+B15.

   C17 now shows $2,400.

6. **In cell E9, type** =E6-B17.

   E9 now shows –$578. Figure 5-4 shows the worksheet with the formulas entered.

7. **In cell E11, type** =E9/B17.

   The value –24.08% appears in E11. The completed worksheet appears in Figure 5-4.

This worksheet was set up to use the appropriate formatting for each cell so that the formulas make sense. You learn to do this for yourself in Chapter 7.

	A	B	C	D	E	F
1	**Budget**					
2						
3	**Fixed Expense**			**Income**		
4	Rent	$850		Paycheck	$1,822	
5	Car Payment	$325				
6	Student Loan	$250		**Total Income**	$1,822	
7	**Total Fixed**	$1,425				
8						
9	**Variable Expense**			**Overall**	-$578	
10	Utilities	$175				
11	Food	$450		Correction %	-24%	
12	Entertainment	$150				
13	Clothes	$100				
14	Miscellaneous	$100				
15	**Total Variable**	$975				
16						
17	**Total Expenses**	$2,400				
18						
19						

Figure 5-4

Referencing a cell on another sheet

When referring to a cell on the same sheet, you can simply use its column and row: A1, B1, and so on. However, when referring to a cell on a different sheet, you have to include the sheet name in the formula.

The syntax for doing this is to list the sheet name, followed by an exclamation point, followed by the cell reference, like this:

```
=Sheet1!A2
```

In the following exercise, you practice using this notation by creating some multisheet formulas.

Files needed: `Chapter 5 Sheets.xlsx`

1. **Open `Chapter 5 Sheets.xlsx` from the data files for this lesson and save it as `Chapter 5 Budget Sheets.xlsx`.**

   This workbook has the same data that you worked with in the last exercise, except it's split out into multiple worksheets.

2. **Click the Expenses tab and look at the data there.**

   When calculating the overall budget amount, you want to refer to B15 there. See Figure 5-5.

3. **Click the Income tab and look at the data there.**

   On this sheet, you want to refer to B4. See Figure 5-6.

4. **Click the Overall tab and, in B3, type** =Income!B4-Expenses!B15**.**

   Cell B3 displays –$578.

   If you hadn't looked beforehand at the cells to reference on the other tabs, you might have been at a loss as to what to type when constructing the formula in Step 4. You have another way to refer to cells when writing a formula. The following steps practice that method.

5. **Click B5 and type** =**.**

6. **Click cell B3 and then type /.**

7. **Click the Expenses tab.**

	A	B	C
1	**Fixed Expense**		
2	Rent	$850	
3	Car Payment	$325	
4	Student Loan	$250	
5	**Total Fixed**	$1,425	
6			
7	**Variable Expense**		
8	Utilities	$175	
9	Food	$450	
10	Entertainment	$150	
11	Clothes	$100	
12	Miscellaneous	$100	
13	**Total Variable**	$975	
14			
15	**Total Expenses**	$2,400	
16			
17			

Figure 5-5

	A	B	C
1	**Income**		
2	Paycheck	$1,822	
3			
4	**Total Income**	$1,822	
5			
6			
7			

Figure 5-6

8. Click cell B15 and press Enter.

The display jumps back to the Overall tab and completes the formula. See Figure 5-7.

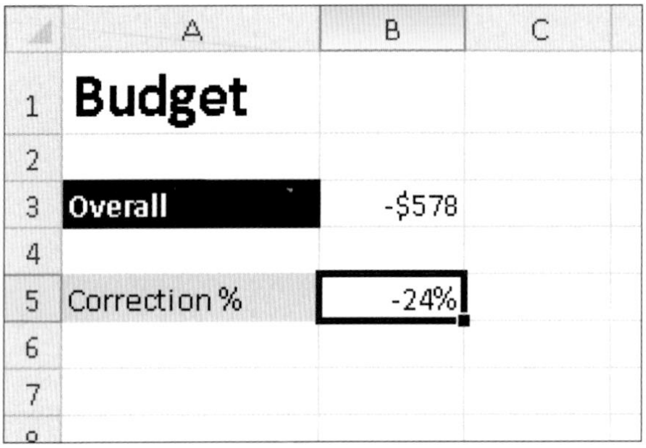

Figure 5-7

9. Save the changes to the workbook and close it.

Leave Excel open for the next exercise.

Moving and Copying Formulas

In Chapter 4, you learn how to move and copy text and numbers between cells, but when it comes to copying formulas, there are a few gotchas. The following sections explain relative and absolute referencing in formulas and how you can use them to get the results you want on the copies.

Copying formulas with relative referencing

When you move or copy a formula, Excel automatically changes the cell references to work with the new location. That's because by default, cell references in formulas are *relative references.* For example, in Figure 5-8, suppose you wanted to copy the formula from B5 into C5. The new formula in C5 should refer to values in column C, not to column B; otherwise, it wouldn't make much sense. So, when B5's formula is copied to C5, it becomes =C3+C4 there.

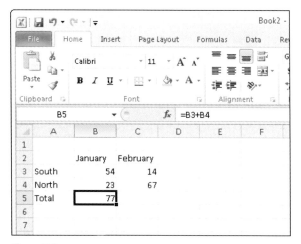

Figure 5-8

In this exercise, you copy formulas using relative referencing (the default) and examine the results.

Files needed: `Chapter 5 Appliance.xlsx`

1. **Open Chapter 5 Appliance.xlsx from the data files for this lesson and save it as Chapter 5 Appliance Sales.xlsx.**

2. **On Sheet1, click cell B13 and examine the formula in the formula bar.**

   It contains references to values in column B. See Figure 5-9.

Figure 5-9

3. **Press Ctrl+C to copy the formula to the Clipboard.**

   A dotted outline appears around B13.

4. **Select C13:E13 and press Ctrl+V.**

   The formula is pasted into those cells.

5. **Click cell C13 and examine the formula in the formula bar.**

   It contains references to values in column C. See Figure 5-10.

	A	B	C	D	E	F	G
C13				=C4+C5+C6+C7+C8+C9+C10+C11			
1			**Appliance Sales**				
2							
3	Item	Q1	Q2	Q3	Q4	Total	Bonus
4	Blenders	90	49	81	76	296	
5	Dishwashers	99	80	38	91		
6	Ranges	66	91	59	42		
7	Refrigerators	95	69	39	60		
8	Mixers	71	42	75	75		
9	Toasters	34	55	44	75		
10	Bread Makers	87	74	73	63		
11	Food Processors	77	86	42	74		
12							
13	Total	619	546	451	556		
14							
15	Sales Bonus Per Item	$10					
16							

Figure 5-10

6. **Click cell F4 and drag the fill handle down to F13.**

   The formula from F4 is copied into that range, with the row numbers changed to refer to the new positions. See Figure 5-11.

7. **Click each of the cells in the F column and examine their formulas in the formula bar.**

TIP

Note that each cell uses the correct row number.

8. **Save the changes to the workbook.**

Leave the workbook open for the next exercise.

	A	B	C	D	E	F	G	H
1	**Appliance Sales**							
2								
3	**Item**	Q1	Q2	Q3	Q4	**Total**	**Bonus**	
4	Blenders	90	49	81	76	296		
5	Dishwashers	99	80	38	91	308		
6	Ranges	66	91	59	42	258		
7	Refrigerators	95	69	39	60	263		
8	Mixers	71	42	75	75	263		
9	Toasters	34	55	44	75	208		
10	Bread Makers	87	74	73	63	297		
11	Food Processors	77	86	42	74	279		
12						0		
13	**Total**	619	546	451	556	2172		
14								
15	Sales Bonus Per Item	$10						
16								
17								

Drag Fill handle

Figure 5-11

Copying formulas with absolute referencing

If you want to "lock down" only one dimension of the cell reference, you can place a dollar sign before only the column, or only the row. These are called *mixed references.* For example, =$C1 would make only the column letter fixed, and =C$1 would make only the row number fixed.

In this exercise, you create absolute references and copy formulas that contain them.

Files needed: Chapter 5 Appliance Sales. xlsx, already open from the previous exercise

1. **In Chapter 5 Appliance Sales.xlsx, click G4 and type** =F4*B15.

   This formula multiplies F4 by B15, referring to F4 with a relative reference and referring to B15 with an absolute reference.

2. **Click G4 again, and drag the fill handle down to G11, copying the formula to that range.**

3. **Click cell G11 and examine its formula in the formula bar, as shown in Figure 5-12.**

   Notice that the reference to column F is updated to show F11, but the reference to B15 has remained fixed.

LINGO

You might not always want the cell references in a formula to change when you move or copy it. In other words, you want it to be an **absolute reference** to that cell. To make a reference absolute, you add dollar signs before the column letter and before the row number. So, for example, an absolute reference to C1 would be =C1. You can mix relative and absolute references in the same formula.

	Chapter 7 Appliance Sales.xlsx - Microsoft
File	Home	Insert	Page Layout	Formulas	Data	Review	View

Insert Function

Σ AutoSum ▾
Recently Used ▾
Financial ▾

Logical ▾
Text ▾
Date & Time ▾

Lookup & Reference ▾
Math & Trig ▾
More Functions ▾

Function Library

Name Manager

Define Name ▾
Use in Formula ▾
Create from Selection

Defined Names

G11 =F11*B15

	A	B	C	D	E	F	G	H
1	Appliance Sales							
2								
3	Item	Q1	Q2	Q3	Q4	Total	Bonus	
4	Blenders	90	49	81	76	296	$2,960	
5	Dishwashers	99	80	38	91	308	$3,080	
6	Ranges	66	91	59	42	258	$2,580	
7	Refrigerators	95	69	39	60	263	$2,630	
8	Mixers	71	42	75	75	263	$2,630	
9	Toasters	34	55	44	75	208	$2,080	
10	Bread Makers	87	74	73	63	297	$2,970	
11	Food Processors	77	86	42	74	279	$2,790	
12								
13	Total	619	546	451	556			
14								
15	Sales Bonus Per Item	$10						
16								
17								

Figure 5-12

Next, you copy the formulas from F11 and G11 into row 13.

4. **Select F11:G11 and press Ctrl+C to copy.**

5. **Select F13:G13 and press Ctrl+V to paste.**

6. **Click G13 and examine the formula in the formula bar to confirm it's correct.**

TIP

You could have dragged the fill handle all the way down to G13 in Step 2, so you wouldn't have to copy the formula into G13 in Step 5. However, there still would have been another step because you would have had an extraneous function in cell G12 that you would have had to delete.

7. **Save the changes to the workbook.**

Leave the workbook open for the next exercise.

Getting to Know Functions

Sometimes, as shown in earlier exercises in this chapter, writing a formula can be awkward or lengthy. For example, suppose you want to sum the values in cells A1 through A10. To express it as a formula, you would have to write out each cell reference individually, like this:

```
=A1+A2+A3+A4+A5+A6+A7+A8+A9+A10
```

Instead of the using the preceding formula, you can sum, using the SUM function like this:

```
=SUM(A1:A10)
```

With a function, you can represent a range with the upper-left corner's cell reference, a colon, and the lower-right corner's cell reference. In the case of A1:A10, there's only one column, so the upper left is A1 and the lower right is A10.

REMEMBER

Range references cannot be used in simple formulas. They work only in functions. For example, the formula =A6:A9 is invalid because no math operation is specified in it. There's no way to insert math operators within a range. To use ranges in a calculation, you must use a function.

Each function has one or more arguments. An *argument* is a placeholder for a number, text string, or cell reference. For example, the SUM function requires at least one argument: a range of cells. So in the preceding example, A1:A10 is the argument. The arguments for a function are enclosed in a set of parentheses.

Each function has its own rules as to how many required and optional arguments it has and what they represent. You don't have to memorize the sequence of arguments (the *syntax*) for each function; Excel asks you for them. It can even suggest a function to use for a certain situation if you aren't sure what you need.

Using the SUM function

The SUM function is by far the most popular function. It sums (that is, adds up) a data range consisting of one or more cells, like this:

```
=SUM(D12:D15)
```

You don't *have* to use a range in a SUM function; you can specify the individual cell addresses if you want. Separate them by commas, like this:

```
=SUM(D12, D13, D14, D15)
```

If the data range is not a contiguous block, you need to specify the individual cells that are outside the block. The main block is one argument, and each individual other cell is an additional argument, like this:

```
=SUM(D12:D15, E22)
```

In this exercise, you replace some formulas with equivalent functions.

Files needed: Chapter 5 Appliance Sales.xlsx, *already open from the previous exercise*

1. **In** Chapter 5 Appliance Sales.xlsx, **click B13 and type** =SUM(B4:B11) **and press Enter.**

    The function replaces the formula that was previously there, and the value in the cell shows as 619.

    Typing a function is one way of entering it. The following steps show some other ways.

2. **Click C13, and type** =SUM(.

3. **Drag across the range C4:C11 to select it, and press Enter to enter that range into the function in C13. The value in the cell shows as 546.**

    The AutoSum button is yet another way to get a sum.

4. **Click D13, and then click the Formulas tab and click the AutoSum button. See Figure 5-13.**

    A dotted outline appears around B13:C13. However, this isn't the range you want to sum.

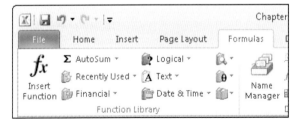

Figure 5-13

5. **Drag across D4:D11 to select that range and then press Enter.**

    The value in D13 shows 451.

6. **Click C13, and drag the fill handle to F13, copying the function to the adjacent cells.**

    Figure 5-14 shows the finished sheet. Note that it doesn't look any different than before; the functions perform the exact same calculations that the formulas did previously.

	A	B	C	D	E	F	G
1				**Appliance Sales**			
2							
3	Item	Q1	Q2	Q3	Q4	Total	Bonus
4	Blenders	90	49	81	76	296	$2,960
5	Dishwashers	99	80	38	91	308	$3,080
6	Ranges	66	91	59	42	258	$2,580
7	Refrigerators	95	69	39	60	263	$2,630
8	Mixers	71	42	75	75	263	$2,630
9	Toasters	34	55	44	75	208	$2,080
10	Bread Makers	87	74	73	63	297	$2,970
11	Food Processors	77	86	42	74	279	$2,790
12							
13	Total	619	546	451	556	2172	$21,720
14							
15	Sales Bonus Per Item	$10					

Figure 5-14

7. **Save the changes to the workbook.**

Leave the workbook open for the next exercise.

Inserting a function

Typing a function and its arguments directly into a cell works fine if you happen to know the function you want and its arguments. Many times, though, you may not know these details. In those cases, Insert Function can help you.

Insert Function enables you to pick a function from a list based on descriptive keywords. Then after you've made your selection, it provides fill-in-the-blank prompts for the arguments.

In this exercise, you find an appropriate function and use Insert Function to create it.

Files needed: Chapter 5 Appliance Sales.xlsx, *already open from the previous exercise*

1. **In** Chapter 5 Appliance Sales.xlsx, **click A16 and type** Average Per Item/Qtr.

2. **Click in B16 and then click the Formulas tab and click the Insert Function button.**

   The Insert Function dialog box opens.

3. **In the Search For a Function text box, delete the placeholder text, type
average, and click Go.**

A list of all the functions that have something to do with averages
appears. See Figure 5-15.

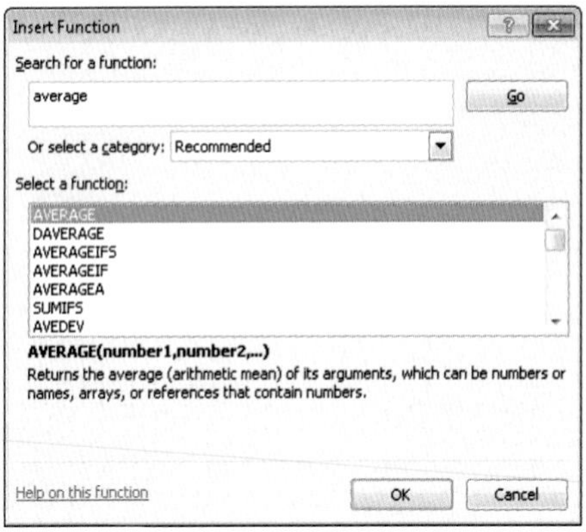

Figure 5-15

4. **In the Select a Function list, select Average and then click OK.**

The Function Arguments dialog box opens.

5. **If a cell reference already appears in the Number1 box, delete it.**

6. **Click the Collapse Dialog button next to the Number1 text box.**

See Figure 5-16.

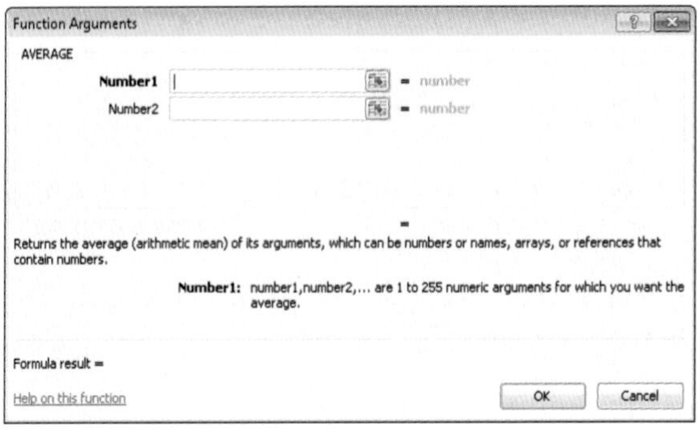

Figure 5-16

7. Drag across B4:E11 to select that range, as shown in Figure 5-17.

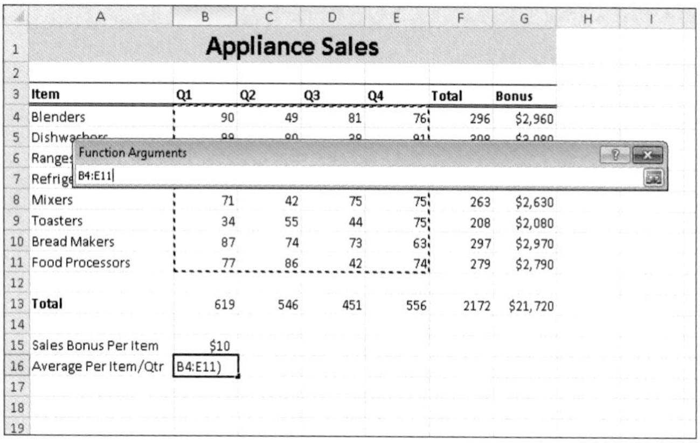

	A	B	C	D	E	F	G	H	I
1		**Appliance Sales**							
2									
3	Item	Q1	Q2	Q3	Q4	Total	Bonus		
4	Blenders	90	49	81	76	296	$2,960		
5	Dishwashers	99	90	20	91	200	$2,000		
6	Ranges								
7	Refrig								
8	Mixers	71	42	75	75	263	$2,630		
9	Toasters	34	55	44	75	208	$2,080		
10	Bread Makers	87	74	73	63	297	$2,970		
11	Food Processors	77	86	42	74	279	$2,790		
12									
13	Total	619	546	451	556	2172	$21,720		
14									
15	Sales Bonus Per Item	$10							
16	Average Per Item/Qtr	B4:E11)							
17									
18									
19									

Function Arguments
B4:E11

Figure 5-17

8. Press Enter or click the Expand Dialog button to return to the Function Arguments dialog box.

9. Click OK.

The function is entered into B16. The result is 67.875.

10. Click B16 and examine the function in the formula bar.

It appears as =AVERAGE(B4:E11).

11. Save the changes to the workbook.

Leave the workbook open for the next exercise.

Touring some basic functions

Excel has hundreds of functions, but most of them are very specialized. The basic set that the average user works with is much more manageable.

Start with the simplest functions of them all: those with no arguments. Two prime examples are

✔ **NOW:** Reports the current date and time.

✔ **TODAY:** Reports the current date.

Even though neither uses any arguments, you still have to include the parentheses, so they look like this:

```
=NOW ( )
=TODAY ( )
```

Another basic kind of function performs a single, simple math operation and has a single argument that specifies what cell or range it operates on. Table 5-2 summarizes some important functions that work this way.

Table 5-2	Simple, One-Argument Functions	
Function	**What It Does**	**Example**
SUM	Sums the values in a range of cells.	=SUM(A1:A10)
AVERAGE	Averages the values in a range of cells.	=AVERAGE(A1:A10)
MIN	Provides the smallest number in a range of cells.	=MIN(A1:A10)
MAX	Provides the largest number in a range of cells.	=MAX(A1:A10)
COUNT	Counts the number of cells that contain numeric values in the range.	=COUNT(A1:A10)
COUNTA	Counts the number of non-empty cells in the range.	=COUNTA(A1:A10)
COUNTBLANK	Counts the number of empty cells in the range.	=COUNTBLANK(A1:A10)

In this exercise, you add some basic functions to a worksheet.

Files needed: Chapter 5 Appliance Sales.xlsx, *already open from the previous exercise*

1. **In** Chapter 5 Appliance Sales.xlsx, **click A17 and type Lowest.**

2. **Click A18 and type** Highest.

3. **Click in B17 and type** =MIN. **Then drag across** B4:E11 **to select the range. Press Enter to complete the function.**

You don't need to type the closing parenthesis; Excel fills it in for you.

The result shows as 34.

4. Click in B18 and type =MAX(B4:E11).

The result shows as 99.

5. Click cell H1 and type As of.

6. Click cell I1 and type =TODAY( ).

Today's date appears there. Figure 5-18 shows the completed worksheet.

	A	B	C	D	E	F	G	H	I	J
1				**Appliance Sales**				As of	1/19/2011	
2										
3	Item	Q1	Q2	Q3	Q4	Total	Bonus			
4	Blenders	90	49	81	76	296	$2,960			
5	Dishwashers	99	80	38	91	308	$3,080			
6	Ranges	66	91	59	42	258	$2,580			
7	Refrigerators	95	69	39	60	263	$2,630			
8	Mixers	71	42	75	75	263	$2,630			
9	Toasters	34	55	44	75	208	$2,080			
10	Bread Makers	87	74	73	63	297	$2,970			
11	Food Processors	77	86	42	74	279	$2,790			
12										
13	Total	619	546	451	556	2172	$21,720			
14										
15	Sales Bonus Per Item	$10								
16	Average Per Item/Qtr	67.875								
17	Lowest	34								
18	Highest	99								
19										
20										

Figure 5-18

7. Save the changes to the workbook and close it.

Leave Excel open for the next exercise.

Exploring Financial Functions

Financial functions are some of the most useful tools for home and small business worksheets because they're all about the money: borrowing it, lending it, and monitoring it.

Here's the basic set:

✔ **PV:** Calculates the present value or principal amount. In a loan, it's the amount you're borrowing; in a savings account, it's the initial deposit.

✔ **FV:** The future value. This is the principal plus the interest paid or received.

✔ **PMT:** The payment to be made per period. For example, for a mortgage, it's the monthly payment; in a savings account, it's the amount you save each period. A period can be any time period, but it's usually a month.

✔ **RATE:** The interest rate to be charged per period (for a loan) or the percentage of amortization or depreciation per period.

✔ **NPER:** The number of periods. For a loan, it's the total number of payments to be made or the points in time when interest is earned if you're tracking savings or amortization.

These financial functions are related. Each is an argument in the others; if you're missing one piece of information, you can use all the pieces you *do* know to find the missing one. For example, if you know the loan amount, the rate, and the number of years, you can determine the payment.

Take a look at the PMT function as an example. The syntax for the PMT function is as follows, with the optional parts in italics:

```
PMT(RATE, NPER, PV, FV, Type)
```

TIP

The Type argument specifies when the payment is made: 1 for the beginning of the period or 0 at the end of the period. It's not required. (I don't use it in the examples here.)

So, for example, say the rate is 0.833% per month (that's 10% per year), for 60 months, and the amount borrowed is $25,000. The Excel formula looks like this:

```
=PMT(.00833,60,25000)
```

If you enter that into a worksheet cell, the monthly payment will be $531.13. You can also enter those values into cells and then refer to the cells in the function arguments, like so (assuming you entered them into B1, B2, and B3):

```
=PMT(B1,B2,B3)
```

Here's the syntax for each of the preceding functions. As you can see, they're all intertwined with one another:

```
FV(RATE, NPER, PMT, PV, Type)
PMT(RATE, NPER, PV, FV, Type)
RATE(NPER, PMT, PV, FV, Type)
NPER(RATE, PMT, PV, FV, Type)
```

Using the PMT function

The PMT function calculates the payment amount on a loan, given the rate, number of periods, and present value. Use this function to answer the question "What would my monthly payment be?"

In this exercise, you calculate the interest rate on a loan.

Files needed: `Chapter 5 Loans.xlsx`

1. Open `Chapter 5 Loans.xlsx` and save it as `Chapter 5 Loans Practice.xlsx`.

2. On the PMT worksheet, click in cell B5.

3. Click the Formulas tab and then the Insert Function button.

4. In the Insert Function dialog box, open the Or Select a Category drop-down list and select Financial.

5. Scroll through the Select a Function list and select PMT.

   See Figure 5-19.

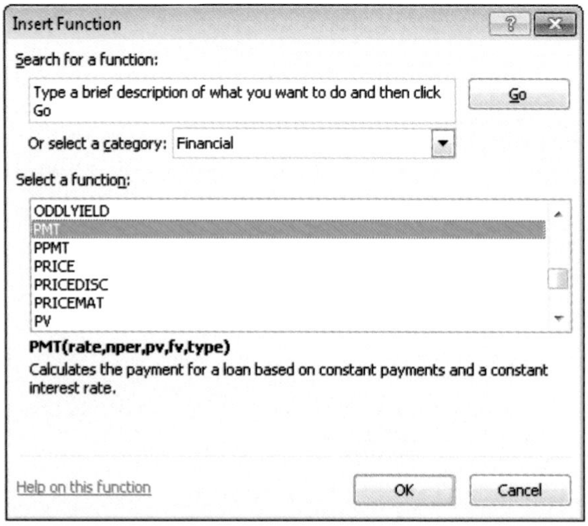

Figure 5-19

6. Click OK.

   The Function Arguments dialog box opens.

7. Drag the dialog box to the side so you can see columns B through D on the worksheet.

8. In the dialog box, click in the Rate text box and then click D6 on the worksheet.

TIP

Interest rates on loans are commonly discussed as a yearly rate, but when calculating a payment, you need to use the monthly rate. The amount in D6 is the yearly rate (B6) divided by 12.

9. **In the dialog box, click in the Nper text box and then click B4 on the worksheet.**

10. **In the dialog box, click in the Pv text box and then click B3 on the worksheet.**

The completed dialog box appears in Figure 5-20.

Function Arguments				?	X

PMT

Rate	D6		=	0.004166667
Nper	B4		=	60
Pv	B3		=	30000
Fv			=	number
Type			=	number

= -566.1370093

Calculates the payment for a loan based on constant payments and a constant interest rate.

Pv is the present value: the total amount that a series of future payments is worth now.

Formula result = -566.1370093

Help on this function   [OK]   [Cancel]

Figure 5-20

11. **Click** OK.

The calculated payment appears in cell B5: –$566.14. It's a negative number because the amount entered in B3 is positive.

PRACTICE

If you want the value in B5 to appear as a positive number, make the amount in B3 negative. If you want them both to appear as positives, enclose the function in B5 in an ABS function (absolute value). To do this, change the entry in B5 to =ABS(PMT(D6,B4,B3)).

12. **Save the changes to the workbook.**

Leave the workbook open for the next exercise.

Using the NPER function

The NPER function calculates the number of payments (in other words, the length of the loan) given the rate, present value, and payment amount. Use this function to answer the question "How long will it take to pay this off?"

In this exercise, you calculate the number of periods for a loan.

Files needed: Chapter 5 Loans Practice.xlsx, already open from the previous exercise

1. **In Chapter 5 Loans Practice.xlsx, click the NPER worksheet tab.**

2. **Click in B4 and type** =NPER(.

   A ScreenTip appears below the cell to prompt you for the arguments. See Figure 5-21. The first argument, rate, is bold in the ScreenTip.

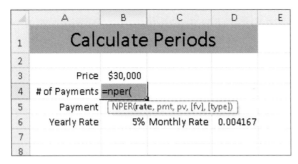

Figure 5-21

3. **Type** D6 **and then type a comma.**

   The ScreenTip makes the next argument prompt bold (pmt).

4. **Type** B5 **and then type a comma.**

   The ScreenTip makes the next argument prompt bold (pv).

5. **Type** B3 **and press Enter.**

   The function is complete. The number of payments is 69.18744.

You can't have a fractional payment in real life, so you might want to use the ROUNDUP function to round up the value in B4 to the nearest whole number. To do so, enclose the current function in a ROUNDUP function like this: =ROUNDUP(NPER(D6,B5,B3),0). The comma and zero near the end are required; the zero says to use no decimal places.

6. **Click the PMT worksheet tab and note the payment amount calculated for a loan of 60 months: $566.14.**

7. **Click the NPER worksheet tab and change the value in B5 to $566.14.**

   The number of payments in B4 changes to 60. Figure 5-22 shows the completed worksheet.

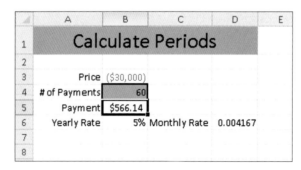

Figure 5-22

    8. Save the changes to the workbook.

Leave the workbook open for the next exercise.

Using the PV function

The PV function calculates the starting value of a loan (assuming it's starting in the present moment) given the rate, number of periods, and payment amount. Use this function to answer the question "How much can I borrow?"

In this exercise, you calculate the present value for a loan.

Files needed: Chapter 5 Loans Practice.xlsx, *already open from the previous exercise*

    1. In Chapter 5 Loans Practice.xlsx, **click the PV worksheet tab.**

    2. Click cell B3 and type =PV(.

    3. Click cell D6 and type a comma.

    4. Click cell B4 (or type B4**) and type a comma.**

    5. Click cell B5 and press Enter.

        The function is now complete. The value shown is ($26,495.35). It's negative.

    6. Click cell B3 to select it.

        The function in B3 shows in the formula bar as =PV(D6,B4,B5).

    7. Change the value in B6 to 3.5%.

        The amount in B3 changes to ($27,484.99), which means that you can borrow more money if you get a lower interest rate.

8. Change the value in B3 to 72.

The amount in B3 changes to ($32,428.79), which means that you can borrow more money if you increase the length of the loan. Figure 5-23 shows the completed worksheet.

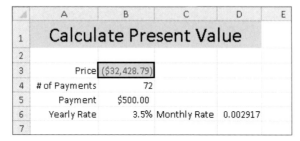

	A	B	C	D	E
1	Calculate Present Value				
2					
3	Price	($32,428.79)			
4	# of Payments	72			
5	Payment	$500.00			
6	Yearly Rate	3.5%	Monthly Rate	0.002917	
7					

Figure 5-23

9. Save the changes to the workbook and close it. Exit Excel.

Summing Up

Here are the key points you learned about in this chapter:

- ✓ A formula is a math calculation. Formulas begin with equals signs.

- ✓ The order of precedence determines the order in which math is processed in a formula: first parentheses, then exponentiation, then multiplication and division, and finally addition and subtraction.

- ✓ Formulas can contain cell references that substitute the cell's value for the reference when the formula is calculated.

- ✓ When you copy a formula, by default the cell references in it are relative, so they change based on the new position.

- ✓ Placing dollar signs in a cell reference (for instance, A1) makes it an absolute reference so it doesn't change when the formula is copied.

- ✓ A function is a word or string of letters that refers to a certain math calculation. A function starts with an equals sign, followed by the function name and a set of parentheses. Arguments for the function go in the parentheses.

- ✓ In functions you can refer to ranges of cells, such as =SUM(A1:A4).

- ✓ If you don't know which function you want, click Formulas, Insert Function.

- ✓ The NOW function shows the current date and time; the TODAY shows the current date.

- ✓ SUM sums a range of cells. AVERAGE averages a range of cells.

- ✓ MIN shows the smallest number in a range, and MAX shows the largest number in the range.

- ✓ COUNT counts the number of cells in a range that contain numeric values. Two related functions are COUNTA, which counts the number of non-empty cells, and COUNTBLANK, which counts the number of empty cells.

- ✓ The functions PV, FV, PMT, RATE, and NPER are all for calculating different parts of a loan's terms. PV is present value; FV is future value. PMT is payment amount. RATE is interest rate. NPER is number of periods.

Try-it-yourself lab

For more practice with the features covered in this chapter, try the following exercise on your own.

1. **Start Excel and create a worksheet that uses the RATE function to cal-culate the interest rate on a loan, given a present value of $150,000, a term of 360 payments, and a payment of $1,000. Make the present value negative in the worksheet so the rate will come out positive.**

TIP

In the cell where you place the RATE function, you may need to increase the number of decimal places shown in order to see the rate correctly. Click the Home tab and then the Increase Decimal button. You may also want to format the rates as percentages; click the Home tab and then the Percentage button.

2. **(Optional) As an extra challenge, look up the PPMT function in the Excel Help system, and then use it to create an amortization table for the loan. If you don't know what an amortization table is, research it online. Figure 5-24 shows an example of the completed project.**

	A	B	C	D	E	F
1	Loan					
2						
3	Rate	0.59%	Yearly	7%		
4	Value	($150,000)				
5	Periods	360				
6	Payment	$1,000				
7						
8						
9	#	Payment	Principal	Interest	Balance	
10					($150,000)	
11	1	$1,000	$122.46	$877.54	($149,877.54)	
12	2	$1,000	$123.08	$876.92	($149,754.46)	
13	3	$1,000	$123.70	$876.30	($149,630.76)	
14	4	$1,000	$124.32	$875.68	($149,506.45)	
15	5	$1,000	$124.94	$875.06	($149,381.51)	
16	6	$1,000	$125.57	$874.43	($149,255.94)	
17	7	$1,000	$126.19	$873.81	($149,129.74)	
18	8	$1,000	$126.83	$873.17	($149,002.92)	
19	9	$1,000	$127.46	$872.54	($148,875.46)	
20	10	$1,000	$128.10	$871.90	($148,747.36)	
21	11	$1,000	$128.73	$871.27	($148,618.63)	
22	12	$1,000	$129.37	$870.63	($148,489.26)	
23	13	$1,000	$130.02	$869.98	($148,359.24)	
24	14	$1,000	$130.66	$869.34	($148,228.57)	
25	15	$1,000	$131.31	$868.69	($148,097.26)	
26	16	$1,000	$131.96	$868.04	($147,965.30)	
27	17	$1,000	$132.62	$867.38	($147,832.68)	
28	18	$1,000	$133.27	$866.73	($147,699.40)	

Sheet1 / Sheet2 / Sheet3

Figure 5-24

Excel has an interest calculation function, IPMT, but you don't have to use it to calculate the interest. You can just subtract the principal amount from the payment.

As you're entering the arguments for the PPMT function, make sure you use absolute references for any of the cells that shouldn't change when that function is copied. That way you can easily fill in the rest of the amortization table by copying. For example, for the worksheet shown in Figure 5-24, the formula in C11 is =PPMT(B3,A11,B5,E10).

Know this tech talk

absolute reference: A cell reference that doesn't change if copied to another cell.

argument: A placeholder for a number, text string, or cell reference in a function.

AVERAGE: A function that averages a range of values.

COUNT: A function that counts the number of cells that contain numeric values in a range.

COUNTA: A function that counts the number of non-empty cells in the range.

COUNTBLANK: A function that counts the number of empty cells in the range.

formula: A math calculation performed in a cell.

function: A text name that represents a math calculation, such as SUM or AVERAGE.

FV: A function that calculates the future value of a loan or savings account.

MAX: A function that provides the largest number in a range of cells.

MIN: A function that provides the smallest number in a range of cells.

NOW: A function that reports the current date and time

NPER: A function that calculates the number of periods in a loan.

PMT: A function that calculates the payment to be made per period for a loan.

PV: A function that calculates the present value or principal amount for a loan or savings account.

RATE: A function that calculates the interest rate to be charged per period, or the percentage of amortization or depreciation per period.

relative reference: A cell reference that changes if copied to another cell.

SUM: A function that sums a range of values.

syntax: The rules that govern how arguments are written in a function.

TODAY: A function that reports the current date.

Manage E-Mail with Outlook

- ✔ Outlook allows you to *send and receive e-mail* from your e-mail accounts at specified intervals.

- ✔ You can *compose an e-mail message in Outlook* to anyone whose e-mail address you have.

- ✔ You can *include file attachments* along with text-based e-mail messages.

- ✔ The Reading pane, which you can set to appear either at the bottom or right of the message list, enables you to *preview message content.*

- ✔ When you reply to a message, *the subject and recipient are prefilled* into the message composition window.

- ✔ You can *manage incoming messages efficiently* by organizing them into folders.

- ✔ Creating message handling rules automatically sorts messages into the folders you specify.

1. **How do you set up an e-mail account in Outlook?**

Look out for page 183

2. **Can you use Outlook to get mail from web accounts like Gmail?**

The web is woven on page 187

3. **How do you compose an e-mail message?**

Find composed creations on page 197

4. **How do you attach a file to a message?**

Attach yourself to page 201

5. **Can you change the interval that Outlook checks for new mail?**

The mail is delivered on page 203

6. **How do you save a received e-mail attachment to your hard drive?**

Treasure these words on page 206

7. **How do you configure the Junk Mail filter in Outlook?**

Filter through the content on page 215

*O*utlook is a multipurpose program. It's an address book, a calendar, a to-do list, and an e-mail handling program, all in one. The most popular Outlook feature, though, is the e-mail handling. Millions of people use Outlook as their primary e-mail program, and for good reason! It's fast, full-featured, and easy to use and customize.

In this chapter, I show you how to set up an e-mail account in Outlook and then how to use it to send and receive e-mail messages.

Discovering Microsoft Outlook

Outlook 2010 is like other Office 2010 applications in many ways. For example, it has a Ribbon, a File tab that opens Backstage View, and a status bar that shows status messages and provides a Zoom slider for changing the magnification of the application's content.

The unique thing about Outlook is that it has several diverse areas, and each area has a different interface. These areas are Mail, Calendar, Contacts, Tasks, and Notes. (Two other items are also listed that aren't really separate areas: Folder List and Shortcuts.) You click a button in the lower-left corner of the Outlook application window to switch to the area you want to work with. See Figure 6-1.

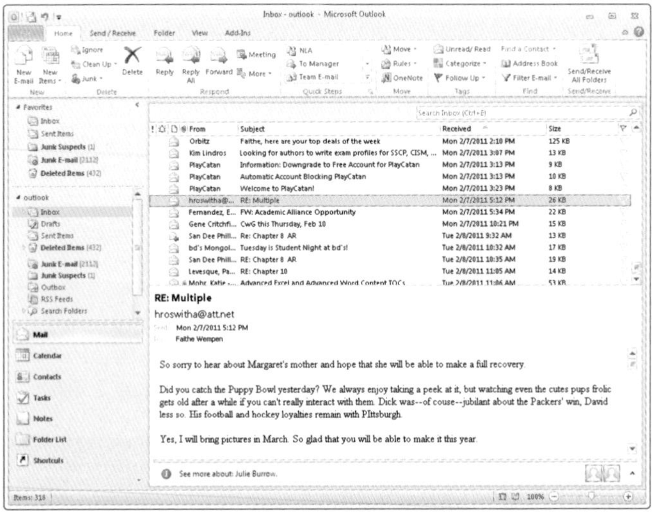

Figure 6-1

Touring the Outlook interface

Even though this chapter covers only the e-mail component of Outlook, it's a good idea to familiarize yourself with the entire application so you can get an idea of how the areas fit together.

> **TIP**
>
> If you've never used Outlook before on the PC you're currently working with, you might be prompted to set up an e-mail address before Outlook starts working normally. If you get such a prompt, skip this tour for now and come back to it after you've worked through the next several sections, which cover e-mail account setup.

In the following exercise, you switch among the different areas of Outlook to see what Outlook has to offer.

Files needed: None

1. **Start Outlook from the Start menu. (Choose Start⇨All Programs⇨Microsoft Office⇨Microsoft Outlook 2010.)**

   If Outlook hasn't been used previously on this PC, the Microsoft Outlook 2010 Startup dialog box opens. Skip to the "Setting Up Outlook for E-Mail" section, later in this chapter; then come back here to finish the tour after you've set up your e-mail.

If anyone has used Outlook previously on this PC, you see the area of the program that was displayed the last time the program was closed.

2. **In the lower-left part of the Outlook window, click Mail. The Mail interface appears, as shown in Figure 6-2.**

The messages will be different, obviously, and you'll probably have different folders than those shown.

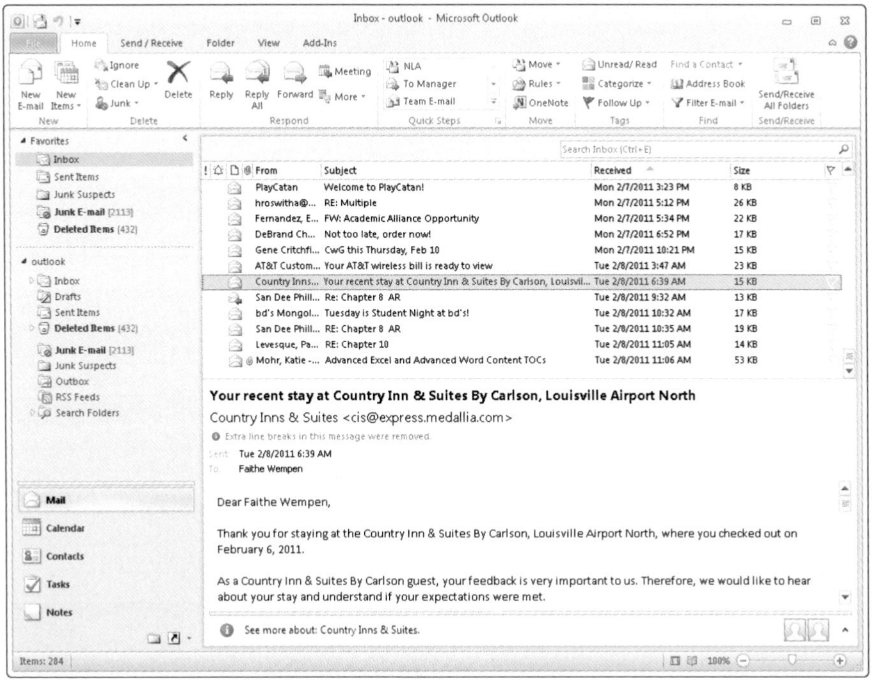

Figure 6-2

When viewing Mail, a mail folder's content appears in the upper-right pane. By default, it shows the Inbox folder, as in Figure 6-2. You can switch to viewing a different folder, such as Sent Items, by clicking the folder name, either in the Favorites list or the Folders list.

The Folders list shows all the available mail folders; the Favorites list shows a subset of those that you (or some other users on this PC) have hand-picked to be placed there. Your Favorites list may not have any folders in it yet. You can drag and drop a folder from the Folders list to the Favorites list to place it there.

3. **Click one of the messages in the Inbox listing. A preview of that message appears in the Reading pane, as shown in Figure 6-2. The Reading pane may also show vertically rather than horizontally on your screen.**

You can optionally switch the orientation of the Reading pane by clicking the View tab and then the Reading Pane button. (Choose Right, Bottom, or None.)

4. **Click the Calendar button in the lower-left corner of the Outlook window.**

A calendar appears, as shown in Figure 6-3. In Figure 6-3 there is an additional calendar, called !Calendar, that appears in the calendar list on the left; you probably don't have that on yours. Figure 6-3 shows a dentist appointment on February 8th. This is how appointments appear on the monthly calendar.

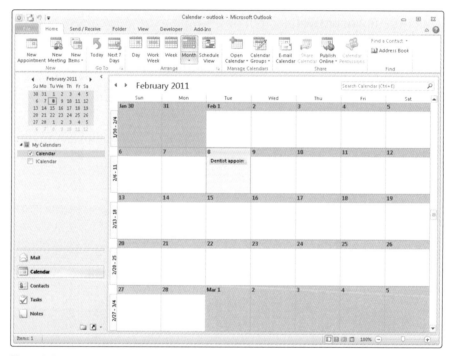

Figure 6-3

5. On the Home tab of the Ribbon, click the Day button.

This step changes the calendar to Day view. See Figure 6-4. Each calendar has a number of different views available.

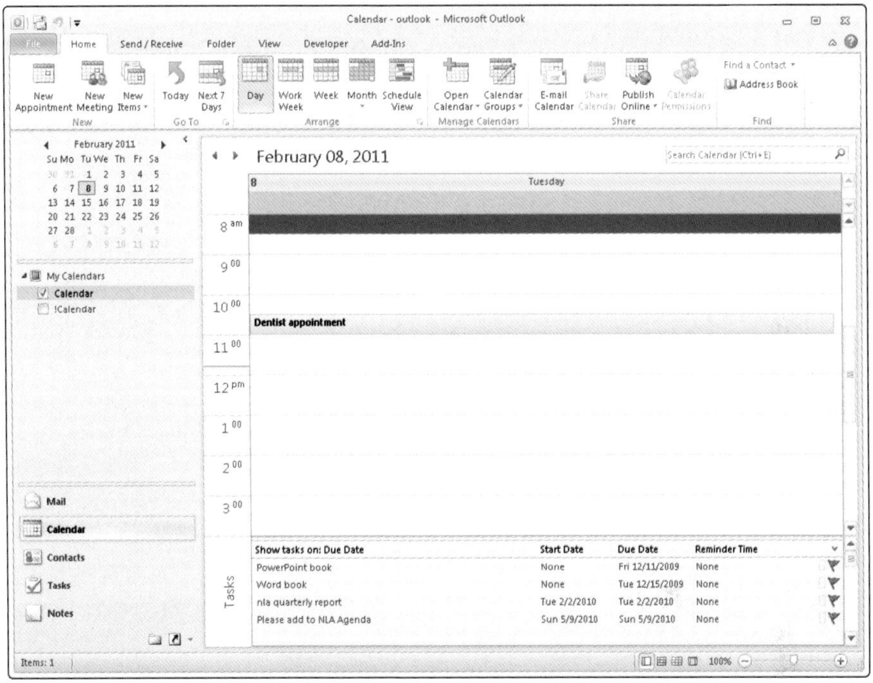

Figure 6-4

For more practice, click each of the other views in the Arrange group on the View tab to see how they display a calendar.

6. Click the Contacts button.

A list of any contacts you've already set up in Outlook appears. Contact listings provide names, addresses, e-mail addresses, phone numbers, and so on for people you want to keep in touch with. Notice the letters along the right side of the listing, as in Figure 6-5:

- You can click a letter to jump quickly to the people with last names starting with that letter.

- You can double-click any listing to see its full record in a separate window.

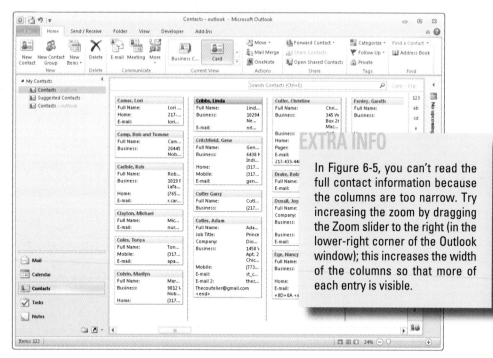

In Figure 6-5, you can't read the full contact information because the columns are too narrow. Try increasing the zoom by dragging the Zoom slider to the right (in the lower-right corner of the Outlook window); this increases the width of the columns so that more of each entry is visible.

Figure 6-5

For more practice, double-click one of the contacts to browse its full information. Then close its window.

7. Click the Tasks button.

A list of any to-do items you have already set up in Outlook appears.

8. Click the Notes button.

A list of any notes you have already set up in Outlook appears.

9. Click the Mail button to return to the Mail folders.

Leave Outlook open for the next exercise.

Setting Up Outlook for E-Mail

The first time you start Outlook, you're prompted to complete several setup operations. The most important of these is to set up your e-mail account. The following exercise walks you through the process.

Outlook supports POP3 and IMAP mail accounts. These are two different kinds of mail servers. You need to know which type you have before you start setting it up in Outlook.

TIP

There's a third kind of e-mail account out there: a web-based account, such as Hotmail, Yahoo! Mail, Gmail, and so on. These are also known as HTTP accounts (HyperText Transfer Protocol). Outlook doesn't support this type of e-mail account. (Some workarounds can force Outlook to recognize certain HTTP mail accounts, but they aren't covered in this chapter.)

Most of the exercises in this book use fictional information and scenarios, but in this case, I ask you to use your own e-mail information. After all, it's *your* e-mail that you want to send and receive, and not some fictional person's, right?

In this exercise, you configure Outlook to send and receive e-mail from your primary e-mail address.

Files needed: None

1. **Start Outlook if it isn't already open. To do so, choose Start⇨All Programs⇨Microsoft Outlook⇨Microsoft Outlook 2010.**

2. **If this is the first time you've started Outlook, the Microsoft Outlook 2010 Startup dialog box opens. Click Next.**

LINGO

Your **e-mail account** is the unique e-mail address that you use to send and receive messages. Your **Internet service provider (ISP)** probably provided you with at least one e-mail account, and you may have other accounts too.

LINGO

POP3 (Post Office Protocol 3) is the most common for home use, and for most offices too. With a POP3 account, mail is stored on the server until you retrieve it, and then downloaded to your PC (and deleted from the server). This is called a store-and-forward system.

With an **IMAP** (Internet Mail Access Protocol) account, the mail stays on the server at all times. This is convenient because you can get your e-mail from anywhere (and review old messages from anywhere), but it's slower than POP3 to access and more labor-intensive for the company managing the server. Some companies provide IMAP to their employees who travel a lot, so they can get their e-mail from different PCs.

If you don't see that dialog box, someone might have already started Outlook on this PC before. Choose File⇨Account Settings⇨Account Settings to open a list of the accounts that are already set up. If your e-mail account is listed, you're done; close the dialog box. If not, click New, click Next, and then pick up at Step 4.

3. **At the E-Mail Accounts screen, you're asked whether you want to configure an e-mail account. You do, so click Next.**

4. **In the Add New Account dialog box, fill in your name, e-mail address, and password, and click Next. See Figure 6-6.**

Add New Account	✕
Auto Account Setup
Click Next to connect to the mail server and automatically configure your account settings.
⦿ **E-mail Account**
Your Name:
Example: Ellen Adams
E-mail Address:
Example: ellen@contoso.com
Password:
Retype Password:
Type the password your Internet service provider has given you.
◯ **Text Messaging (SMS)**
◯ **Manually configure server settings or additional server types**
< Back   Next >   Cancel

Figure 6-6

Outlook attempts to determine the name of your mail server and then contact it to set up your accounts, using an encrypted connection.

- *If the encrypted connection works,* a message appears, telling you so.

- *If the encrypted connection doesn't work,* a message to that effect appears. Click Next, and it tries to connect unencrypted.

If Outlook can determine the right settings (and it does in most cases), it logs into the mail server and sends a test message to you. Wait while all this goes on.

5. **Check to make sure Outlook correctly detected the account type (probably POP3). You should see a message that says Your POP3 account has been successfully configured. If it says IMAP, as in Figure 6-7, do not proceed to Step 6 (unless, of course, you**

actually do have an IMAP mail account). Instead, see the next section, "Changing the Mail Server Type during Setup."

6. **Only if the mail server type was correctly identified, click Finish; otherwise, see the next section.**

If the test message fails, see the later section "Troubleshooting Mail Setup."

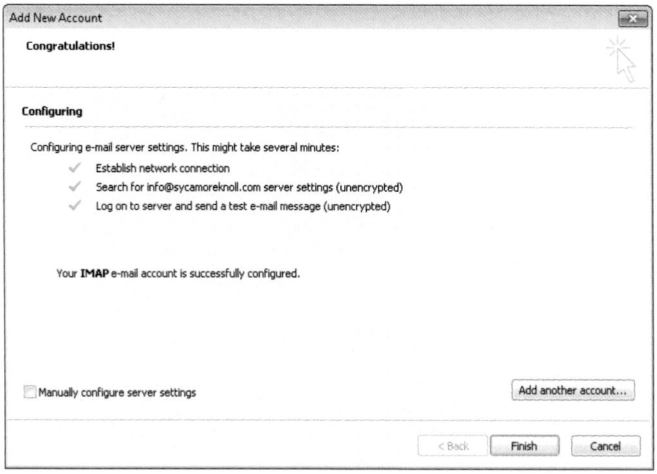

Add New Account

Congratulations!

Configuring

Configuring e-mail server settings. This might take several minutes:

✓   Establish network connection

✓   Search for info@sycamoreknoll.com server settings (unencrypted)

✓   Log on to server and send a test e-mail message (unencrypted)

Your **IMAP** e-mail account is successfully configured.

☐ Manually configure server settings   [Add another account...]

    [< Back] [**Finish**] [Cancel]

Figure 6-7

Changing the mail server type during setup

If you see a message saying "Your IMAP account has been successfully configured" as you're configuring a POP3 e-mail account, as shown in Figure 6-7, you need to change the account type. You also need to specify a data file in which to store the messages. (IMAP accounts don't require a data file because they store messages only on the server.)

You must change the mail server type before clicking Finish as you are configuring the new account. Outlook won't let you change the server type afterwards.

From the screen shown in Figure 6-7, follow these steps to change the server type:

1. **Select the Manually Configure Server Settings check box and click Next.**

   The Internet E-Mail Settings page of the dialog box appears. See Figure 6-8.

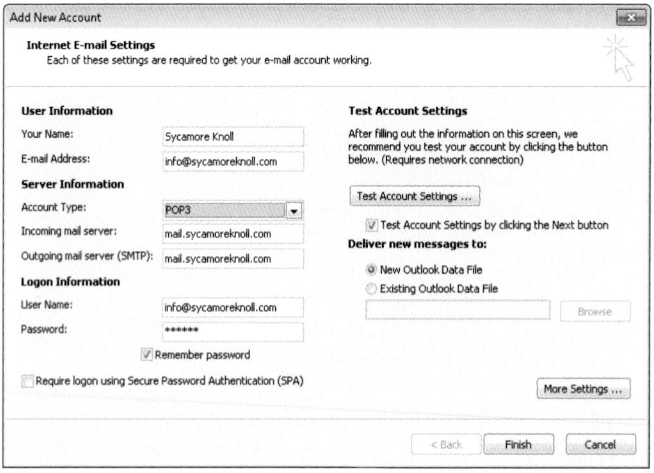

Figure 6-8

2. **Open the Account Type drop-down list and select POP3.**

3. **In the Deliver New Messages To area, select Existing Outlook Data File.**

4. **Click the Browse button.**

   The Open Outlook Data File dialog box appears.

5. **Navigate to the folder containing your Outlook data file, select it, and click OK.**

   - If Outlook 2010 was installed from scratch on this PC and it didn't replace an earlier version of Outlook, the path is probably `C:\ Users\`*`username`*`\Documents\Outlook Files\Outlook.pst` (where *username* is your login name in Windows).

   - If you upgraded to Outlook 2010 from an earlier version, the path is `C:\users\`*`username`*`\AppData\Local\Microsoft\Outlook` (where *username* is your login name in Windows).

If the AppData folder doesn't appear, you have to enable the display of hidden files and folders in Windows. To do so, open a Computer window (Start➪Computer) and choose Organize➪Folder and Search Options. The Folder Options dialog box appears. On the View tab, select the option labeled Show Hidden Files, Folders, and Drives and then click OK.

6. **Click the Finish button to complete the setup using the correct server type.**

Setting up additional mail accounts

If you have other e-mail accounts, you can set them up in Outlook, too. If you have a separate account for a home-based business or hobby, for example, you might want to be able to get the mail for that address at the same time you retrieve the mail for your main account.

In this exercise, you set up an additional e-mail account in Outlook. You need an additional account of your own for this exercise, as it doesn't provide a sample one.

Files needed: None

1. Choose File⇨Account Settings⇨Account Settings.

The Account Settings dialog box opens.

2. On the E-Mail tab, click New.

The Choose Service options appear. The E-Mail Account option is selected by default. See Figure 6-9.

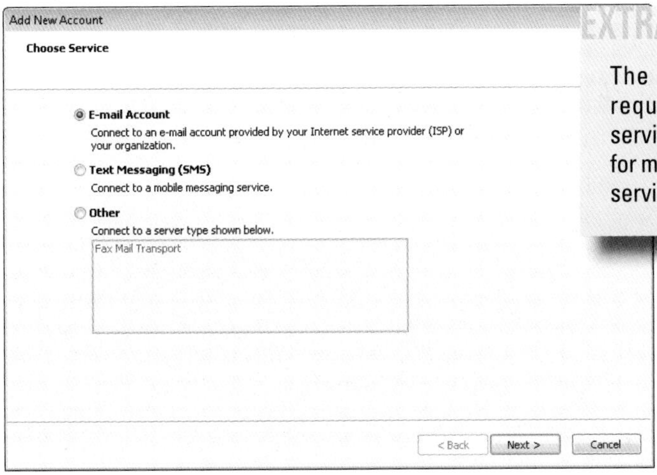

> **EXTRA INFO**
>
> The Text Messaging option requires a Microsoft Mobile service provider; it can't be used for most cellphone text messaging services.

Figure 6-9

3. Click Next to accept the default setting.

4. Jump to Step 4 in the section "Setting Up Outlook for E-Mail," earlier in the chapter, to complete the setup process.

5. When you finish setting up the account, click Close to close the Account Settings dialog box.

Troubleshooting mail setup problems

Each e-mail service has its own quirks in how you have to set up the account in Outlook (or any mail program) to properly send and receive messages. Outlook can automatically detect the settings in many cases, but it can't always detect every service correctly.

If Outlook wasn't able to successfully send a test message (see the earlier section, "Setting Up Outlook for E-Mail"), you need to do some troubleshooting. Don't panic, though. It's not that difficult. If you get stuck, you can always call your ISP's tech support line and get help.

If you're using a web-based e-mail provider such as Yahoo!, Gmail, or Hotmail, it probably won't work with Outlook. This is a known issue. Some services have workarounds that you can follow to make them work in Outlook; check the tech support section at the website where you get your web-based mail to see whether there is anything you can do.

To troubleshoot mail problems, make sure you have the following information handy. If you don't have it, contact your ISP. It may also be available on the ISP's website.

- ✔ **Your e-mail address and password:** You probably have this already from your earlier attempt.

- ✔ **The incoming and outgoing mail server addresses:** They both might be the same.

The server address is usually whatever comes after the @ sign in your e-mail address, preceded by the word mail. For example, if your e-mail address is `tom@myprovider.com`, the mail server might be `mail.myprovider.com`. If there are separate servers for incoming and outgoing mail, the incoming one might be `pop.myprovider.com`, and the outgoing one might be `smtp.myprovider.com`. Those are just guesses, though; you need to get that information from your ISP.

- ✔ **Information about whether an encrypted connection should be used.**

- ✔ **Information about whether your outgoing mail server requires authentication:** If it does require authentication, you also need to know whether the outgoing server requires a different username and password than your regular one.

Armed with all that information, follow these steps to troubleshoot:

1. **Choose File➪Account Settings➪Account Settings.**

    The Account Options dialog box opens.

2. **Double-click the e-mail account you want to troubleshoot.**

    The Change Account dialog box opens. See Figure 6-10.

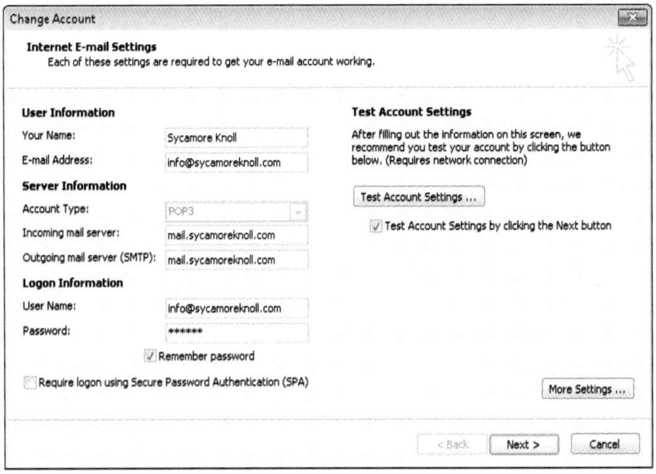

Figure 6-10

3. **Check all the information in the dialog box to make sure it matches the information you have about your account.**

    In particular, check the Account Type, Incoming Mail Server, and Outgoing Mail Server (SMTP).

You may not be able to change the account type. If you can't, and it's wrong, you need to delete that account from Outlook and set it up again, as if it were a new account.

4. **Mark or clear the Require Login Using Secure Password Authentication (SPA) check box, whichever is different from the current setting.**

Click Test Account Settings to see whether that fixed the problem. If it didn't, go back to the original setting.

5. **Click the More Settings button.**

The Internet E-Mail Settings dialog box opens.

6. **Click the Outgoing Server tab and then select the My Outgoing Server (SMTP) Requires Authentication check box.**

See Figure 6-11.

7. **Try each of the three options. After each one, click OK and then click the Test Account Settings button to check whether it helped.**

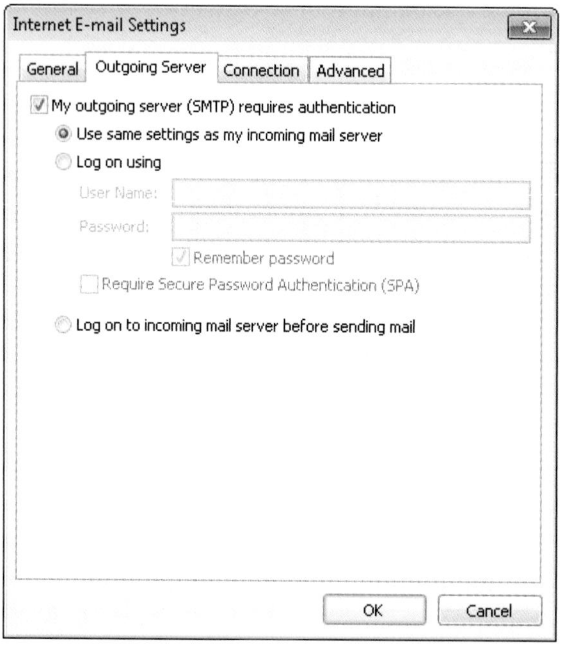

Internet E-mail Settings

| General | Outgoing Server | Connection | Advanced |

☑ My outgoing server (SMTP) requires authentication

- ◉ Use same settings as my incoming mail server
- ○ Log on using

  User Name: [ ]

  Password: [ ]

  ☑ Remember password

  ☐ Require Secure Password Authentication (SPA)

- ○ Log on to incoming mail server before sending mail

[OK]   [Cancel]

Figure 6-11

If you select the Log On Using radio button, fill in your username and password in the boxes provided. For the username, use your complete e-mail address. If that doesn't work, try using only the part of your e-mail address before the @ sign. Try it with the Require Secure Password Authentication (SPA) check box deselected, and then try it with that check box selected.

8. **If you closed the Internet E-mail Settings dialog box, click the More Settings button again to reopen it. Then on the Advanced tab (see Figure 6-12), drag the Server Timeouts slider closer to the word *Long* (that is, farther to the right).**

This change can help give more time to a mail server that is slow to respond. A timeout delay of more than two minutes isn't usually needed.

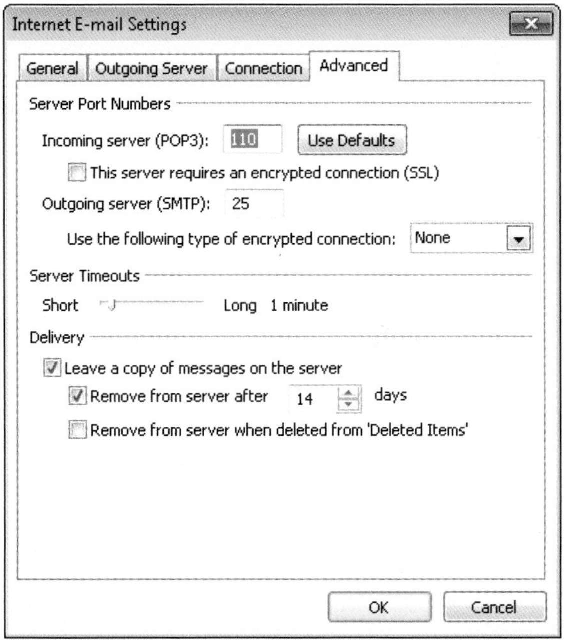

Internet E-mail Settings

General | Outgoing Server | Connection | Advanced

Server Port Numbers

Incoming server (POP3): 110   Use Defaults

☐ This server requires an encrypted connection (SSL)

Outgoing server (SMTP): 25

Use the following type of encrypted connection: None ▼

Server Timeouts

Short ⎯⎯J⎯⎯⎯⎯ Long   1 minute

Delivery

☑ Leave a copy of messages on the server

   ☑ Remove from server after   14 ⬍ days

   ☐ Remove from server when deleted from 'Deleted Items'

OK   Cancel

EXTRA INFO

Some mail servers use different port numbers for incoming and/or outgoing mail. Check with your service provider to make sure that it uses the defaults of 110 for incoming and 25 for outgoing, and make changes on the Advanced tab if needed.

Figure 6-12

9. **Click OK and click the Test Account Settings button.**

10. **If you got Outlook to successfully complete a test message, great. Close all dialog boxes.**

If not, contact your e-mail service provider's tech support and find out what setting you need to change to make it work.

Receiving and Reading Your Mail

After you configure your e-mail account(s) in Outlook, receiving mail is an automatic process. Outlook automatically sends and receives mail when you start it and also at 30-minute intervals (by default) whenever Outlook is running. Your incoming mail comes automatically into the Inbox folder. You can also initiate a manual send/receive operation at any time.

Sending and receiving e-mail manually

Manually sending and receiving mail connects to the mail server(s), sends any mail you have in queue, and downloads any waiting mail for you.

In the following exercise, you manually send and receive e-mail.

Needed: An e-mail account set up in Outlook

1. Click the Send/Receive All Folders button on the Quick Access Toolbar.

See Figure 6-13.

MORE INFO

Alternative methods: You can click the Send/Receive tab and then click the Send/Receive All Folders button, or press F9.

Figure 6-13

Leave Outlook open for the next exercise.

 If the Send/Receive All Folders button doesn't appear on the Quick Access Toolbar, click the Send/Receive tab, right-click the Send/Receive All Folders button, and choose Add to Quick Access Toolbar.

Setting the send/receive interval

By default, the automatic send/receive interval is 30 minutes. You might prefer a different interval. For example, because I need to respond quickly to business requests via e-mail, I have mine set to check every 5 minutes.

In the following exercise, you change the interval at which Outlook automatically sends and receives mail.

1. **Click the Send/Receive tab, click the Send/Receive Groups button, and then choose Define Send/Receive Groups.**

TIP

Alternatively, you can press Ctrl+Alt+S.

The Send/Receive Groups dialog box opens.

2. **Under the Setting for Group "All Accounts" section, make sure that the Schedule an Automatic Send/Receive Every *X* Minutes check box is selected.**

3. **Click the down increment arrow on the text box to change the number of minutes to 5.**

See Figure 6-14.

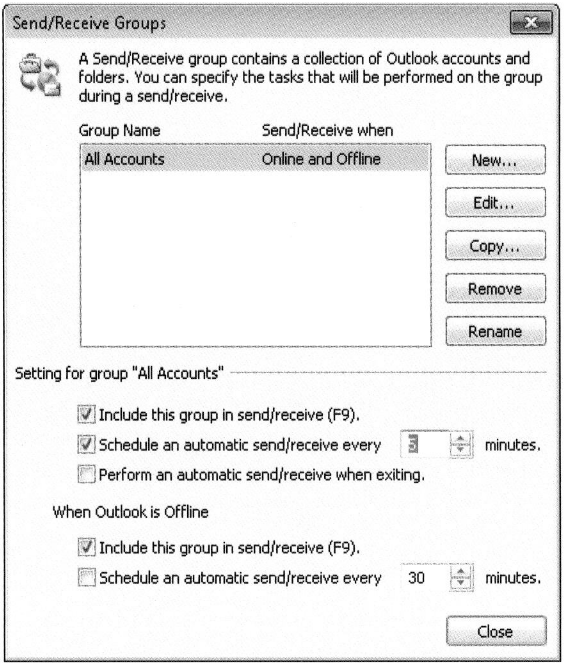

EXTRA INFO

In the dialog box, under the When Outlook Is Offline heading, there is a duplicate of the Schedule an Automatic Send/Receive Entry Every *X* Minutes option. That setting applies only when you aren't connected to the Internet. You can have a different interval when offline than when online.

Figure 6-14

4. Click the Close button.

Leave Outlook open for the next exercise.

Reading an e-mail message

You can read messages in the Reading pane, or you can open each message in its own separate window.

In the following exercise, you read an e-mail message.

Needed: An e-mail account set up in Outlook, and the Reminder e-mail message that you sent yourself earlier in the chapter

1. **Click the View tab, click the Reading Pane button, and choose Right to turn on the Reading pane at the right if it isn't already there.**

2. **Click the Reading Pane button again and choose Bottom to move the Reading pane below the Inbox.**

3. **Click the Reminder message in the Inbox pane.**

   The message appears in the Reading pane. See Figure 6-15.

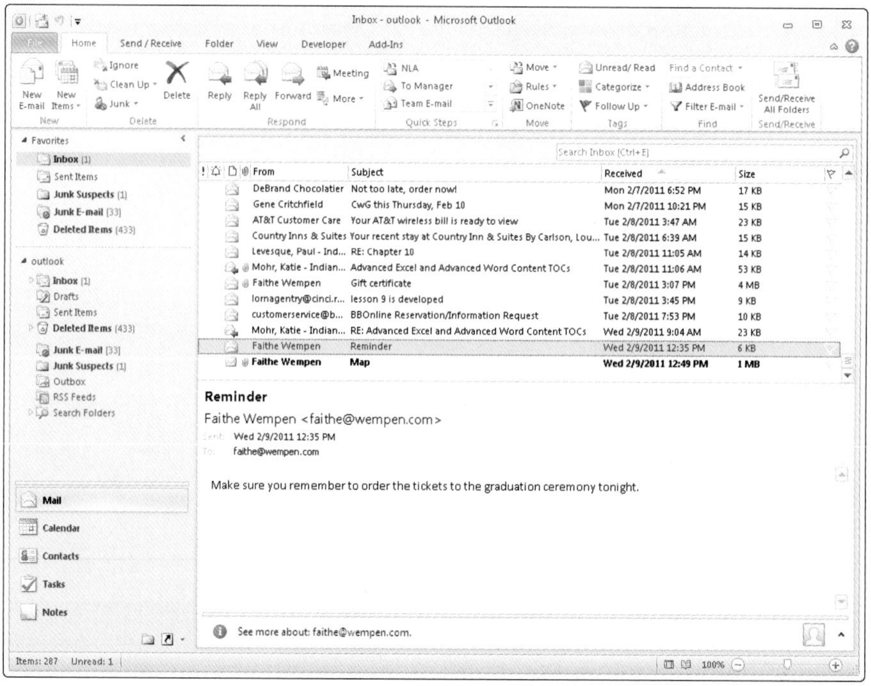

Figure 6-15

4. **Double-click the message in the Inbox pane to display the message in a separate window.**

See Figure 6-16.

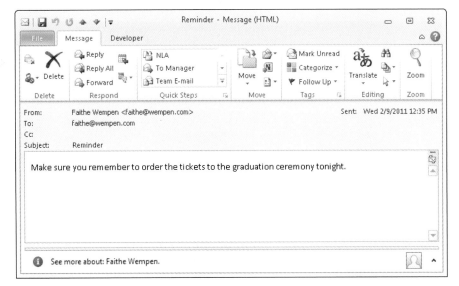

Figure 6-16

TIP

Click the Close (X) button in the message window to close it.

Leave Outlook open for the next exercise.

Viewing an e-mail attachment

Using attachments, people can exchange all types of files with one another, such as files from other Office applications like Word, Excel, and PowerPoint.

WARNING!

Some types of attachments can carry viruses. (Pictures are generally safe, though.) If you have any doubts about the safety of any file you receive, do not open it.

LINGO

Some e-mail messages have **attachments**, which are additional files that travel along with the e-mail message as it is sent and received.

In the following exercise, you read an e-mail message that has an attachment, and save the attachment to your hard disk.

Needed: An e-mail account set up in Outlook, and the Map e-mail that you sent yourself earlier in the chapter

1. In the Inbox pane, click the Map message to select it.

The paper clip icon indicates that the e-mail has an attachment. See Figure 6-17.

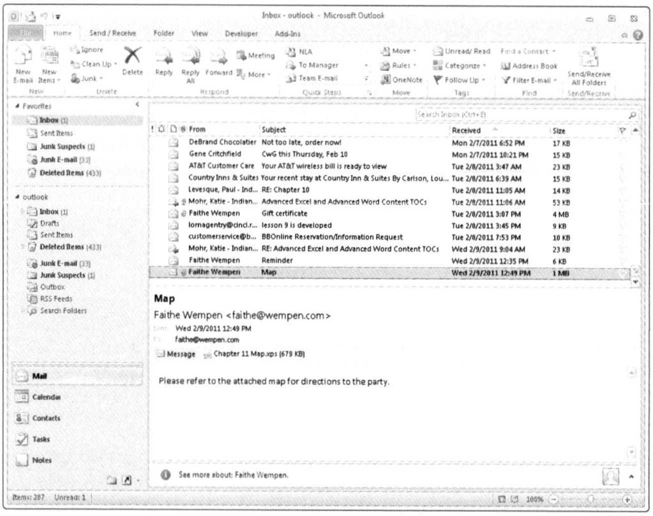

Figure 6-17

In the Reading pane, notice that there are two files listed above the message. One is called Message, and the other is the attached file's name (Chapter 6 Map.xps).

2. Click Chapter 6 Map.xps in the Reading pane.

A warning appears, stating that you should preview files only if they come from a trustworthy source.

3. Click the Preview File button.

A preview of the attachment appears in the Reading pane.

TIP

If the file type isn't one that Outlook can preview, a message appears and tells you This file cannot be previewed because there is no previewer installed for it.

4. **Click Message to return to seeing the message in the Reading pane.**

5. **Double-click** `Chapter 6 Map.xps`**.**

   An Opening Mail Attachment dialog box appears. See Figure 6-18.

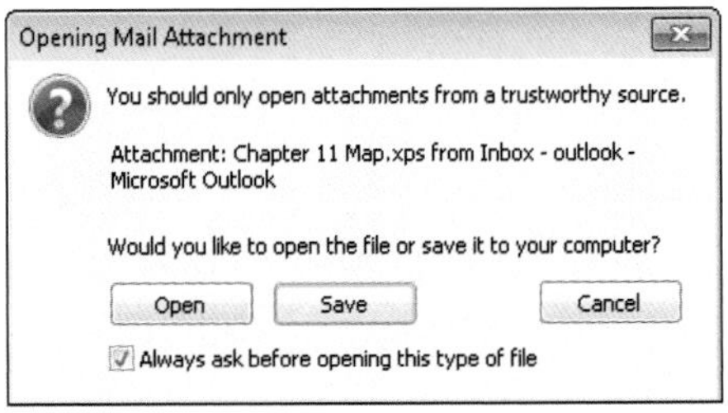

Opening Mail Attachment

You should only open attachments from a trustworthy source.

Attachment: Chapter 11 Map.xps from Inbox - outlook - Microsoft Outlook

Would you like to open the file or save it to your computer?

[Open] [Save]   [Cancel]

☑ Always ask before opening this type of file

Figure 6-18

6. **Click the Open button.**

   The map opens in the XPS Viewer application.

TIP

The XPS Viewer comes free with Windows Vista and Windows 7. If you're using Windows XP, you can download a free copy of the XPS Viewer from Microsoft.com, or you can skip Steps 5–7 of this exercise.

7. **Click the Close button (X) to close the XPS Viewer application.**

8. **In the Reading pane, right-click the** `Chapter 6 Map.xps` **file and choose Save As.**

   The Save As dialog box opens.

9. **Navigate to the location where you're storing your completed work for this lesson.**

10. **Click Save.**

   The attachment is saved.

Leave Outlook open for the next exercise.

Composing and Sending E-Mail

You can compose and send your own e-mail messages from your e-mail account. To do so, you start a new message with the New E-Mail command and then fill in the form that appears with the appropriate recipient, subject, and body information. Then click Send, and off it goes.

Replying to a message

Replying to a message is quick and easy because you don't have to look up the recipient's e-mail address. It's already filled in for you.

In the following exercise, you reply to an e-mail message.

Needed: An e-mail account set up in Outlook, and the Reminder e-mail that you sent yourself earlier in this chapter

> 1. **In the Inbox pane, click the Reminder e-mail message.**
>
> 2. **On the Home tab, click the Reply button.**

TIP

If multiple people had received the e-mail and you wanted to reply to them all, you could click the Reply to All button in Step 2. In this exercise, you were the only recipient, so it's a moot point.

A new window opens with the original message quoted in the body area, your e-mail address filled in on the From text box, and the original sender (also you) filled in on the To line. In the Subject text box, the original subject appears with RE: in front of it.

> 3. **At the top of the message body area, type your reply:** Thank you, I will.
>
> See Figure 6-19.

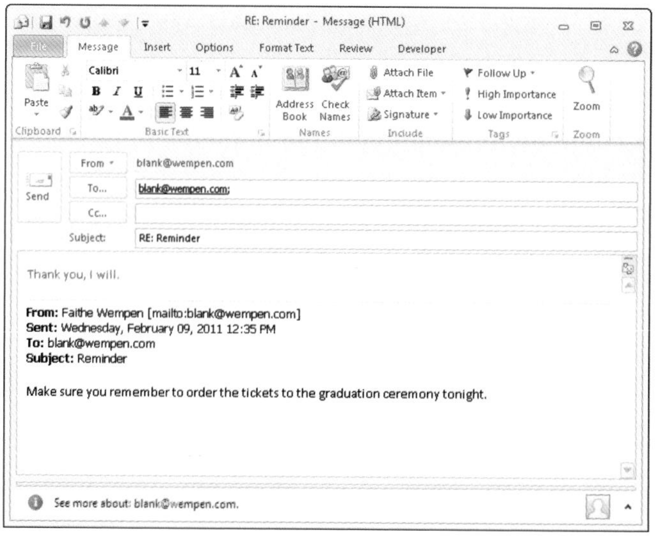

![Outlook reply message window titled "RE: Reminder - Message (HTML)" showing the ribbon with Message, Insert, Options, Format Text, Review, Developer tabs. The From field shows blank@wempen.com, To field shows blank@wempen.com, Subject shows RE: Reminder. The message body begins "Thank you, I will." followed by the quoted original message: From: Faithe Wempen [mailto:blank@wempen.com], Sent: Wednesday, February 09, 2011 12:35 PM, To: blank@wempen.com, Subject: Reminder, Make sure you remember to order the tickets to the graduation ceremony tonight.]

Figure 6-19

4. Click the Send button.

The reply is sent.

Composing a new message

You can send a new e-mail message to anyone for whom you have an e-mail address. Just fill in the recipient, subject, and message, and send it off.

In the following exercise, you send yourself an e-mail message. By doing so, you'll then have a received message later to practice reading and replying to.

Needed: An e-mail account set up in Outlook

1. With the Inbox displayed onscreen, click the Home tab and then click the New E-Mail button.

A new Untitled – Message window appears. Your default e-mail address is already filled in on the From text box. See Figure 6-20.

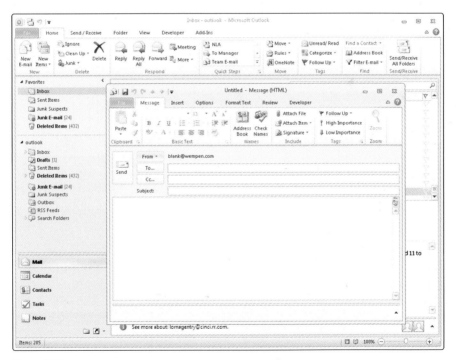

Figure 6-20

2. In the To text box, type your own e-mail address.

If you want to send mail to multiple recipients, separate their e-mail addresses with commas in the To box. You can use the Cc box for additional recipients who should get a courtesy copy. (Both To and Cc recipients get identical messages.)

You can choose a recipient from Outlook's Address Book by clicking the To button. I don't cover that skill in this chapter, but you can experiment with it on your own.

3. In the Subject text box, type Reminder.

Including an appropriate subject line is important to alert the recipient about the topic you're writing about.

4. In the body area, type the following:

Make sure you remember to order the tickets to the graduation ceremony tonight.

If you want to, you can format the body text in your message. Use the formatting buttons in the message composition window, such as Bold, Italic, Font, Font Size, and so on, just as you do in Word and other Office applications.

5. Check the message to make sure it looks like Figure 6-21 (except with your own e-mail address in both the From and To boxes, rather than the dummy one shown in the figure).

6. Click the Send button.

The message is sent. Depending on your Outlook settings, it may go out immediately, or it may wait until the next scheduled send/receive operation.

7. To make sure that the message goes out, click the Send/Receive tab and then click the Send/Receive All Folders button.

The message should appear in your Inbox as a new message. If the message doesn't appear, repeat the Send/Receive operation after a few minutes' wait.

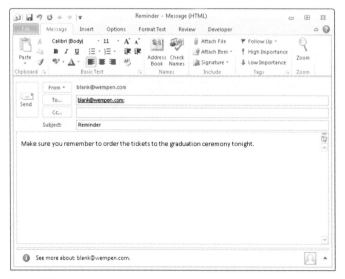

Figure 6-21

Attaching a file to a message

You can attach a file to an e-mail, so that the file travels along with the message to the recipient. The recipient can then open the attachment directly from the Inbox, or save it to their hard disk for later use.

In the following exercise, you send yourself an e-mail message that contains an attachment. By doing so, you'll then have a received message with an attachment later to practice reading.

Needed: An e-mail account set up in Outlook

1. **With the Inbox displayed onscreen, click the Home tab and then click the New E-Mail button.**

   A new Untitled – Message window appears. Your default e-mail address is already filled in on the From text box.

2. **In the To text box, type your own e-mail address.**

3. **In the Subject text box, type** Map.

4. **In the body area, type the following:**

   Please refer to the attached map for directions to the party.

5. **Click the Message tab and then the Attach File button.**

   The Insert File dialog box opens.

6. **Navigate to the folder containing the data files for this lesson and select** `Chapter 6 Map.xps`.

See Figure 6-22.

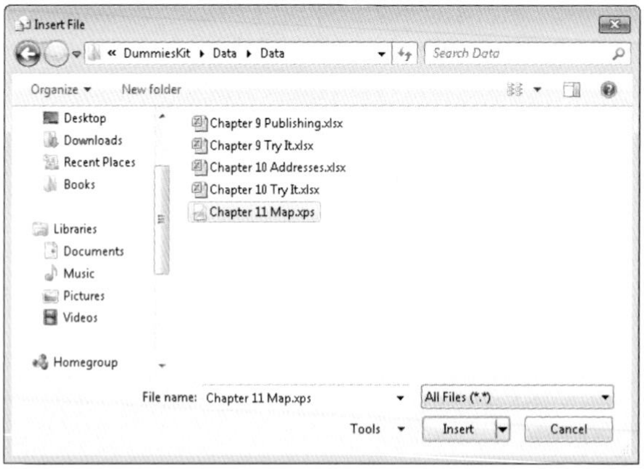

Figure 6-22

7. **Click the Insert button.**

8. **Check the message to confirm that it looks like Figure 6-23 (except with your own e-mail address in the From and To boxes).**

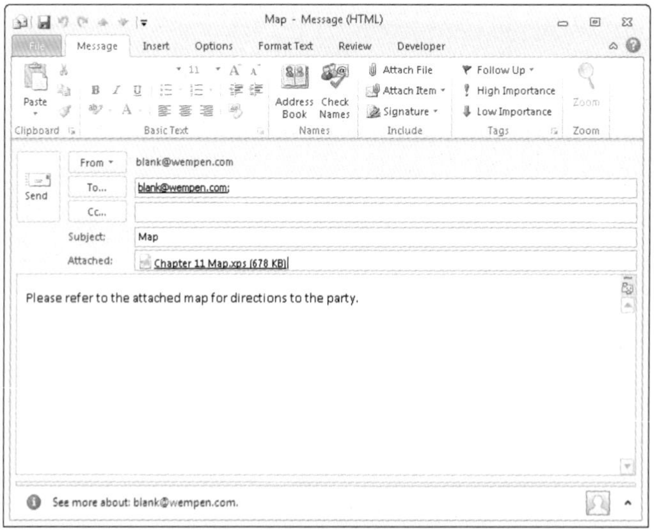

Figure 6-23

9. **Click the Send button.**

   The message is sent. Depending on your Outlook settings, it may go out immediately, or it may wait until the next scheduled send/receive operation.

10. **To make sure that the message goes out, click the Send/Receive tab and then click the Send/Receive All Folders button.**

    The message should appear in your Inbox as a new message. If it doesn't, repeat the Send/Receive operation after a few minutes' wait.

Managing Incoming Mail

If you receive a lot of e-mail, you may want to set up some systems for keeping it organized. Your system can include creating folders to store e-mail that you want to keep for later reference, moving messages from one folder to another, deleting e-mail that you no longer need, and flagging an e-mail for later follow-up. You can also configure Outlook's Junk E-mail filter to be more or less aggressive in trying to filter out unwanted advertisements.

Creating folders for managing mail

Outlook starts with a basic set of folders, which you can see on the Folders list when viewing the Inbox:

- ✔ **Inbox:** Incoming mail

- ✔ **Outbox:** Messages waiting to be sent

- ✔ **Sent Items:** Copies of sent messages

- ✔ **Junk E-Mail:** Messages Outlook's Junk Mail filter has identified as possible junk

- ✔ **Deleted Items:** Messages you have deleted from other folders

- ✔ **RSS Feeds:** Any RSS feeds you've subscribed to

LINGO

RSS (Really Simple Syndication) feeds enable you to receive updated content from Web sites automatically in Outlook, without having to visit those sites.

You can create new folders if you like and then either manually drag and drop messages into them for storage or create mail-handling rules that automatically place messages into those folders upon receipt.

In the following exercise, you create a mail folder.

Needed: An e-mail account set up in Outlook

1. **In the Folder List to the left of the Inbox pane, right-click Inbox and choose New Folder.**

   See Figure 6-24. The Create New Folder dialog box opens.

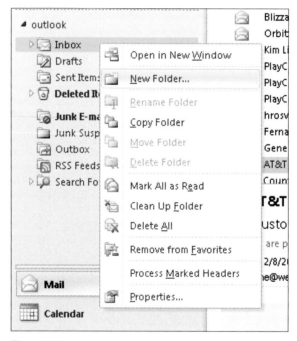

Figure 6-24

2. **Click in the Name box and type Short-Term.**

3. **Make sure that Inbox is selected in the folder list at the bottom of the dialog box.**

   See Figure 6-25.

4. **Click OK.**

The new folder is created below the Inbox folder on the folder list. There may also be other folders already beneath the Inbox folder, depending on whether anyone has created others on this PC already. In Figure 6-26, for example, there are four other folders besides Short-Term.

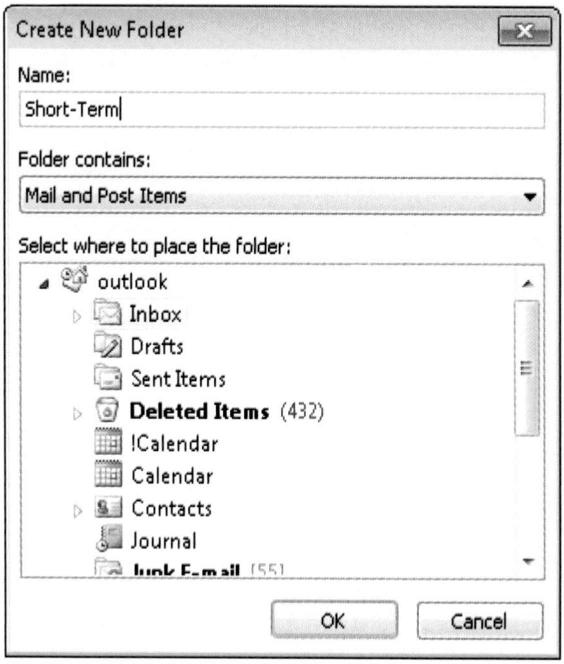

Figure 6-25

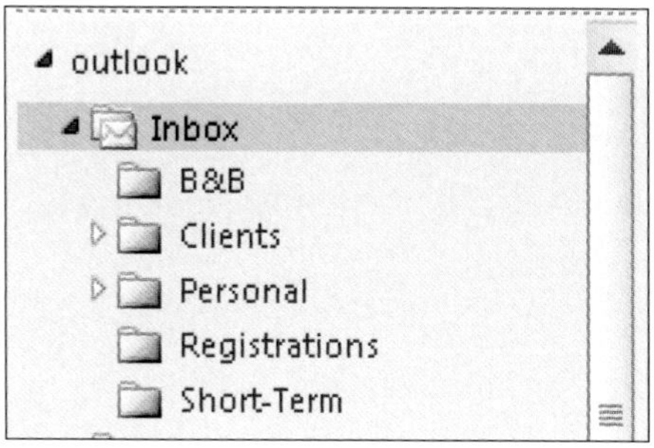

Figure 6-26

5. **Click the new Short-Term folder to select it.**

   Its content appears. It's empty, so both of the panes on the right are blank.

Leave Outlook open for the next exercise.

Moving a message to a folder

One way to move messages to another folder for storage is to drag and drop them there. You can drag individual messages or select multiple messages at once and drag them as a group.

In the following exercise, you move a message into a different folder.

Needed: An e-mail account set up in Outlook, the Short-Term folder created in the previous exercise, and the Reminder e-mail that you sent yourself earlier in this chapter

1. **In the Folder List to the left of the Inbox pane, click Inbox to return to the Inbox folder.**

2. **If the Short-Term folder isn't visible below the Inbox folder in the folder list on the left, click the triangle to the left of Inbox to expand its list of subfolders.**

   See Figure 6-26.

3. **In the Inbox, click the Reminder e-mail that you sent yourself earlier in the lesson.**

4. **Drag the Reminder e-mail to the Short-Term folder and drop it there.**

   The message is moved into that folder.

5. **Click the Short-Term folder to display its content.**

   It now contains the message you just placed there. See Figure 6-27.

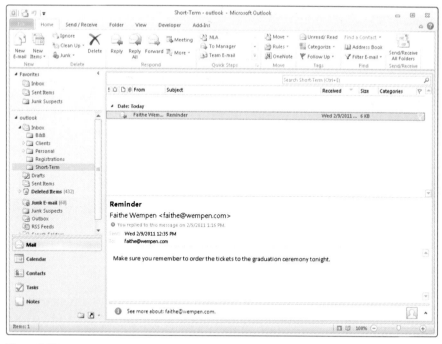

Figure 6-27

Leave Outlook open for the next exercise.

Creating a rule that moves messages

You can create message-handling **rules**, which are instructions that execute automatically to carry out your wishes for certain situations. For example, a rule can move message from a certain person or with a certain word in the subject line to a specified folder.

In the following exercise, you create a message-handling rule that moves messages based on a word in the subject line.

Needed: An e-mail account set up in Outlook, the Short-Term folder created in an earlier exercise, and the Map e-mail that you sent yourself earlier in this chapter

1. **Choose File⇨Info⇨Manage Rules & Alerts.**

   The Rules and Alerts dialog box opens.

2. **Click the New Rule button.**

   The Rules Wizard dialog box opens.

3. **In the Stay Organized section of the Step 1: Select a Template pane, select Move Messages with Specific Words in the Subject to a Folder.**

   See Figure 6-28.

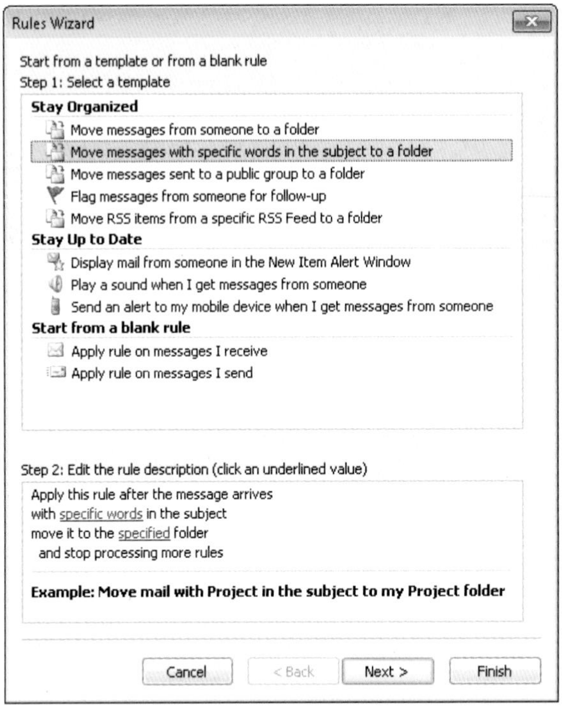

Figure 6-28

4. **In the Step 2 pane, click the underlined phrase <u>specific words</u>.**

   The Search Text dialog box opens.

5. **In the text box labeled Specify Words or Phrases to Search For in the Subject, type Map and then click the Add button to add it to the Search list.**

   Figure 6-29 shows the word already added to the search list.

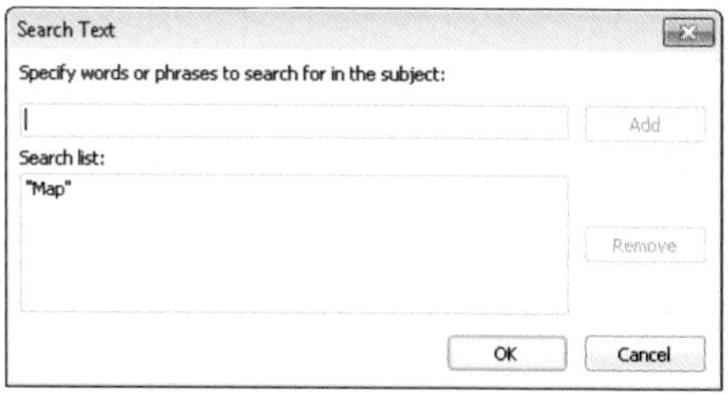

Search Text

Specify words or phrases to search for in the subject:

| | Add |

Search list:

"Map"

| | Remove |

| OK | Cancel |

Figure 6-29

6. Click OK to return to the Rules Wizard dialog box.

The word *Map* appears underlined in the Step 2 pane.

7. In the Step 2 pane, click the underlined word specified.

The Rules and Alerts dialog box appears, showing a folder list.

8. Click the triangle to the left of Inbox to expand the list of subfolders and then click Short-Term.

See Figure 6-30.

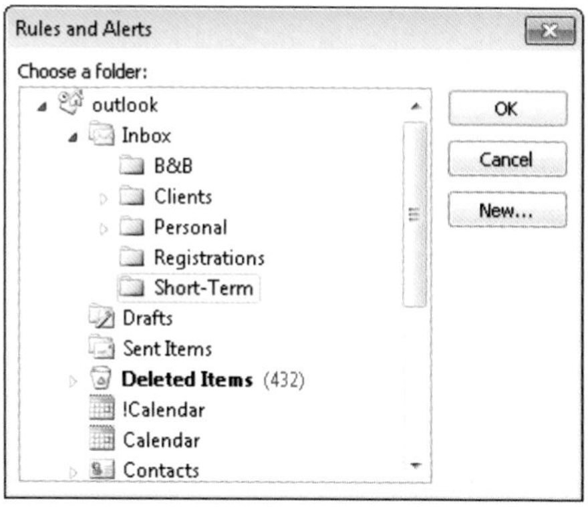

Rules and Alerts

Choose a folder:

- ▲ outlook — [OK]
  - ▲ Inbox — [Cancel]
    - B&B — [New...]
    - ▷ Clients
    - ▷ Personal
    - Registrations
    - Short-Term
  - Drafts
  - Sent Items
  - ▷ **Deleted Items** (432)
  - !Calendar
  - Calendar
  - ▷ Contacts

Figure 6-30

9. Click OK to return to the Rules Wizard dialog box.

Now in the Step 2 pane, the rule appears as shown in Figure 6-31.

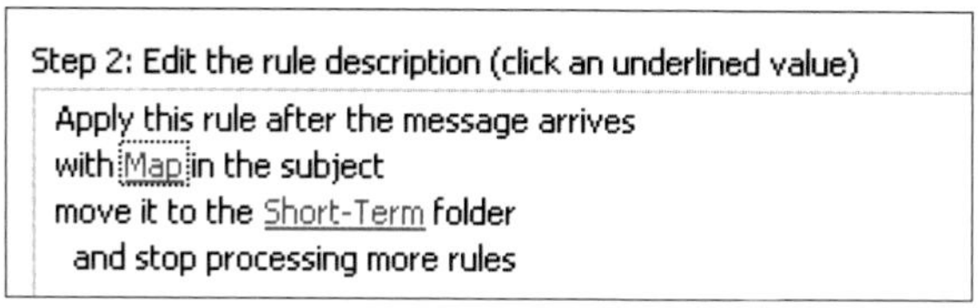

Step 2: Edit the rule description (click an underlined value)

Apply this rule after the message arrives
with Map in the subject
move it to the Short-Term folder
and stop processing more rules

Figure 6-31

10. **Click the Finish button.**

The rule is created, and it appears in the Rules and Alerts dialog box.

11. **Click the Run Rules Now button.**

The Run Rules Now dialog box opens.

12. **Click to mark the Map check box, selecting the Map rule.**

See Figure 6-32.

Figure 6-32

13. **Click the Run Now button.**

The rule is run, and the message with the Map subject line is moved into the Short-Term folder.

14. **Click Close to close the Run Rules Now dialog box.**

15. **Click OK to close the Rules and Alerts dialog box.**

16. **Click the Home tab to return to the Inbox.**

    Notice that the Map message is no longer there.

17. **In the folder list at the left, click the Short-Term folder.**

    The Map message appears there.

Leave Outlook open for the next exercise.

Customizing the Favorites list

You can place shortcuts in the Favorites list to the mail folders you use most frequently, so you do not have to wade through a long list of folders every time you want them.

In the following exercise, you add a folder to the Favorites list.

Needed: An e-mail account set up in Outlook, and the Short-Term folder created in an earlier exercise

LINGO

The **Favorites list** is a shortcut area that appears at the top of the folder list pane in Outlook when in the Mail area of the application.

1. **In the Folder list on the left, click the Short-Term folder to select it.**

2. **Drag the Short-Term folder up to the Favorites area and drop it at the top of the list.**

    A shortcut to the Short-Term folder now appears on the Favorites list. See Figure 6-33.

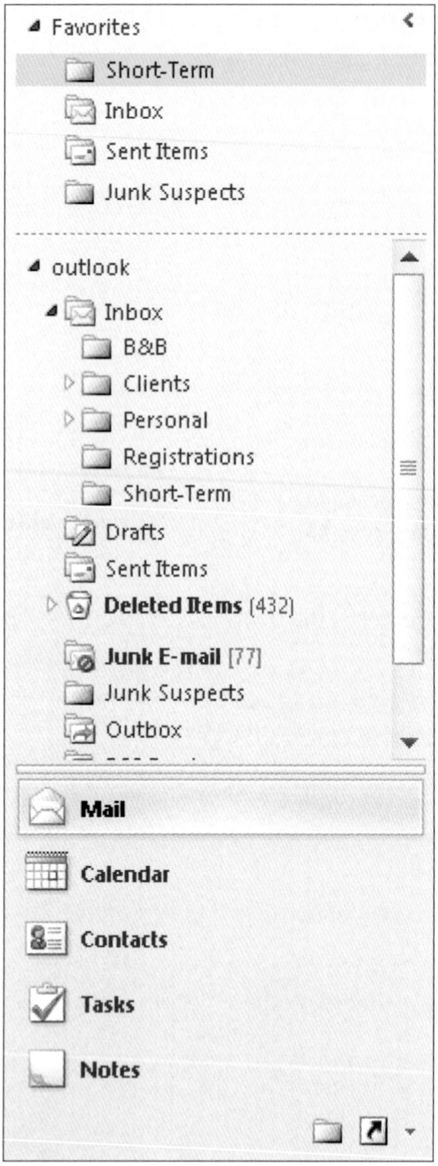

Figure 6-33

3. **Right-click the Short-Term folder on the Favorites list.**

    A shortcut menu opens.

4. Choose Remove from Favorites.

The Short-Term folder no longer appears on the Favorites list.

Leave Outlook open for the next exercise.

Deleting e-mail

Even though so far you've been focusing on how to save e-mail for later reference, there's nothing wrong with deleting e-mail after you read it. In fact, as time goes by, you'll accumulate way too much e-mail if you don't delete most of it.

In the following exercise, you delete an e-mail message and then retrieve it again from the Deleted Items folder.

Needed: An e-mail account set up in Outlook, and the Short-Term folder created in an earlier exercise, containing the Map and Reminder e-mails sent to yourself earlier in the lesson

1. **In the Folders list on the left, click Short-Term to display that folder if it isn't already displayed.**
2. **Click the Map e-mail message.**
3. **Press the Delete key on the keyboard to delete it.**
4. **Click the Reminder e-mail message.**
5. **Click the Home tab and click the Delete button to delete it.**
6. **In the Folders list, click the Deleted Items folder.**

   The display switches to that folder.
7. **Click the Received column heading to sort by that column.**

   A down-pointing triangle should appear on that column heading.

> If an up-pointing triangle appears there, click the Received column heading a second time to change the sort order.

8. **Scroll to the bottom of the list of messages.**

   Your two deleted messages appear there. See Figure 6-34.
9. **Click the Reminder e-mail to select it.**
10. **Hold down the Ctrl key and click the Map e-mail to select it.**

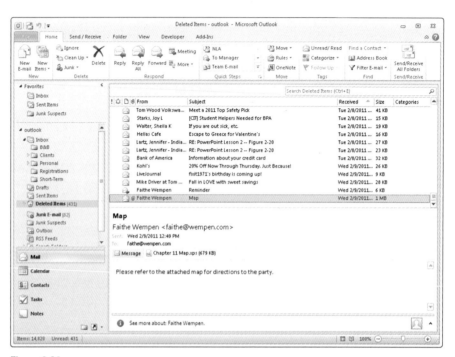

Figure 6-34

11. **Drag the selected e-mail messages to the Short-Term folder in the Folders list on the left.**

    The messages are moved back into the Short-Term folder.

12. **Click the Short-Term folder to display its content and confirm that the two messages now appear there.**

    Leave Outlook open for the next exercise.

Flagging an e-mail

You can assign different flags to a message depending on when follow-up is due. When a flagged message is overdue, the entire message appears in red text on the message list.

In the following exercise, you flag an e-mail and then mark it as completed.

LINGO

Sometimes when you receive an e-mail, you don't have time to deal with it appropriately at that time. You can **flag** an e-mail to remind yourself that you need to take action on it later. You can then mark it as Completed after you've done whatever it was you needed to do.

Needed: An e-mail account set up in Outlook, and the Short-Term folder containing the Map and Reminder e-mails sent to yourself earlier in the lesson

1. **In the Short-Term folder, click the Map message to select it.**

2. **Click the flag outline in the Flag column (on the far left edge of the message list).**

   The flag changes from transparent to bright red, as shown in Figure 6-35. The default flag is a Today flag, indicating you should follow up on it today.

!	☆	D	⑧	From	Subject		Received	▽	Size	Categories		▽	▲

   ◢ **Date: Today**

   | | Faithe Wem... | Map | Wed 2/9/2011 ... | 1 MB | ▼ |
   | | Faithe Wem... | Reminder | Wed 2/9/2011 ... | 6 KB | |

Figure 6-35

3. **Click the red flag.**

   It changes to a check mark, indicating the action has been completed on the message.

4. **Right-click the check mark, and from the shortcut menu that appears, choose Next Week.**

   The flag reappears, and changes to a pink flag, indicating a lower priority.

PRACTICE

For more practice, try selecting each of the other flags on the shortcut menu to assign them to the message.

5. **Right-click the flag, and on the shortcut menu, choose Clear Flag.**

   The flag goes back to being transparent, as it was when you began.

Leave Outlook open for the next exercise.

Configuring the Junk Mail filter

You can adjust the sensitivity of the Junk Mail filter in Outlook's options. If you set it to be very aggressive, fewer junk messages will get through, but it might sometimes mark legitimate messages as junk. If you set it to be less aggressive, you'll get more junk in your Inbox.

LINGO

Outlook comes with a **Junk Mail filter** that removes some of the more obvious junk messages from your Inbox before they have a chance to annoy you. The Junk Mail filter relies on internal rules that Outlook receives from Microsoft; occasionally Microsoft sends out updates for it, which you receive as Windows Updates. The Junk Mail filter is far from perfect, but it does catch some items.

In the following exercise, you configure the Junk Mail filter in Outlook.

Needed: An e-mail account set up in Outlook

1. **Click the Home tab, click the Junk button, and choose Junk E-Mail Options.**

   The Junk E-Mail Options dialog box appears.

2. **On the Options tab, click the option button that best represents the level of filtering you want. See Figure 6-36.**

   • *No Automatic Filtering:* Turns off the filter.

   • *Low:* Moves most obvious junk e-mail.

   • *High:* Catches almost all junk e-mail but also may catch some regular mail.

   • *Safe Lists Only:* Allows only e-mail on your Safe Senders List. (If you choose this option, you must then configure the lists on the Safe Senders and Safe Recipients tabs.)

3. **Click OK to accept the new setting.**

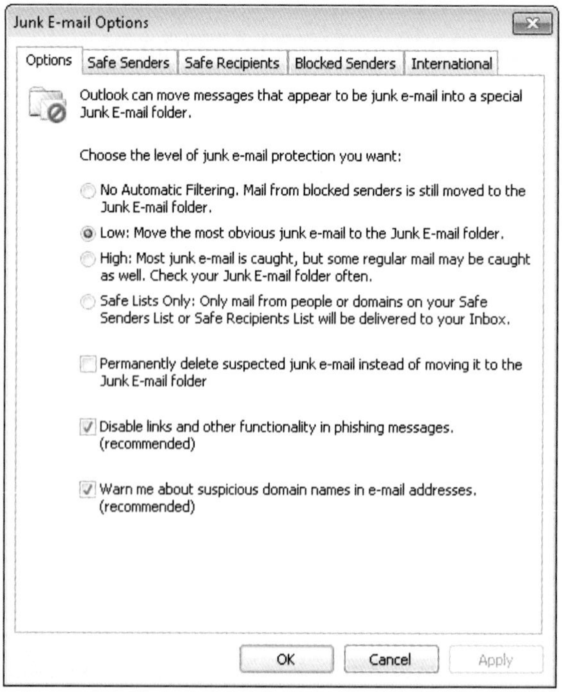

Figure 6-36

Summing Up

Here are the key points you learned about in this chapter:

- ✔ Sending and receiving e-mail in Outlook requires a valid e-mail account.
- ✔ Most e-mail accounts are of the POP3 type; IMAP is a less common but also supported type.
- ✔ Outlook does not work with a web mail account.
- ✔ To compose a new e-mail message, click Home, New E-Mail.
- ✔ To attach a file, from the e-mail composition window, click Message, Attach File.
- ✔ To manually send and receive, click the Send/Receive All Folders button on the Quick Access Toolbar or on the Send/Receive tab, or press F9.
- ✔ You can set the Reading pane to appear below or to the right of the message list. Click View and then Reading Pane to change its position.
- ✔ To save an e-mail attachment, right-click it and choose Save As.
- ✔ To create new e-mail folders, right-click the Inbox folder and choose New Folder.
- ✔ To move a message to a folder, drag it there.
- ✔ To add a folder to the Favorites list, drag it there.
- ✔ To create message handling rules, choose File⇨Info⇨Manage Rules & Alerts.
- ✔ To delete an e-mail, press the Delete key or click Home, Delete.
- ✔ To flag an e-mail, click the flag symbol to its right on the message list.
- ✔ To configure the junk mail filter, click Home, Junk, Junk E-Mail Options.

Try-it-yourself lab

For more practice with the features covered in this chapter, try the following exercise on your own.

1. **Ask several friends for their e-mail addresses.**

2. **In Outlook, compose a new e-mail message and address it to at least three people. Separate the addresses with commas in the To box.**

3. **In the Subject text box, type** Best Joke Ever.

4. In the message body, type your favorite joke. (Keep it clean.) End the message by asking your friends to send a joke back to you using Reply All. Ask them to put the word *Joke* in the subject line.

5. Click Send.

6. Create a new folder called Jokes.

7. Create a message-handling rule that sends any incoming jokes to that folder. (Hint: Use the word *Joke* in the subject line as the criterion.)

8. Sit back and enjoy the jokes that your friends send back to you!

Know this tech talk

attachment: A file that travels along with an e-mail message.

e-mail account: The unique e-mail address that you use to send and receive messages.

Favorites list: A shortcut area that appears at the top of the folder list pane in Outlook when in the Mail area of the application.

flag: To mark an item to remind yourself to take action on it later.

HTTP: Hypertext Transfer Protocol, a web-based Internet protocol. This is the protocol that most web-based mail services use, such as Hotmail and Gmail.

IMAP: Internet Mail Access Protocol, an alternative to POP3 where the messages remain on the server.

Internet service provider (ISP): The company that provides your Internet service.

Junk Mail filter: A feature in Outlook that removes some of the more obvious junk messages from your Inbox.

POP3: Post Office Protocol 3, the most common type of e-mail account. This type works on a store-and-forward basis, with messages transferred from the server to your local PC and then deleted from the server.

rule: A message-handling instruction that executes to carry out your wishes for sorting and managing e-mail.

Chapter 7

Using Contacts, Notes, and Tasks

✔ Contacts *store information you need to keep in touch* with people.

✔ The File As property for a contact *controls how it is alphabetized in* the Contacts list.

✔ E-mailing contact information to others can *save them time in data entry*.

✔ Creating tasks for the things you need to accomplish helps you *prioritize tasks and track your progress toward their completion*.

✔ You can *set a reminder so that a pop-up box opens* and lets you know when it's time to work on a task.

1. **How do you add a contact to Outlook?**

Contact page... 221

2. **Can you alphabetize a contact by the company name rather than the person?**

Information keeps you company on page... 228

3. **How do you get a contact back after accidentally deleting it?**

Find your contacts on page 229

4. **How do you e-mail a contact to someone who doesn't have Outlook?**

Send yourself to page.. 234

5. **How do you create a Tasks list that includes multiple priorities?**

Prioritize page 237

6. **How do you set a reminder to complete a task?**

Reminders are remembered on page... 241

*O*utlook is much more than just an e-mail program. It excels at storing information that you need for your daily business and personal dealings, such as contact information, notes, and to-do lists. If you can't keep yourself organized with all these tools available to you, don't blame Outlook!

In this chapter, I show you how to enter and use contact information in the Contacts area of Outlook. I also show how to create and manage tasks and to-do items in the Tasks area.

Storing Contact Information

Outlook stores complete contact information about the people you want to keep in touch with. You can store not only mailing addresses, but also phone numbers, e-mail addresses, pager numbers, and personal information such as birthdays, spouse names, departments, and professions.

Adding and editing a contact

You may not have any contacts yet in the Contacts area of Outlook. Don't worry about that, though, because it's easy to add one.

In the following exercise, you create a contact in Outlook.

Files needed: None

LINGO

The Contacts area of Outlook stores a **contact** (also called a **record**) for each person or business that you want to save for later use.

1. **In Outlook, click the Contacts button in the lower-left corner of the application window.**

   The Contacts pane appears. You may or may not have any contacts in it.

2. **Click the Home tab and then the New Contact button.**

   The Untitled – Contact window opens.

3. **Enter the information shown in Figure 7-1.**

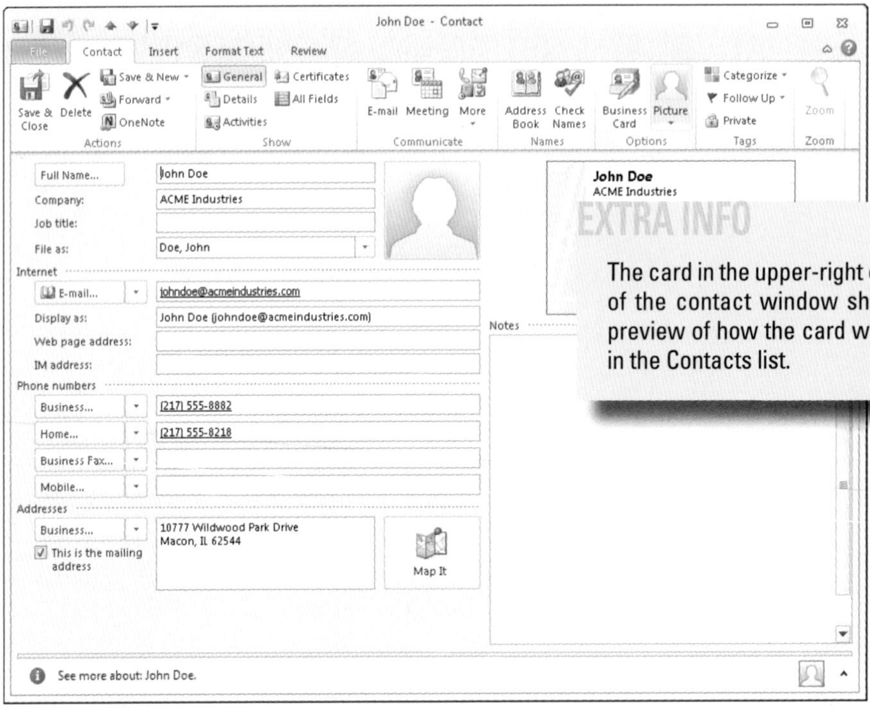

The card in the upper-right corner of the contact window shows a preview of how the card will look in the Contacts list.

Figure 7-1

4. **On the Contact tab of the Ribbon, click the Details button.**

   Additional fields appear.

5. **Enter the additional information shown in Figure 7-2.**

6. **Click the Save & Close button on the Ribbon.**

   The contact closes, and a card for it appears on the Contacts list. See Figure 7-3. If you've already entered other contacts, they appear there also.

7. **Double-click the contact you just created.**

   It reopens.

8. **Add a job title of Vice President for the contact.**

9. **Click the Save & Close button.**

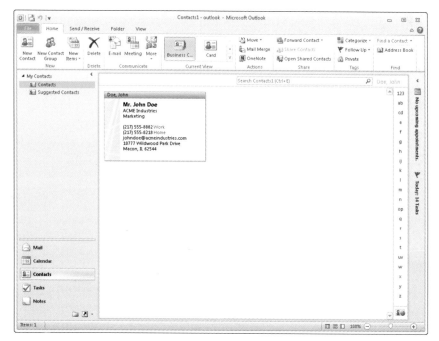

Figure 7-2

> **EXTRA INFO**
>
> Depending on the view you're using, the card may look different than shown here. On the Home tab, in the Current View group, click Card or Business Card to switch between the two types of cards you can display. Figure 7-3 shows Business Card view.

Figure 7-3

10. **If you don't already have other contacts entered, enter the contacts shown in Figure 7-4.**

Later exercises assume you have multiple contacts entered.

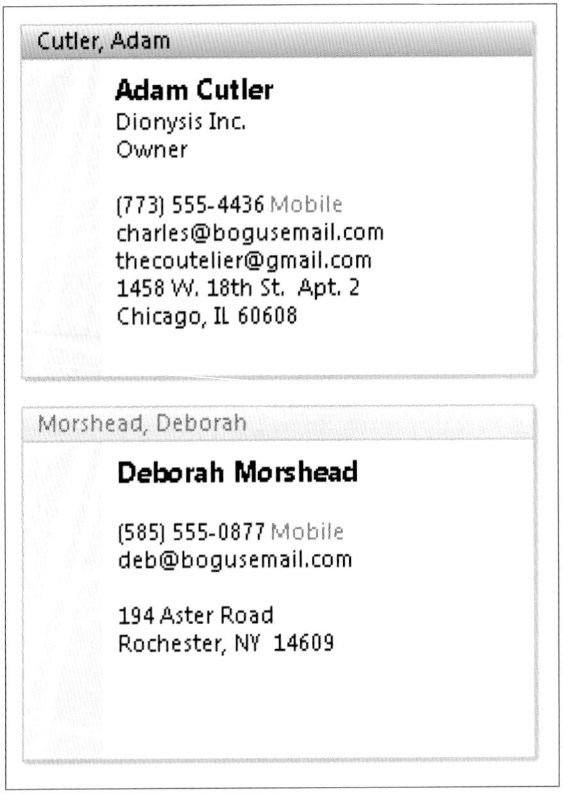

Cutler, Adam

Adam Cutler
Dionysis Inc.
Owner

(773) 555-4436 Mobile
charles@bogusemail.com
thecoutelier@gmail.com
1458 W. 18th St. Apt. 2
Chicago, IL 60608

Morshead, Deborah

Deborah Morshead

(585) 555-0877 Mobile
deb@bogusemail.com

194 Aster Road
Rochester, NY 14609

Figure 7-4

Leave Outlook open for the next exercise.

Navigating the Contacts list

Depending on the view you're using at the moment, each contact may be displayed as a card, a business card, or an item in a list. You can change the view of the Contacts list in several ways. You can jump to a particular letter of the alphabet by clicking a letter along the right side of the display. You can switch between views on the View tab, and you can display or hide the Navigation pane. The following exercise practices all those skills.

In the following exercise, you change the way contacts are displayed in Outlook.

1. **Click the View tab, click the Navigation Pane button, and choose Minimized.**

   This minimizes the Navigation pane so that it appears only as a thin bar on the left side of the screen. You can expand it any time you need it by clicking the arrow in its top-right corner. See Figure 7-5.

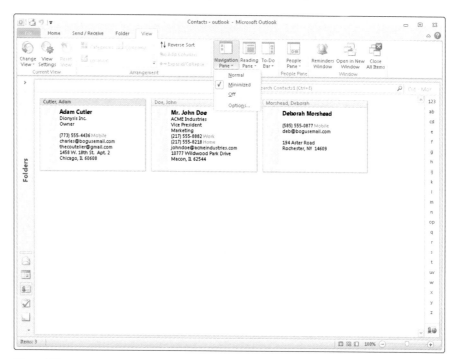

Figure 7-5

2. **Click the Home tab, and click the More button in the Current View group.**

   A gallery appears that contains four options: Business Card, Card, Phone, and List.

3. **Click each of the views to try them out. Apply the Card view last so that you end up in Card view.**

TIP

Notice the gray vertical bar that's separating the columns in Card view. You can drag this bar to increase or decrease the width of the column so that each card's details shows fully or partially.

4. Drag the vertical bar to the right until all the text in each card is fully displayed.

See Figure 7-6.

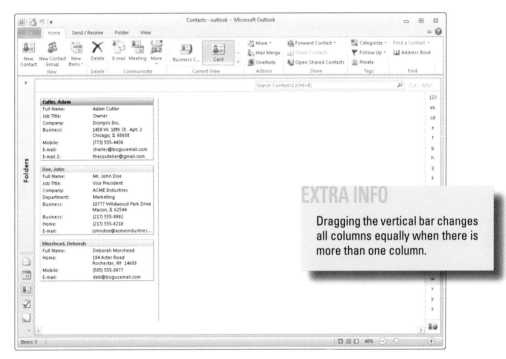

EXTRA INFO

Dragging the vertical bar changes all columns equally when there is more than one column.

Figure 7-6

5. On the View tab, click the Reading Pane button and choose Right to turn on the Reading pane.

The selected contact's full information appears in the Reading Pane to the right of the list. See Figure 7-7.

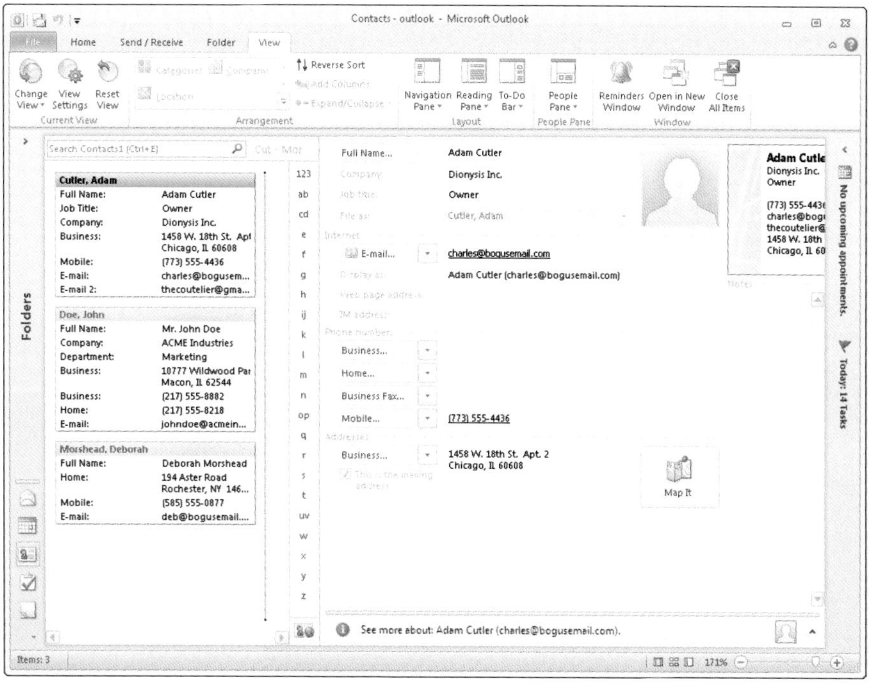

Figure 7-7

6. **Click the Reading Pane button and choose Off to turn off the Reading pane again.**

7. **Still on the View tab, click the To-Do Bar button and choose Normal to turn on the To-Do Bar.**

   It shows a monthly calendar and lists any items you have set up in your To-Do list (covered later in this chapter). See Figure 7-8.

8. **Click the To-Do Bar button and choose Off to turn off the To-Do Bar.**

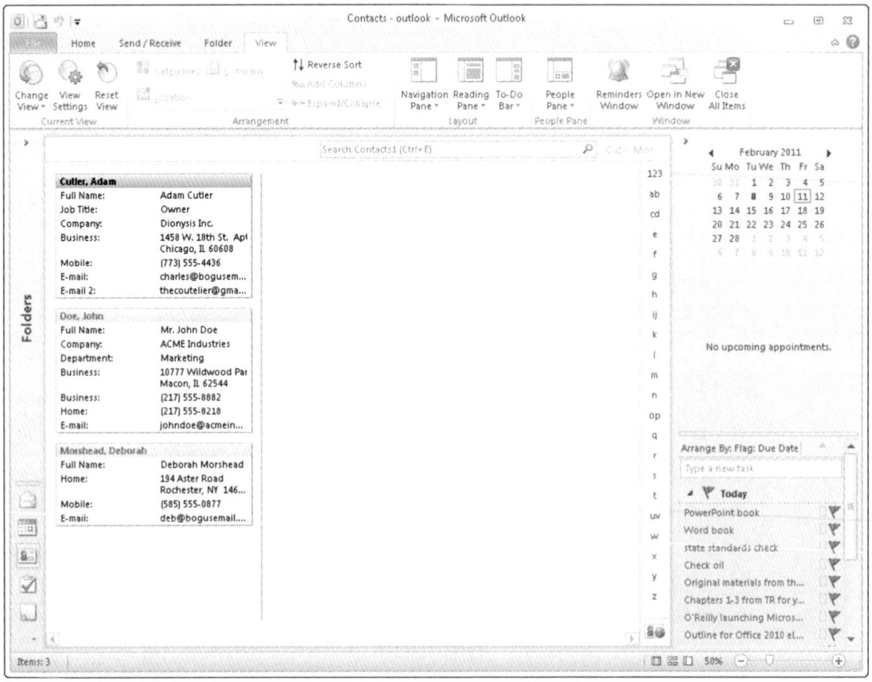

Figure 7-8

9. On the View tab, click the Reverse Sort button to change the sort order of the contacts to Z to A.

10. Click the Reverse Sort button again to change the sort order back to the default (A to Z).

Leave Outlook open for the next exercise.

Changing how a contact is filed

If someone asked you how contacts were alphabetized in Outlook, you would probably say that they're done by last name, right? And you'd be absolutely . . . *wrong.*

Yes, so far the contacts you've worked with have been alphabetized by last name, but that's just a coincidence. They've been done that way because that's how they're set to be filed. The **File As** setting determines the sort order in the Contacts list. By default, when you create a new contact, the File As setting for it is set to *Last Name, First Name.* But you can change that to some other setting if you prefer, such as the company name or the first name. Set it to whatever way you think you will search for that contact in the future.

In this exercise, you change a contact's File As setting to the business name.

1. **Double-click the Doe, John contact to reopen it.**
2. **Open the File As drop-down list and select ACME Industries.**

   See Figure 7-9.

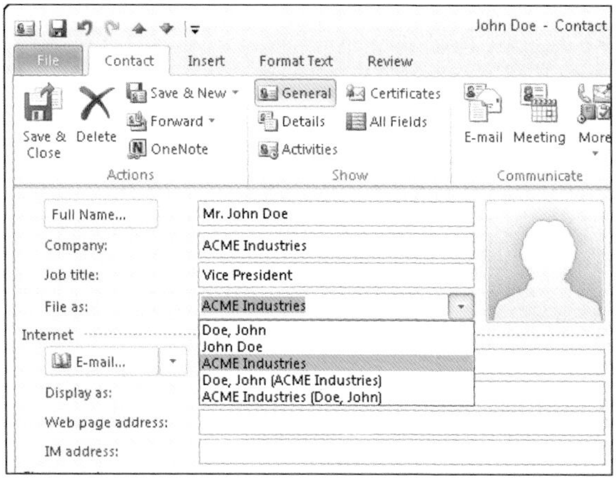

Figure 7-9

EXTRA INFO

If you want both the company name and the person's name to show, choose one of the File As options that includes both. The one that appears first will be how it is alphabetized. For example, Doe, John (ACME Industries) alphabetizes by Doe, but also includes ACME Industries in the title.

3. **Click the Save & Close button.**

   The contact closes. Notice that it now appears alphabetized in the A section, at the top of the contact list, and that ACME Industries appears as the top line.

Leave Outlook open for the next exercise.

Deleting and restoring a contact

With an Outlook Contacts list, you don't have to tear pages out of a paper address book to get rid of a person's information; just delete the contact.

REMEMBER

Deleted contacts go to the Deleted Items folder in Outlook until the next time you empty the Deleted Items folder, so you can retrieve them from there if you make a mistake.

In this exercise, you delete a contact, and then retrieve it from the Deleted Items folder.

1. **Click the ACME Industries contact to select it.**

2. **Press the Delete key on the keyboard or click the Home tab and then the Delete button.**

3. **If the Navigation pane is minimized, click the arrow in the upper-right corner of it to expand it to normal size.**

4. **At the bottom of the Navigation pane, click the Folder List icon (or press Ctrl+6).**

   The Navigation pane changes to show the Folder list.

5. **In the Folder list, click Deleted Items.**

   See Figure 7-10.

TIP

If you see the deleted ACME contact on the list, skip to Step 7. Otherwise, continue to Step 6 to find it.

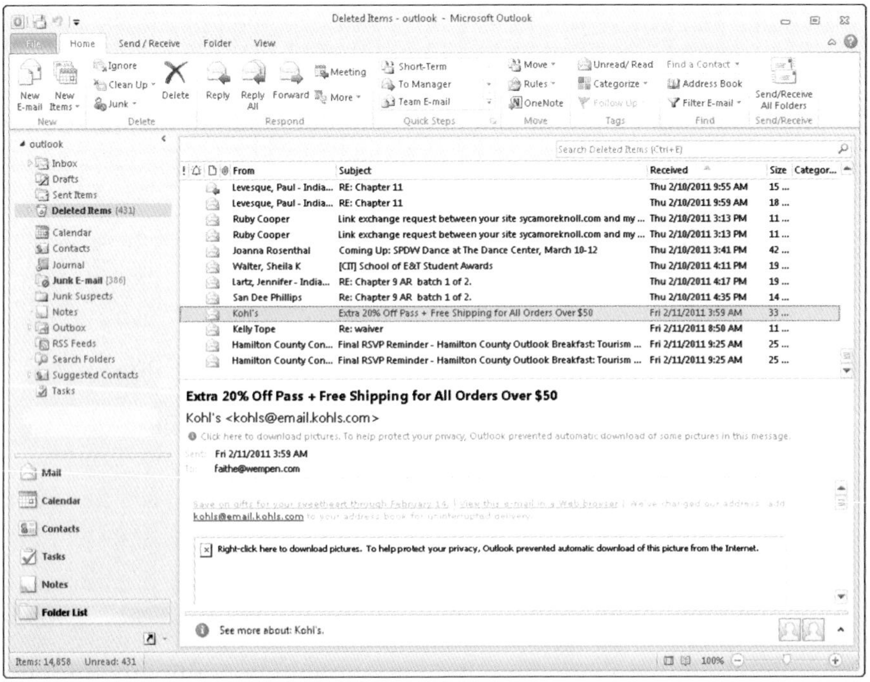

Figure 7-10

6. **Click in the Search text box and type** ACME. **Press Enter.**

The list of deleted items is filtered to show items containing that word. The deleted contact is included on that list. See Figure 7-11.

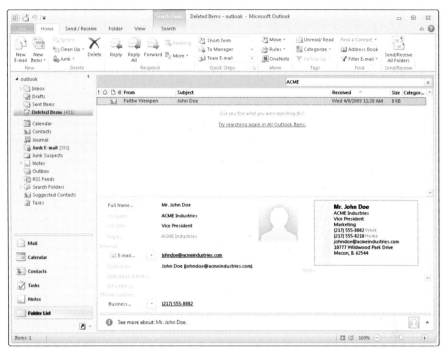

Figure 7-11

7. **Drag the contact to the Contacts folder in the Navigation pane and drop it there.**

It is moved from the Deleted Items folder back to the Contacts folder.

8. **Click the Contacts folder in the Navigation pane to display its contents.**

Note that the ACME contact is restored.

Leave Outlook open for the next exercise.

Using Contact Information

Storing contact information is all well and good, but you'll probably want to do something useful with it.

If you need the information for some offline task, such as addressing an envelope by hand or looking up a phone number to dial, you can just browse through the Contacts list and double-click the desired content to open all its details.

You can also perform some actions on the PC with the stored contact information. For example, you can use contact information to address e-mail messages, and you can send contact information to other people.

Sending an e-mail message to a contact

You can easily address an e-mail message to a contact in your Contacts list. You can initiate this process either from the Contacts area of the program or from the Mail area.

In this exercise, you start an e-mail message to a contact using two different methods.

1. **In the Navigation pane, click Contacts.**

2. **Click the ACME contact to select it.**

3. **On the Home tab, click the E-Mail button.**

   A new e-mail message opens with the ACME contact's e-mail address filled in.

4. **Click the Close (X) button on the new e-mail message's window to close it without sending it.**

5. **When prompted to save changes, click No.**

6. **In the Navigation pane, click Mail.**

7. **Click the New E-Mail button.**

   A new e-mail message window opens.

8. **Click the To button.**

   The Select Names: Contacts window opens. Scroll through the list to find John Doe and then double-click it. The address is added to the To line. See Figure 7-12.

9. **Click OK.**

   The address is added to the To line in the new message window.

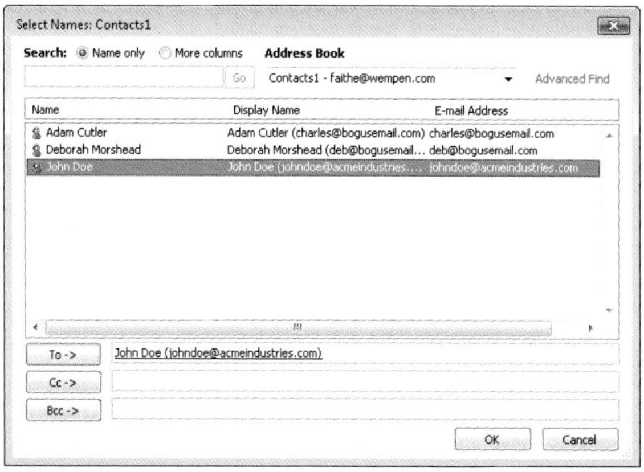

Figure 7-12

EXTRA INFO

Notice that the names are listed in *First, Last* order, without the business name, regardless of the File As setting.

10. Select the address in the To text box and press Delete to remove it.

11. In the To text box, start typing John.

A drop-down list appears with the names that include John. Click John Doe to choose that person's address, as shown in Figure 7-13.

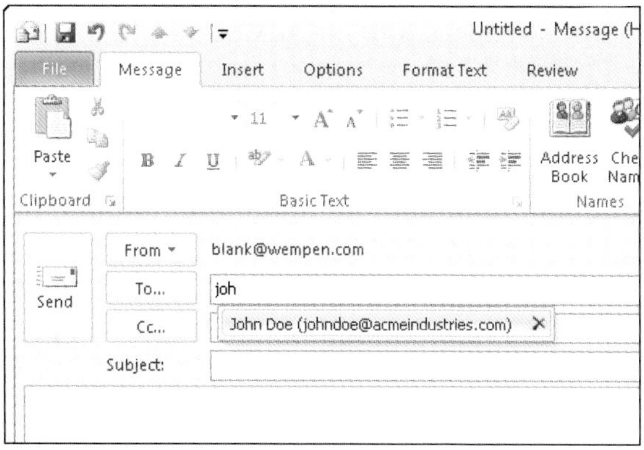

Figure 7-13

12. Click the Close (X) button on the new e-mail message's window to close it without sending it.

When prompted to save changes, click No.

Leave Outlook open for the next exercise.

Attaching contact info to an e-mail

You can share a contact with another e-mail user by attaching the contact record to an e-mail.

In this exercise, you attach a vCard to an e-mail you are composing.

1. **In the Contacts list, select the ACME Industries contact.**

2. **Click the Home tab, click the Forward Contact button, and choose As a Business Card.**

   See Figure 7-14. A vCard version of the contact is inserted in the message. See Figure 7-15.

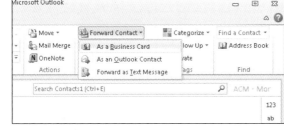

Figure 7-14

3. **Type your own e-mail address in the To text box.**

4. **Click the Send button.**

   The contact is sent via e-mail (to you).

5. **On the Quick Access Toolbar, click the Send/Receive All Folders button.**

   The e-mail containing the attached contact should arrive within a few minutes. Repeat the Send/Receive operation if needed.

6. **When you receive the e-mail containing the contact, double-click the message to open it.**

7. **Double-click the Mr. John Doe.vcf attachment to view it.**

8. **Click the Save & Close button.**

   If a Duplicate Contact Detected dialog box opens, click Cancel.

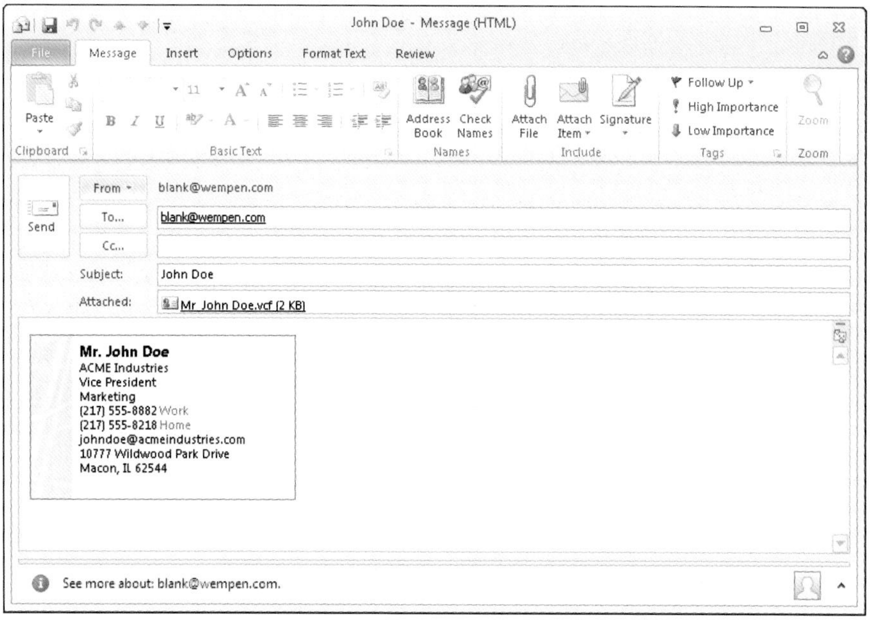

Figure 7-15

For more practice, send yourself copies of the contact in the other two formats: Outlook Contact and Text Message.

Leave Outlook open for the next exercise.

Using Tasks and the To-Do List

The Tasks area in Outlook helps you create and manage action items for yourself and others. Not only can Outlook keep track of what you need to do, but it can remind you of upcoming deadlines, record what percentage of a large job you've completed, and even send e-mails that assign certain tasks to other people.

Displaying the Tasks list

To view the Tasks area of Outlook, click Tasks in the lower-left part of the Navigation pane. Any tasks or to-do items that you may have already created appear there.

In the upper part of the Navigation pane, in the My Tasks section, you can click either To-Do list or Tasks to specify which set of activities you want to look at. For the purposes of this book, I assume that you choose Tasks.

In the following exercise, you display Tasks items in the Tasks area of Outlook.

1. **In the lower-left corner of the Outlook window, click Tasks.**
2. **Under My Tasks in the upper-left corner, click Tasks.**

   The list changes to show only tasks, not other to-do items.
3. **Click the View tab, click the Reading Pane button, and choose Right to open a reading pane on the right side of the screen.**

   If you already have some tasks created, they appear; if not, both panes appear blank, as shown in Figure 7-16.

LINGO

It's important to understand the difference in Outlook between Tasks and the To-Do list.

Tasks are specific items you created in the Tasks area of Outlook. Something isn't technically a *task* unless it was created in the Tasks section.

The To-Do list contains everything from the Tasks list, plus other items you have marked for action, such as e-mail messages you flag for follow-up.

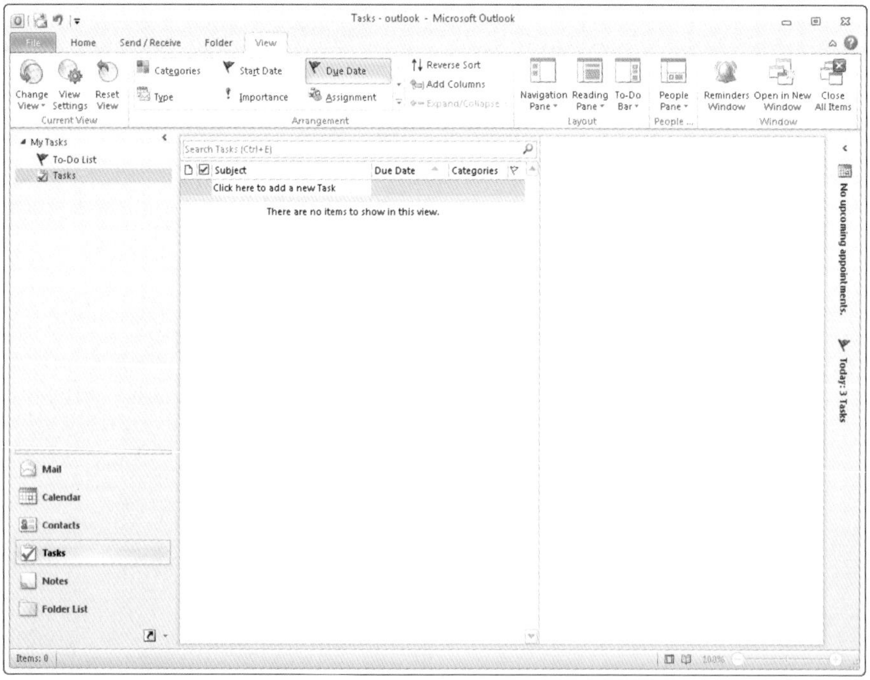

Figure 7-16

Leave Outlook open for the next exercise.

Creating a task

In this exercise, you create a task.

> **LINGO**
>
> A **task** is a database record that contains information about something that you need to accomplish. For example, when I was writing this book, I used a task in Outlook to keep track of my deadlines and progress.
>
> Like with Contacts, you can enter as much or as little information as you like about each task, depending on what you want to track and how closely you want to monitor it.

1. **With the Tasks area of Outlook displayed, click the Home tab and then the New Task button.**

   An Untitled – Task window opens.

2. **In the Subject text box, type** Data Conversion Project**.**
3. **Click the down arrow in the Start Date box, then click today's date on the calendar.**
4. **Click the down arrow on the Due Date box and click a date two weeks from today.**
5. **Open the Status drop-down list and click In Progress.**
6. **In the Body area of the task window, type** Data conversion between the UNIVAC system and Windows Server**.**
7. **Open the Priority drop-down list and select High.**

   Higher priority tasks appear at the top of the list in certain views, or if you sort by priority.

   Figure 7-17 shows the completed task window.

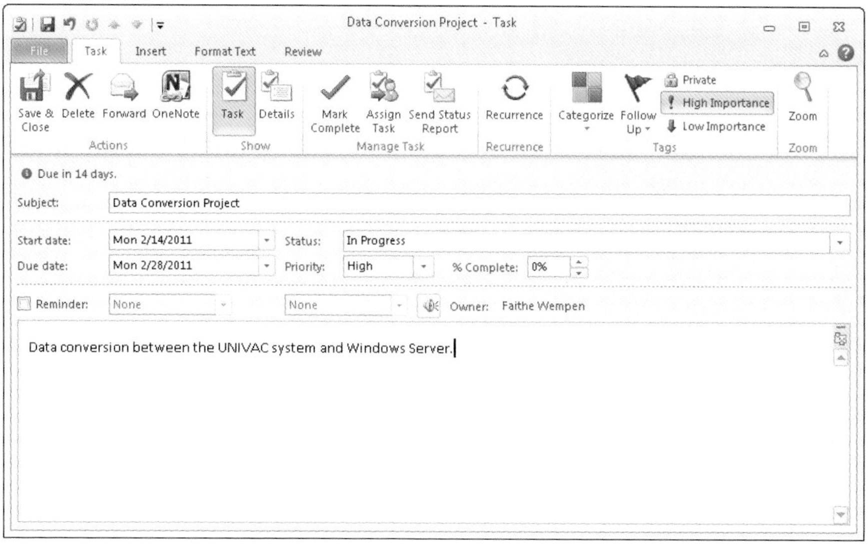

Figure 7-17

8. **Click the Save & Close button.**

The task appears in the Tasks list.

9. **Click the new task.**

Its details appear in the Reading pane, as shown in Figure 7-18.

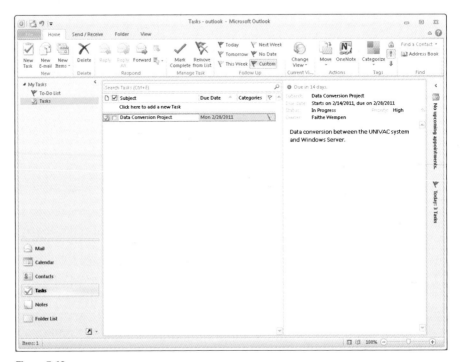

Figure 7-18

10. **On the View tab, click the Change View button and choose Detailed to switch to Detailed view.**

This action enables you to see the task's priority in the Priority column.

High-priority tasks appear with a red exclamation point in that column; low-priority tasks show a blue down-pointing arrow there. See Figure 7-19. Notice that in Detailed view, the Reading pane no longer appears. You earlier displayed it for Simple List view, but the setting doesn't carry over when you switch views.

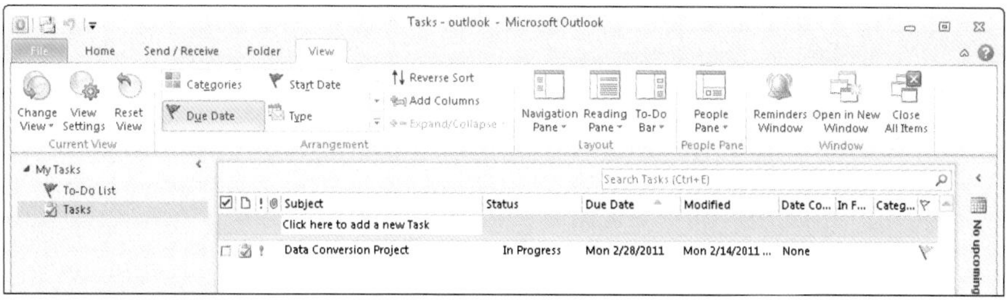

Figure 7-19

Leave Outlook open for the next exercise.

Updating a task

As your work on a task progresses, you may want to update its status in Outlook. You may also want to flag it for follow-up, change its due date, or mark it as completed.

In this exercise, you change a task's settings, including updating its progress and changing its due date.

1. **In the Tasks area of Outlook, click the task you created in the previous exercise if it isn't already selected.**

2. **Click the check mark to the left of the task.**

   It's marked as completed. It turns gray, and a strikethrough line is drawn through it. See Figure 7-20.

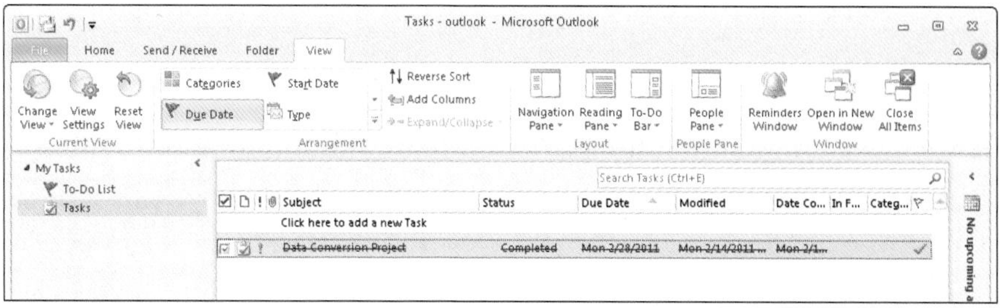

Figure 7-20

Completing a task does not automatically delete it. Depending on the view, a completed task may disappear from the Tasks list, but it's not gone.

3. **Click the View tab, click the Change View button, and choose Active.**

This view displays only active tasks, and the completed task is no longer active, so it doesn't appear.

4. **Click the Change View button again and choose Detailed.**

This view returns to showing detailed information about each task. The completed task appears here.

5. **Click the task's check mark again to toggle the task's status back to being incomplete.**

6. **Double-click the task to reopen its window.**

7. **Open the Status drop-down list and click In Progress.**

8. **Click the up increment arrow on the % Complete box to set the percent to 25%.**

Figure 7-21 shows the task at this point.

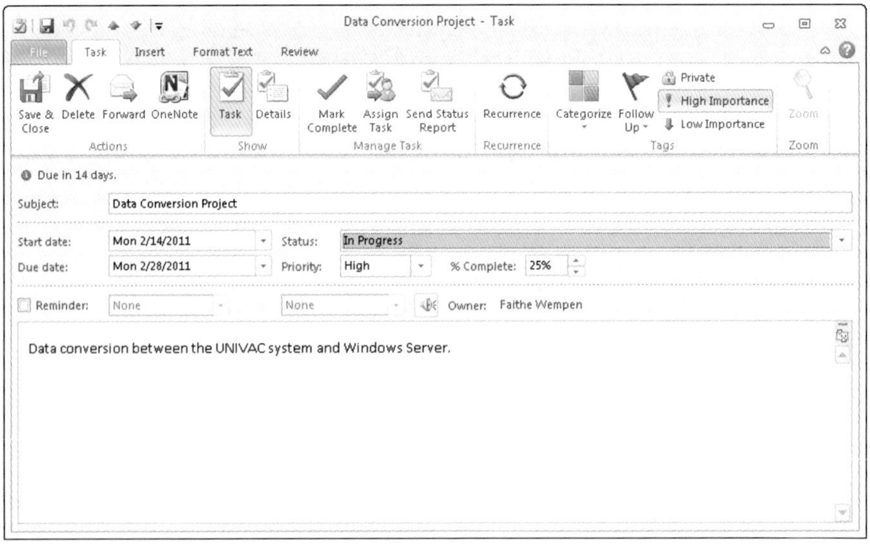

Figure 7-21

9. **Click the Save & Close button.**

The task closes.

10. **On the Tasks list, click the task's status (In Progress). A menu opens. From the menu, choose Deferred.**

    See Figure 7-22.

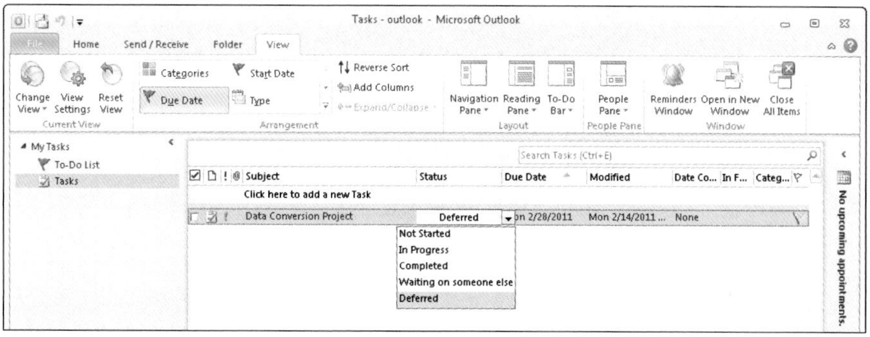

Figure 7-22

11. **Click the Home tab and then the This Week.**

    This changes the follow-up flag on the task to this week. It also changes the Due Date field.

12. **On the Home tab, click the No Date button.**

    This sets the task to have no due date at all. (That's appropriate because its status is now Deferred.)

You can also right-click the flag in the Flag column on the task list and choose a different follow-up flag if you prefer that method.

Leave Outlook open for the next exercise.

Setting a task reminder

You may want to set a reminder to help you stay on top of your task assignments. Reminders pop up at the time you specify to let you know it's time to pay attention to a task. You can also enter your own custom reminder text.

Set your reminder to occur before the task's actual due date to give yourself some time to work on it. For example, set a budget's reminder for two weeks prior to the date.

In this exercise, you set a reminder for a task.

1. **In the Tasks area of Outlook, double-click the task you created earlier.**

   It opens in its own window.

2. **Select the Reminder check box.**

3. **Today's date may already appear in the Date box. If it doesn't, open the Date drop-down list and click today's date.**

4. **Open the Time drop-down list and click a time that is 3 minutes from now. If the exact time isn't one of the choices, close the drop-down list, click in the Time box, and manually type the time.**

   See Figure 7-23.

TIP

A default-assigned sound plays when the reminder occurs. To change the sound, you can click the Sound button (it looks like a speaker) and browse for a different sound file.

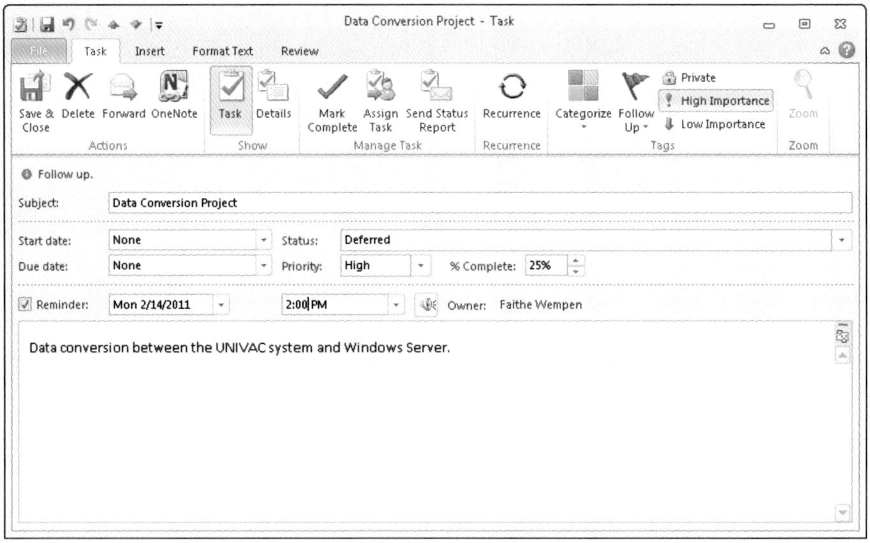

Figure 7-23

5. **Click the Save & Close button.**

6. **Wait 3 minutes for the reminder box to pop up.**

   See Figure 7-24.

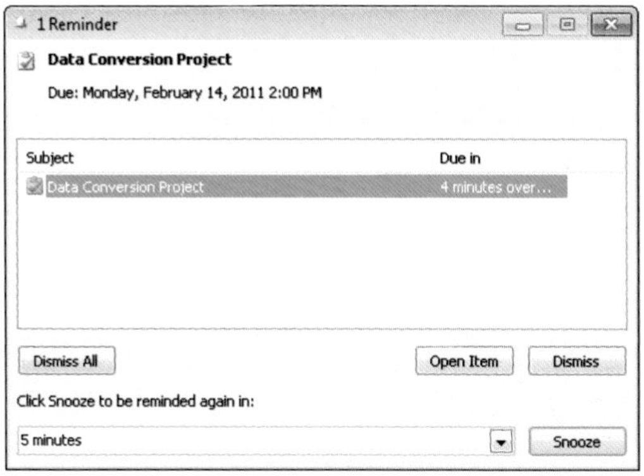

Figure 7-24

7. **Click the Dismiss button.**

   The reminder is dismissed.

TIP

You could have clicked Snooze instead to make it disappear temporarily but pop up again later.

Leave Outlook open for the next exercise.

Deleting a task

As I mention earlier, completing a task doesn't delete it. You might want to keep completed tasks around for later reference. If you don't want to see them, switch to a view that doesn't include completed tasks, such as the Active view. If you're sure you want to delete a task, though, it's easy enough to delete it.

In the following exercise, you delete a task in three different ways.

1. **In the Tasks area of Outlook, select the task you created earlier.**

2. **On the Home tab, click the Delete button.**

   The task is deleted.

3. **Click the Undo button on the Quick Access toolbar to undo the deletion.**

4. **Select the task and then press the Delete key.**

   The task is deleted.

5. **Click the Undo button on the Quick Access toolbar to undo the deletion.**

6. **Right-click the task and choose Delete.**

   The task is deleted.

Close Outlook when you're finished with this exercise.

If you're ready for more on Outlook, there's a bonus chapter on our website!

 *Summing Up*

Here are the key points you learned about in this chapter:

- ✔ A contact (or record) is the information about a single person, business, or family that you store in the Contacts area of Outlook.

- ✔ To add a contact, view the Contacts section of Outlook and then click Home, New Contact.

- ✔ To change the view of the Contacts list, you can click Home, Current View, More and then click the desired view.

- ✔ To turn the Reading pane on or off, click View, Reading Pane and then click the position you want (Right, Bottom, or Off).

- ✔ To change how a contact is filed alphabetically, set its File As setting.

- ✔ To delete a contact, select it and press Delete. You can restore it from the Deleted Items folder if you change your mind.

- ✔ To send an e-mail to a contact, select the contact and then click Home, E-Mail.

- ✔ You can attach contact information to an e-mail in any of three formats: Outlook contact, vCard, or text message. Click Home, Forward Contact and choose the desired format.

- ✔ The Notes area provides space for you to store pieces of information.

- ✔ To create a note, switch to the Notes area and click Home, New Note or double-click an empty area. The first few words you type become the note's title.

- ✔ You can assign color-coded categories to notes with the Categories button.

- ✔ The Tasks area of Outlook can display either Tasks (tasks only) or the To-Do list (tasks plus other items that have due dates or are flagged for follow-up).

- ✔ To create a task, in the Tasks area, click Home, New Task.

- ✔ To update a task, double-click it to reopen its window.

- ✔ To delete a task, select it and press the Delete key.

Try-it-yourself lab

For more practice with the features covered in this chapter, try the following exercise on your own.

1. **In Outlook, use the Tasks section to create a list of all the assignments and readings that are due in your classes in the next two weeks. (If you aren't in any classes, use to-do items for your work or personal commitments instead.) Prioritize them and set appropriate due dates.**

2. **Use the Contacts section to enter contact information for yourself and two other people.**

3. **Use the Notes section to enter at least two notes containing information you want to remember. (For security reasons, don't include passwords if this is a PC that you share with other people.) For example, you could enter a favorite quotation in a note or a favorite Web site URL.**

Know this tech talk

category: A color-coded classification you can assign to notes and other objects.

contact: A set of contact data (name, address, phone, and so on) for a person, family, or business. Also called a *record*.

File As: The setting in a contact's properties that controls how it appears in the alphabetical sort of the Contacts list.

note: A data record in the Notes section of Outlook, containing any text you place in it. It's an electronic equivalent to a yellow sticky note.

record: Same as *contact*.

reminder: A timed pop-up window that reminds you at a certain date and time of a task or other item to deal with.

tasks: Items you create in the Tasks area of Outlook, containing information about a job or responsibility to be accomplished.

To-Do list: A list of things to accomplish in Outlook that includes both tasks and other items that require follow-up, such as e-mail to be answered.

Chapter 8

Getting Started with PowerPoint

✔ Presentations *provide visual aids* for live or remotely delivered speeches.

✔ PowerPoint lets you create presentations you can *print, deliver onscreen, e-mail, or distribute on CD.*

✔ PowerPoint's views enable you to *work with the program in different ways as needed.*

✔ The File➪New command enables you to *create a new presentation,* either blank or based on a template or theme.

✔ Templates *provide a head-start* on both formatting and content.

✔ Adding new slides to a presentation enables you to *expand its scope and add more content.*

✔ Duplicating a slide saves time by avoiding repetitive data entry.

✔ Placeholders *provide guidance* to where to place content on a slide.

✔ Manually created text boxes enable you to *place additional text where no placeholders exist.*

✔ Selection handles enable you to *resize objects on slides.*

1. **Which view is best for viewing the entire presentation at a glance?**

View the entire answer on page.. 253

2. **How do you start a new, blank presentation?**

At least the page isn't blank on page.................................. 255

3. **What's the difference between a template and a theme?**

Decide the difference on page.. 257

4. **How do you create a new slide with a different layout than the default?**

Default to page 261

5. **How do you delete a slide?**

Slide over to page 266

6. **How do you create extra text boxes on a slide?**

Text is extra informative on page...................................... 268

7. **How do you resize a text box?**

You won't box yourself in on page....................................... 273

8. **How do you move an object on a slide?**

This answer is the object of page.. 273

*P*owerPoint is the most popular presentation software in the world. Presentation software creates support materials for people who give speeches. You can project PowerPoint slides on a big screen behind you as you speak, create handouts to distribute to the audience, and print note pages for your own reference. PowerPoint can also create self-running presentations for distribution via CD or online.

This chapter offers you some basics for working with PowerPoint. You learn how to start a new presentation, add slides and text to it, and move and resize the content on a slide. In later chapters, you learn how to add other types of content and how to add animation and special effects to a show.

Exploring the PowerPoint Interface

In PowerPoint, you work with slides and presentations rather than documents (as in Word) or worksheets (as in Excel).

At a big-picture level, PowerPoint's interface is very similar to that in Word and Excel: It has a Ribbon, a File tab, and a status bar. The default view of the presentation, called *Normal view,* consists of three panes, as shown in Figure 8-1. (You may or may not see the rulers onscreen, depending on your settings.)

LINGO

A **slide** is an individual page of the presentation. The term *page* isn't a perfect descriptor, though, because PowerPoint slides are designed to be displayed on a computer screen or with a projector rather than printed. A **presentation** is a collection of one or more slides saved in a single data file.

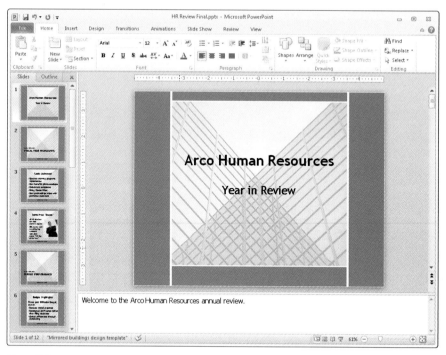

Figure 8-1

✔ The **Slides/Outline pane** is the bar along the left side. It has two tabs: Outline and Slides. When the Outline tab is selected, a text-based outline of the text from the slides appears here. When the Slides tab is selected, thumbnail images of the slides appear here.

✔ The **Slide pane** (that's singular, not plural) in the middle shows the active slide in a large, editable pane. Here's where you do most of your work on each slide.

✔ The **Notes pane** runs along the bottom of the screen. Here you can type any notes to yourself about the active slide. These notes don't show onscreen when you display the presentation, and they don't print (unless you explicitly choose to print them).

Move around in a presentation

You can navigate through a presentation in many of the same ways you moved through other applications' content. The Page Up and Page Down keys scroll one full screen at a time, and you can drag the scroll bars to scroll as well. You can also select slides from the Slides tab of the Slides/ Outline pane.

In the following exercise, you open a presentation file and move around in it.

Files needed: `Chapter 8 Meals.pptx`

1. **Open PowerPoint. To do so, choose Start⇨All Programs⇨Microsoft Office⇨Microsoft PowerPoint.**

   PowerPoint opens.

2. **Open the file `Chapter 8 Meals.pptx`. To do so, take these steps:**

   a. Choose File⇨Open. The Open dialog box appears.

   b. Navigate to the folder containing the data files for this lesson, and click `Chapter 8 Meals.pptx`.

   c. Click Open. The file opens in PowerPoint.

3. **Save the file as `Chapter 8 Meals Tour.pptx`. To do so, here's what you do:**

   a. Choose File⇨Save As. The Save As dialog box opens.

   b. In the File Name box, type **Chapter 8 Meals Tour.pptx**.

   c. Click Save. The file is saved under a new name.

4. **In the Slides/Outline pane, click the Outline tab.**

   A text outline of the presentation appears. See Figure 8-2.

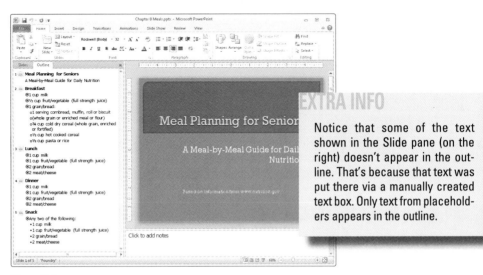

EXTRA INFO

Notice that some of the text shown in the Slide pane (on the right) doesn't appear in the outline. That's because that text was put there via a manually created text box. Only text from placeholders appears in the outline.

Figure 8-2

5. In the Slides/Outline pane, click the Slides tab.

Thumbnail images of each slide appear in that pane.

6. Click the thumbnail image of slide 3.

That slide becomes active. In other words, it appears in the Slide pane (the large pane on the right), where you can edit it. See Figure 8-3.

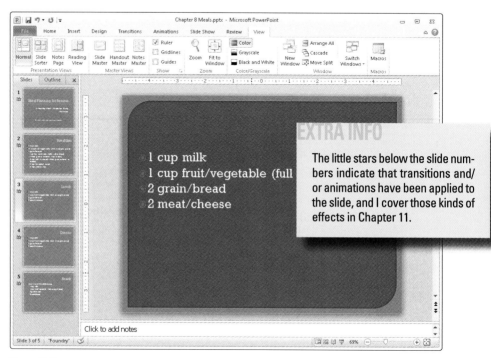

1 cup milk
1 cup fruit/vegetable (full
2 grain/bread
2 meat/cheese

EXTRA INFO

The little stars below the slide numbers indicate that transitions and/or animations have been applied to the slide, and I cover those kinds of effects in Chapter 11.

Figure 8-3

7. Press the Page Down key.

The next slide (slide 4) becomes active.

8. In the vertical scroll bar on the Slide pane, click in the blank area above the scroll box.

The previous slide (slide 3) becomes active.

9. Press the Home key.

Slide 1 becomes active.

10. Press the End key.

Slide 5 (the last slide) becomes active.

11. **Click below slide 5, in the Notes pane, and type** Thank the audience for their attention.

12. **Save the presentation.**

Leave PowerPoint open for the next exercise.

Understand PowerPoint views

PowerPoint provides several views for you to work with. Each view is useful for a different set of activities. Normal view (refer to Figure 8-1), the default, is the most commonly used view. You can switch to one of the other views in either of these ways:

- ✔ Click one of the View buttons in the bottom-right corner of the PowerPoint window. (Not all the views are represented there.)

- ✔ On the View tab, click a button for the view you want.

Figure 8-4 shows Slide Sorter view and also points out the two places where you can switch views: on the View tab and on the status bar. Slide Sorter view is best for rearranging slides and viewing the entire presentation at a glance.

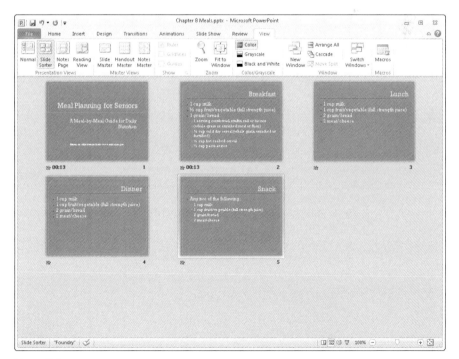

Figure 8-4

In this exercise, you try several views in PowerPoint.

Files needed: `Chapter 8 Meals Tour.pptx`, *already open from the previous exercise*

1. Click the View tab and then the Slide Sorter button.

The presentation changes to Slide Sorter view, as shown in Figure 8-4.

2. On the View tab, click the Notes Page button.

Notes Page view is available only from the View tab (not the status bar). See Figure 8-5. In Notes Page view, you can see any notes that you've entered for the active slide.

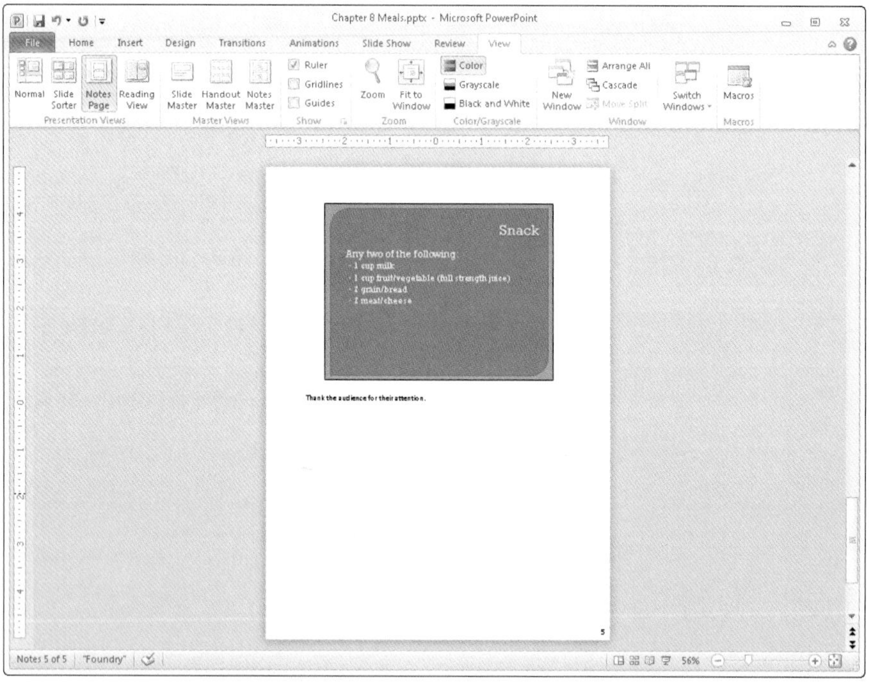

Figure 8-5

3. In the status bar, click the Normal button.

The presentation switches back to Normal view.

4. In the status bar, click the Slide Show button.

The presentation opens in Slide Show view. The slide fills the entire screen.

5. Press Esc to leave Slide Show view.

6. Look on the View tab and notice that there's no button for Slide Show view there.

7. Click the Slide Show tab.

   Notice that there are two buttons here for entering Slide Show view: From Beginning and From Current Slide. See Figure 8-6.

Figure 8-6

8. In the Slides/Outline pane, click slide 4 to make it active.

9. Click the Slide Show tab and then the From Current Slide button.

   Slide 4 appears in Slide Show view.

10. Press Esc to return to Normal view.

11. Click the Save button on the Quick Access Toolbar to save it.

12. Choose File➪Close to close the presentation.

Leave PowerPoint open for the next exercise.

Creating a New Presentation

You can create a new presentation in several ways. You can create a blank one, or you can base a presentation on a template that contains formatting specs, sample content, or both.

Creating a blank presentation

When you start PowerPoint, a new blank presentation appears, containing a single slide. The fastest and simplest way to create a new presentation is to start with a blank one. You can then add text to the presentation, including additional slides.

In this exercise, you create a new blank presentation.

Files needed: None

1. **Choose File⇨New.**

   Backstage view opens, displaying icons for various types of presentations you can create. Blank presentation is automatically selected. See
   Figure 8-7.

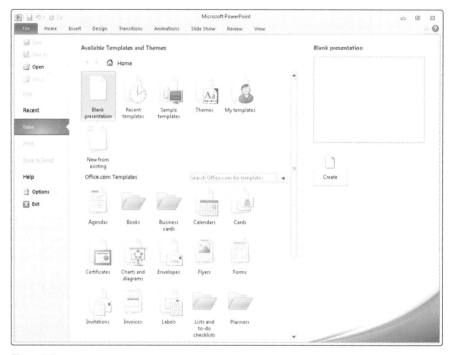

Figure 8-7

2. **Click the Create button.**

   A new, blank presentation opens.

3. **Choose File⇨Close to close the new presentation.**

   Don't save changes if prompted.

4. **Press Ctrl+N.**

   A new, blank presentation opens.

This is an alternative method of doing the same thing as in Steps 1–2.

5. Choose File⇨Close to close the new presentation.

Leave PowerPoint open for the next exercise.

Create a presentation with a template

PowerPoint's templates give you a jump start to creating complete presentations. Each template employs one or more themes. A *theme* is a collection of settings including colors, fonts, background graphics, bullet graphics, and margin and placement settings. PowerPoint has several built-in templates, and you can create your own templates or download new ones from Microsoft Office Online. The templates in the Themes category in the New Presentation window contain no sample content, only formatting. You can insert your own text and objects (such as charts or pictures) and build a finished presentation very quickly.

LINGO

A **template** is a reusable sample file that includes a background, layouts, coordinating fonts, and other design elements that work together to create an attractive finished slide show. Templates may (but are not required to) contain sample content, too.

In this exercise, you create a new presentation based on a theme.

Files needed: None

1. Choose File⇨New.

Backstage View opens, displaying icons for various types of presentations you can create.

2. In the Available Templates and Themes section, click Sample Templates.

The templates stored on your hard drive appear.

3. Click the Introducing PowerPoint 2010 template.

See Figure 8-8.

4. Click the Create button.

A new presentation is created based on that template. It includes a theme and 20 sample slides. See Figure 8-9.

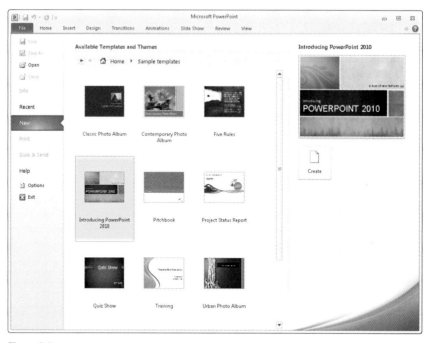

Figure 8-8

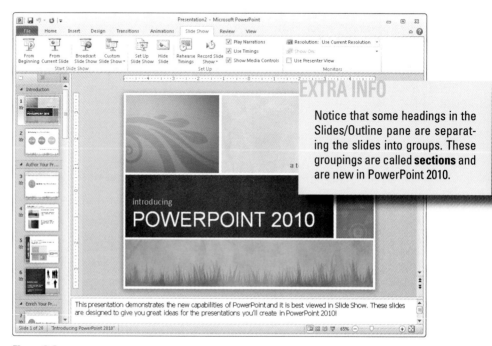

Figure 8-9

5. Save the presentation as Chapter 8 Sample.

6. Close the presentation by choosing File⇨Close.

Leave PowerPoint open for the next exercise.

Creating New Slides

Each new presentation begins with one slide in it: a title slide. You can easily add more slides to the presentation by using the default layout (Title and Content) or any other layout you prefer.

Several methods are available for creating new slides, and each one is best suited for a particular situation. In the following sections, you learn each of the methods.

Creating a new slide with the Ribbon

The most straightforward way to create a new slide is with the New Slide command.

In this exercise, you create three new slides: two using the default layout and one using a different layout.

Files needed: None

1. In PowerPoint, press Ctrl+N to start a new, blank presentation.

A single slide appears in it.

2. Click the Home tab and then the New Slide button.

A new slide appears with the Title and Content layout.

3. Press Ctrl+M.

Another new slide appears with the Title and Content layout.

4. Click the arrow below the New Slide button, opening a menu of other layouts.

See Figure 8-10.

5. Click the Two Content layout.

A new slide appears with a title placeholder and two separate content placeholders. See Figure 8-11.

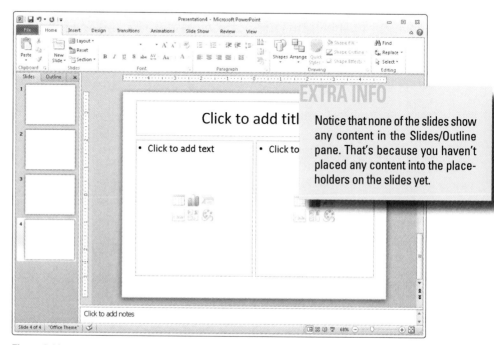

Figure 8-10

Figure 8-11

6. **Close the presentation without saving it.**

Leave PowerPoint open for the next exercise.

Creating a new slide in the Slides/Outline pane

From the Slides/Outline pane, you can create new slides by clicking where you want them and then pressing Enter.

The process is somewhat different depending on which of the tabs is displayed in the pane: Slides or Outline. In the Slides pane, you click to place a horizontal insertion point line between two existing slides or at the bottom of the list of slides and then press Enter. In the Outline pane, you click to place a text insertion point at the beginning of the title of an existing slide, and then you press Enter to create a new title (and a new slide).

In this exercise, you create new slides using both the Slides and the Outline tabs of the Slides/Outline pane.

Files needed: `Chapter 8 Comstar.pptx`

1. **Open the file `Chapter 8 Comstar.pptx` and save it as `Chapter 8 Comstar Practice.pptx`.**
2. **In the Slides/Outline pane, make sure the Slides tab is selected.**
3. **Click between slides 1 and 2 in the Slides/Outline pane.**

   A blinking horizontal line appears there. See Figure 8-12.

4. **Press Enter.**

   A new slide appears there with the Title and Content layout.

Normally a slide inserted this way uses the same layout as the one above it. However, if the slide above it is a Title Slide, the inserted slide takes on the Title and Content layout. This is by design, because PowerPoint anticipates that you probably don't want two title slides in a row.

Figure 8-12

5. Click the Outline tab.

Six small gray rectangles appear, representing each slide. The text from the slides also appears. The slide titles appear in bold on the first line of each slide, and the slide content appears below it. The line for slide 2 (the newly inserted slide) is blank because there's no content in it yet. See Figure 8-13.

6. In the Outline pane, click to place the insertion point after the word *staff* on slide 3.

7. Press Enter.

A new line appears in the content for slide 3.

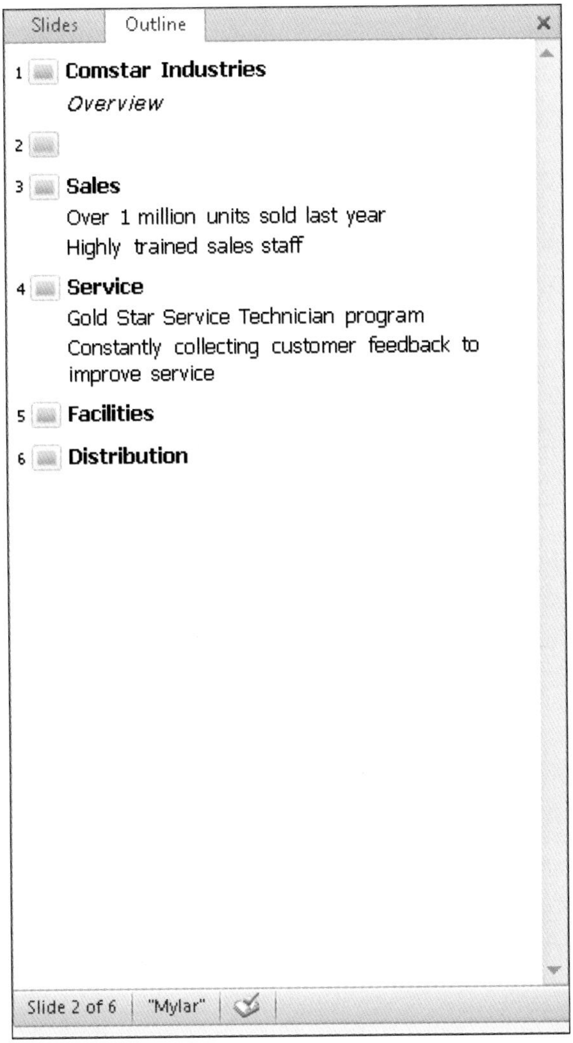

Figure 8-13

8. Press Shift+Tab to promote the new line to being a slide title.

A slide icon (4) appears next to the new line. See Figure 8-14.

Figure 8-14

9. Click to place the insertion point to the left of the slide title (Service) on slide 5.

10. Press Enter.

A new slide appears before the Service slide. It's a new slide because it takes its outline level from the line that the insertion point was on when you pressed Enter.

11. **Save the presentation.**

Leave the presentation open for the next exercise.

Duplicating a slide

If you need to create a series of very similar slides, you may find it easier to copy or duplicate a slide and then make the small modifications to each copy.

Copying and duplicating are two separate commands in PowerPoint, but they have essentially the same result.

When you copy a slide (or multiple slides), you place a copy of it on the Clipboard, and then you paste it from the Clipboard into the presentation. You can paste anywhere in the presentation or into a different presentation (or, for that matter, a different document altogether).

When you duplicate a slide (or multiple slides), go to the Home tab, click the New Slide button, and choose Duplicate Selected Slides. You don't have to paste, because that command accomplishes both a copy and a paste operation at the same time. However, you also don't have a choice of where they're pasted; they're pasted directly below the original selection.

In this exercise, you copy a slide and duplicate a slide.

Files needed: `Chapter 8 Comstar Practice.pptx`, *already open from the previous exercise*

1. **In the Slides/Outline pane click the Slides tab.**

2. **Click slide 6 to select it.**

3. **Click the Home tab and then the Copy button, or press Ctrl+C.**

4. **Click below slide 8 and click the Paste button, or press Ctrl+V.**

    A copy of slide 6 appears as the new slide 9.

5. **Click slide 1 to select it.**

6. **On the Home tab, click the down arrow under the New Slide button and choose Duplicate Selected Slides.**

A copy of slide 1 appears immediately below the original. You should now have 10 slides in the presentation. In the status bar, the message `Slide 2 of 10` appears. See Figure 8-15.

Figure 8-15

7. Save the presentation.

Leave the presentation open for the next exercise.

Deleting a slide

Deleting a slide removes it from the presentation. You can delete a slide either by pressing the Delete key or by right-clicking the slide and choosing Delete Slide from the shortcut menu.

TIP

There's no recycle bin for slides; you can't get them back after you delete them. However, you can undo your last action(s) with the Undo button on the Quick Access toolbar, and that includes undoing deletions. If you haven't saved your work since you made the deletion, you can also get a deleted slide back by closing the file without saving changes and then reopening it.

In this exercise, you delete some slides.

Files already open from the previous exercise

1. **In the Slides/Outline pane, click slide 2 (which is a duplicate of slide 1).**

2. **Press the Delete key.**

   One of the blank slides is now slide 2.

3. **Press the Delete key again.**

   Now slide 2 is the Sales slide.

4. **Click slide 3 (also blank), hold down the Shift key, and click slide 4 (also blank).**

5. **Right-click one of the selected slides (3 or 4) and choose Delete Slide from the shortcut menu.**

   See Figure 8-16.

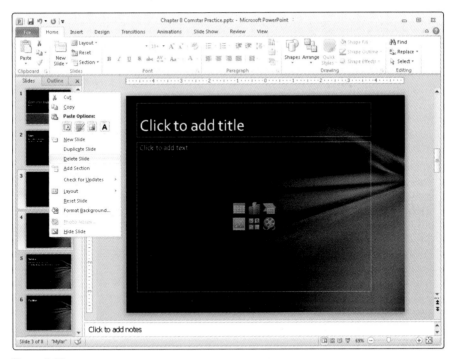

Figure 8-16

6. **Click slide 6 (the last slide) to select it.**

7. **Right-click slide 6 and choose Delete Slide from the shortcut menu.**

   The presentation now contains five slides, all of which have a title.

8. **Save the presentation.**

Leave the presentation open for the next exercise.

Adding Text to a Slide

Adding text to a slide is as easy as clicking in a placeholder box and typing. You can also type text on the Outline tab of the Slides/Outline pane or create your own text boxes in addition to the placeholders.

Typing in a slide placeholder

Some placeholders are specifically for text. For example, the placeholder for each slide's title is text-only. Click in such a placeholder and type the text you want. A content placeholder, such as the large placeholder on the default layout, can hold any *one* type of content: text, table, chart, SmartArt graphic, picture, clip art, or media clip (video or sound). Later chapters explain some of these other types of content in more detail.

You can type either on the slide itself (in the Slide pane) or in the Outline. Either way, the text is placed in the slide's placeholders. Text you type at the highest outline level on the outline is placed in the slide's Title placeholder, and text you type at subordinate outline levels is placed in the Content placeholder.

LINGO

A **slide layout** is a combination of one or more content placeholders. For example, the default slide layout — Title and Content — has two boxes: a text box at the top for the slide's title, and one multipurpose content placeholder in the middle that can be used for text, a graphic, or any of several other content types.

In this exercise, you type text into slide placeholders.

Files needed: `Chapter 8 Comstar Practice.pptx,` *already open from the previous exercise*

1. **In the Slides/Outline pane, click slide 5 to select it.**

2. **In the Slide pane, click in the content placeholder (where it says** `Click to add text`**).**

   See Figure 8-17. The insertion point moves into the content placeholder.

3. **Type Four warehouses totaling over 40,000 square feet.**

4. **Press Enter.**

5. **On the Slides/Outline pane, click the Outline tab.**

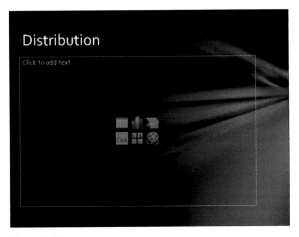

Figure 8-17

6. **Type State-of-the-art environmental controls.**

   The typed text appears both on the slide and in the outline. See Figure 8-18.

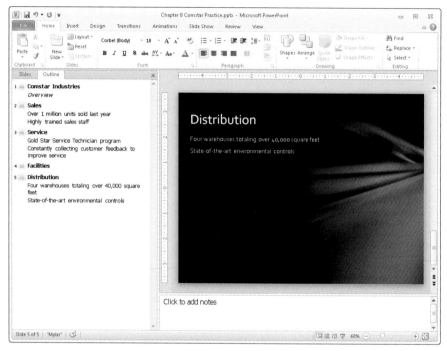

Figure 8-18

7. Save the presentation.

Leave the presentation open for the next exercise.

Manually placing text on a slide

Whenever possible, you should use the layout placeholders to insert slide content. However, sometimes you may not be able to find a layout that's exactly what you want. For example, maybe you want to add a caption or note next to a picture, or you want to create a collage of text snippets arranged artistically on a slide.

TIP

The text in such a text box doesn't appear in the Outline, so use this type of text box sparingly.

When you place a text box manually (click the Insert tab and then the Text Box button), you can use two possible techniques: You can drag to draw the width of the box you want, or you can click the slide and start typing. The properties of the resulting text box are different for each method, as you see in the following steps.

In this exercise, you manually place text on a slide.

Files needed: `Chapter 8 Comstar Practice.pptx`, *already open from the previous exercise*

1. **In the Slides/Outline pane, click the Slides tab.**

2. **Click slide 1 to select it.**

3. **Click the Insert tab and then the Text Box button.**

4. **Click in the gray area at the bottom of the slide.**

   A text box appears there. It starts out collapsed horizontally, with just enough room for one character, but it will expand as you type. See Figure 8-19.

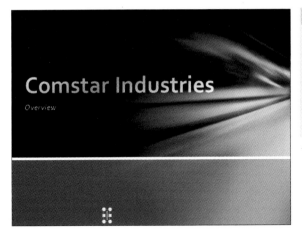

EXTRA INFO

This text box doesn't wrap text automatically to additional lines. If you want additional lines, press Enter to create paragraph breaks, or Shift+Enter to create line breaks without paragraph breaks.

Figure 8-19

5. **Type** Copyright 2012 Comstar Industries.

6. **Click slide 5 to select it.**

7. **On the Insert tab, click the Text Box button.**

8. **Near the bottom of the slide, close to the horizontal center, click and drag to draw a text box that is approximately 2 inches wide.**

See Figure 8-20.

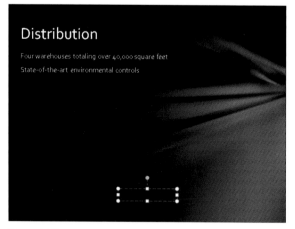

Distribution

Four warehouses totaling over 40,000 square feet

State-of-the-art environmental controls

Figure 8-20

9. **Type** Copyright 2012 Comstar Industries.

The text wraps to multiple lines, and the text box increases in height as needed. See Figure 8-21.

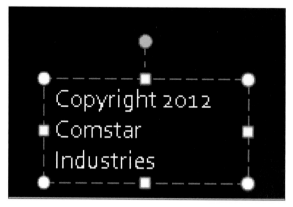

Copyright 2012 Comstar Industries

Figure 8-21

10. **Save the presentation.**

Leave the presentation open for the next exercise.

Manipulating Slide Content

Each placeholder box and each manually created text box or other item is a separate object that you can move around and resize freely. In the next several exercises, you learn how to work with the existing content on a slide.

Moving a slide object

To move a text box, position the mouse pointer over the border of the box, but not over a selection handle. The mouse pointer changes to a four-headed arrow. Click and drag the box to a new location. It works the same when moving nontext objects like pictures except you don't have to be so fussy about pointing at the border when you drag a nontext object; you can point anywhere in the center of the object instead if you like.

> If you want to move or resize a certain placeholder on every slide in your presentation, do so from Slide Master view (covered in Chapter 9). That way, you can make the change to the layout's template, and the change is applied automatically to every slide that uses that layout.

In this exercise, you move some text boxes.

Files needed: `Chapter 8 Comstar Practice.pptx`, *already open from the previous exercise*

1. **In the Slides/Outline pane, click slide 1 to select it.**

2. **Click in the Overview text box to move the insertion point into it, so you can see its boundaries, and then click the border of the text box to select the box itself.**

> When the insertion point is inside the text box, the border of the box appears dashed. When the box itself is selected, the border of the box appears solid.

3. **Position the mouse pointer over the border.**

   The mouse pointer becomes a four-headed arrow.

4. **Drag the text box to the top-left corner of the slide, as shown in Figure 8-22.**

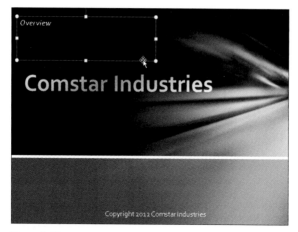

Figure 8-22

5. Click the Comstar Industries text box to select it.

 Make sure the border is solid, indicating that the text box itself is selected.

6. Hold down the Shift key and drag the text box downward so that the words appear to float slightly above the white line.

See Figure 8-23.

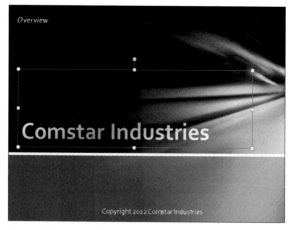

Figure 8-23

> Using the Shift key is optional. Holding down the Shift key constrains the movement to one dimension so you don't accidentally change the box's horizontal position as you drag it vertically.

7. Save the presentation.

Leave the presentation open for the next exercise.

Resizing a slide object

To resize an object, select it and then drag a selection handle. To maintain the height-width proportion for the box — its **aspect ratio** — hold down the Shift key while you drag one of the corner selection handles.

In this exercise, you resize some text boxes.

Files needed: Chapter 8 Comstar Practice. pptx, *already open from the previous exercise*

LINGO

A **selection handle** is a circle or square on the border of an object. Each box has eight selection handles: one in each corner, and one on each side. (The green circle handle at the top of the selected box rotates it when dragged.)

1. **In the Slides/Outline pane, click slide 5 to select it if it isn't already selected.**
2. **Click the text box at the bottom of the slide, which you created in the previous exercise.**
3. **Point to the selection handle in the upper-right corner of the text box.**

   The mouse pointer turns into a double-headed arrow. See Figure 8-24.

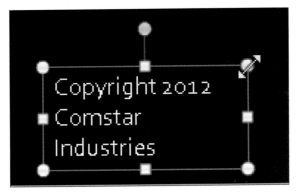

Figure 8-24

4. **Drag diagonally up and to the right, enlarging the text box by about
½ inch in each direction. Use the rulers to gauge the distance. Then
release the mouse button.**

Figure 8-25 shows the resized box.

Figure 8-25

EXTRA INFO

Notice that the height of the text
box actually decreased, even
though you dragged to increase it.
That's because this particular text
box is set to auto-size the height
of the box as needed to fit the text,
and when you widened it, you
caused the text to fit on one fewer
lines. Notice also that the text box
is now about ½ inch higher on the
slide than it was before.

TIP

If you don't want a text box to automatically
resize to fit the content, change its AutoFit
setting. You learn about that in Chapter 9.

5. **Click slide 3 to select it.**

6. **Click the frame of the text box that contains the body content on the
slide.**

As you can see when the frame is selected, the frame is much larger than
it needs to be to contain this content. See Figure 8-26.

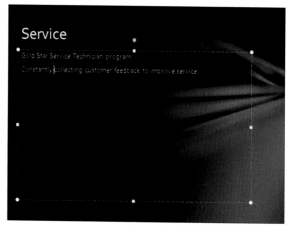

Figure 8-26

There is nothing wrong with leaving the frame at a larger size. Because it has no border, it isn't noticeable to the audience. However, for this exercise, you resize it anyway, just for practice.

7. **Drag the right side (square) selection handle to the left until it aligns with the 0" mark on the horizontal ruler.**

The text in the placeholder wraps to additional lines as needed. See Figure 8-27.

If you resize the placeholder(s) on a slide and then apply a different layout or design to the slide, everything snaps back to the default size and location. So make sure you have the right layout and design chosen before you spend a lot of time resizing or moving placeholders.

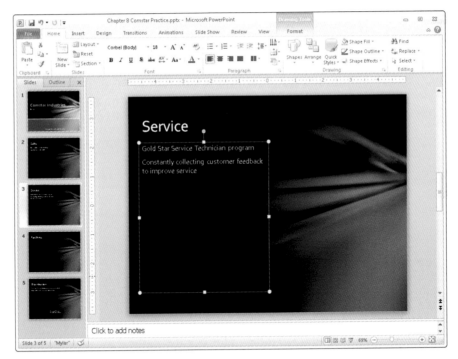

Figure 8-27

8. **Save the presentation.**

Leave the presentation open for the next exercise.

Deleting a slide object

Deleting a slide object is a lot like deleting a slide, except you select the object first, rather than selecting an entire slide. The easiest way to get rid of an object is to select it and press the Delete key. You can also right-click the object's border and choose Cut to cut it to the Clipboard, and then just not paste it anywhere.

In this exercise, you delete a text box.

Files needed: Chapter 8 Comstar Practice.pptx, *already open from the previous exercise*

1. **In the Slides/Outline pane, click slide 5 to select it.**

2. **Click inside the Copyright text box at the bottom of the slide, so the insertion point moves into the box.**

3. **Press the Delete key.**

   Notice that a single character of text was deleted; the entire text box was not.

4. **Click the border of the text box, so the border becomes a solid line, as shown in Figure 8-28.**

Figure 8-28

5. **Press the Delete key.**

   The entire text box is deleted.

6. **Save and close the presentation and exit PowerPoint.**

Summing Up

Here are the key points you learned about in this chapter:

- ✔ A presentation is a collection of one or more slides in a single data file. A slide is an individual page of a presentation.

- ✔ Normal view is the default view for PowerPoint. It consists of three panes: Slides/Outline, Slide, and Notes.

- ✔ Use the scroll bars to move around in a presentation, or use shortcut keys such as Page Up and Page Down.

- ✔ Slide Sorter view is handy for browsing all the slides in the presentation at once and rearranging them.

- ✔ Notes Page view is good for typing and organizing speaker notes.

- ✔ Slide Show view is used to display the presentation onscreen in full-screen mode.

- ✔ Reading View is like Slide Show view except it's in a window rather than full-screen.

- ✔ To create a new blank presentation, press Ctrl+N.

- ✔ To create a presentation based on a template, choose File⇨New and then choose the template you want.

- ✔ A template is a reusable sample file that includes both formatting and sample slides. A theme is like a template except it contains only formatting.

- ✔ To create new slides, click Home, New Slide, or click where you want the new slide in the Slides/Outline pane and press Enter.

- ✔ To delete a slide, select it in the Slides/Outline pane and press Delete.

- ✔ A slide layout contains one or more placeholders. To type text in a placeholder, click in it and begin typing.

- ✔ To manually create an additional text box on a slide, click Insert⇨Text Box.

- ✔ To move an object on a slide, drag it by its border (but not by a selection handle).

- ✔ To resize an object, drag one of its selection handles.

- ✔ To delete an object, select it and press Delete.

Try-it-yourself lab

For more practice with the features covered in this chapter, try the following exercise on your own.

1. **Start PowerPoint and create a new presentation based on a template of your choice.**

2. **Add and edit text in the presentation to deliver information about your favorite hobby or organization.**

   a. Add or delete slides from the presentation as needed to fit the content you want to present.

   b. Add or delete text boxes from slides as needed.

3. **Save the presentation as `Chapter 8 Hobby.pptx`.**

Know this tech talk

Aspect ratio: The proportion of height to width.

Normal view: The default view, consisting of the Slide pane, the Slides/ Outline pane, and the Notes pane.

presentation: A collection of one or more slides saved in a single data file.

selection handle: A circle or square on the border of an object's frame that can be dragged to resize the object.

slide: An individual page of a presentation.

Slide layout: A slide template that contains one or more content placeholders.

template: A reusable sample file that includes a background, layouts, coordinating fonts, and other design elements. Templates may also include sample content.

theme: A template that includes only formatting, and no sample content.

Chapter 9
Formatting a Presentation

✔ You can use themes to *apply consistent formatting* to all the slides in a presentation.

✔ A color theme applies a *preset combination of colors* to a presentation that work well together.

✔ A font theme applies a *preset combination of two fonts* that work well together.

✔ Shape styles provide an *easy shortcut for formatting* an object with a border, a fill, and an effect combination in a single step.

✔ You can use a background fill to make a text box opaque so it *contrasts with the slide background.*

✔ You can use a border to *define the edges of a text box.*

✔ Shape effects *apply special formatting to objects* for a professional look.

✔ Changing the AutoFit setting for a text box lets you *determine what happens when text overflows a text box.*

1. **How can you apply a theme?**

Apply yourself to page 283

2. **Can you use different fonts without changing to a different theme?**

Change your direction to page... 288

3. **What's a shape style?**

The shape of things is on page... 290

4. **How do you add a gradient background fill to a text box?**

Fill in the blank on page 291

5. **How do you make the border around a text box dotted or dashed?**

Dash to the answer on page 294

6. **How do you change the thickness of a border?**

Bound on to page.. 295

7. **What kinds of shape effects can you apply?**

Kindly look at the solutions on page.................................... 296

*F*ormatting can dramatically increase a presentation's effectiveness and impact. In PowerPoint you can use themes to apply preset formatting to the entire presentation at once, or you can format individual elements. You can apply text formatting just as you do in other Office applications, from the Home tab, and you can apply background fills and borders to text boxes as well.

In this chapter, you learn how to apply different themes to a presentation and how to change its color and font theme settings. You also learn how to apply a fill and a border to enhance the impact of a text box.

Understanding and Applying Themes

All presentations have a theme, but the default theme — simply named Blank — is so plain that it's almost like it's not there at all. Blank uses a white background, black Calibri text, and no background or design graphics.

Changing the presentation theme

You can switch to a different theme from the Design tab. You can choose themes stored on your local hard drive (contained in the Built In section) or choose themes from the Office.com online content if you're connected to the Internet when browsing for a theme.

In this exercise, you change a presentation's theme.

Files needed: `Chapter 9 Diner.pptx`

LINGO

A **theme** is a design set that you apply to a PowerPoint presentation to change several elements at once, including background, color scheme, fonts, and the positions of the placeholders on the various layouts. Word and Excel also use themes, but in PowerPoint, the theme feature is exceptionally strong and full featured.

1. Open the file **Chapter 9 Diner.pptx** and save it as **Chapter 9 Diner Formatting.pptx**.

2. Click the Design tab.

3. Click the More button in the Themes group, opening the Themes gallery.

    See Figure 9-1.

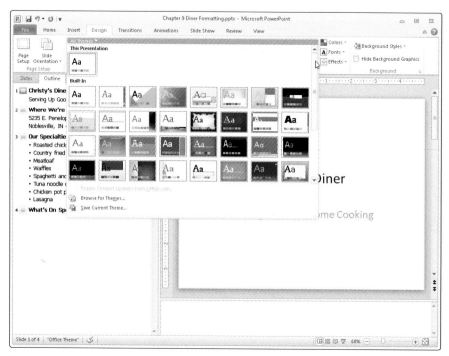

Figure 9-1

4. Point at several different themes with the mouse and watch them previewed on the slide behind the open gallery.

5. Click the Equity theme.

Themes are in alphabetical order. Hover the mouse pointer over a theme to see its name pop up in a ScreenTip.

6. Click the More button again to reopen the Themes gallery.

7. Scroll down the list in the Themes gallery to the From Office.com section and click the Urban Pop theme, applying it to the presentation.

8. **In the Slides/Outline pane, click the Slides tab.**

9. **Click each of the slides in the Slides tab to see the effect that the new theme has on each one's content.**

   Figure 9-2 shows slide 1, for example.

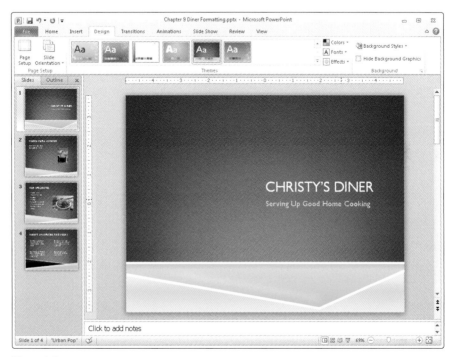

Figure 9-2

10. **Save the presentation.**

Leave the presentation open for the next exercise.

Changing the presentation colors

You can apply each theme in a variety of color combinations, so you don't have to choose between a theme that has the right style and one that has the right colors. You can select the theme first and then change to the colors from any other theme. You can also create your own custom **color themes**.

LINGO

A **color theme** is a preset combination of colors designed to work well together.

In this exercise, you change a presentation's colors and create your own custom color theme.

Files needed: Chapter 9 Diner Formatting.pptx, *already open from the previous exercise*

1. **Click the Design tab and then the Colors button.**

   The Colors gallery opens, listing all the colors for each of the available themes. Each color theme shows the colors it contains and its name. See Figure 9-3.

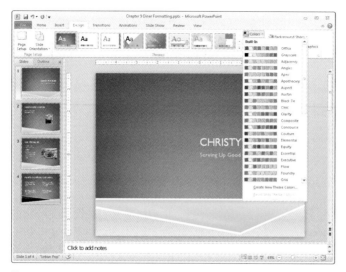

Figure 9-3

2. **Point to several different themes and observe the color changes on the slide behind the open gallery.**

3. **Scroll down through the Colors gallery and select Waveform.**

   The background of each slide turns to navy blue, and the other colors change, too.

4. **On the Design tab, click the Colors button and then choose Create New Theme Colors.**

   The Create New Theme Colors dialog box opens.

5. **Click the Accent 3 color button.**

   A menu opens. See Figure 9-4.

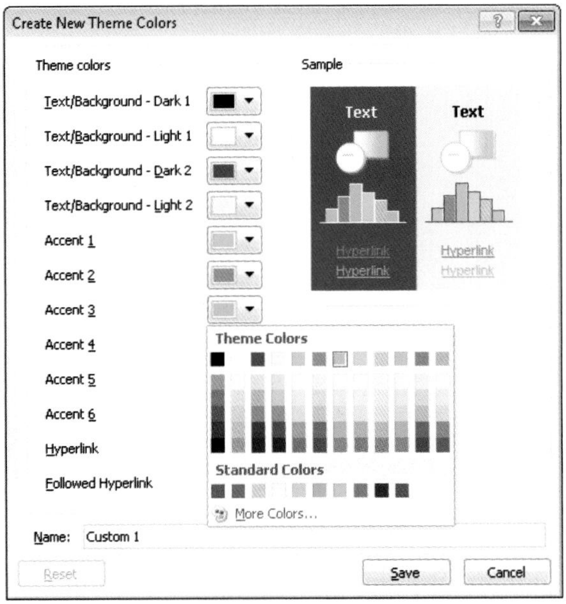

Figure 9-4

6. **Choose More Colors.**

The Colors dialog box opens.

7. **Click the Custom tab in the Colors dialog box if it isn't already displayed.**

8. **In the Color Model drop-down list, make sure RGB is selected.**

9. **Enter the following values: Red: 45, Green: 155, Blue: 71.**

See Figure 9-5.

10. **Click OK to close the dialog box.**

11. **In the Name box at the bottom of the Create New Theme Colors dialog box, change the name to Waveform 2.**

12. **Click the Save button.**

The new color theme is applied to the presentation. Notice that the green areas are now darker.

13. **Save the presentation.**

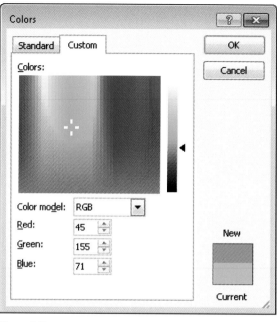

Figure 9-5

Leave the presentation open for the next exercise.

Changing the presentation fonts

Each theme has a set of two fonts that it uses: one designated for headings and one for body text. You can use the fonts from any other theme available if you don't like the ones that your chosen theme provides. You can also create your own custom font theme.

In this exercise, you change a presentation's fonts and create your own custom font theme.

Files needed: Chapter 9 Diner Formatting.pptx, *already open from the previous exercise*

1. **Click the Design tab and then the Fonts button.**

   The Fonts gallery opens, listing all the available themes and showing what fonts they use. See Figure 9-6.

2. **Point to several different font themes and observe the changes in the slide behind the open gallery.**

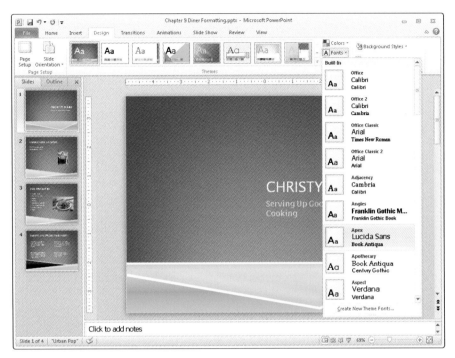

Figure 9-6

3. **Click the Apex theme.**

   The fonts from that theme are applied to the presentation. This theme uses Lucida Sans for the headings and Book Antiqua for the body text.

4. **On the Design tab, click the Fonts button and choose Create New Theme Fonts.**

5. **Open the Body Font drop-down list and select Calibri.**

6. **In the Name text box, type** Apex Custom.

   See Figure 9-7.

Figure 9-7

7. **Click the Save button.**

The body text in the presentation changes to reflect the new font chosen for body text.

8. **Save the presentation.**

Leave the presentation open for the next exercise.

Formatting Text Boxes and Placeholders

In most cases, presentations look best when they're consistently formatted. That means that usually your best bet is to apply formatting to the Slide Master.

Sometimes, however, you may want to format an individual text box or object differently from the rest, to make it stand out. In the following sections, you learn how to format specific text boxes in different ways.

Applying shape styles

The easiest way to apply formatting to an object is with the Shape Styles command. Depending on the style you choose, a shape style can include a border, a fill color, and special effects that make the shape look shiny, matte, or raised. Although from the name you may expect shape styles to apply only to graphical shapes, they still work with text boxes because PowerPoint considers a text box to be a shape (a rectangle).

LINGO

Shape styles are formatting presets that use the theme colors and effects in the presentation to format objects in multiple ways at once.

In this exercise, you apply shape styles to two shapes.

Files needed: Chapter 9 Diner Formatting.pptx, already open from the previous exercise

1. **In the Slides/Outline pane, click slide 4 to select it.**

2. **In the Slide pane, click the Early Morning Eye Opener text box.**

3. **Click the Drawing Tools Format tab.**

4. **In the Shape Styles group, click the More button to open the Shape Styles gallery.**

See Figure 9-8.

Figure 9-8

5. **Select Moderate Effect, Blue, Accent 1. The style is applied to the text box.**

   It's the second style in the fifth row.

6. **In the Slide pane, click the Dessert Special text box.**

7. **Click the More button again to reopen the Shape Styles gallery.**

8. **Select Moderate Effect, Blue, Accent 2.**

   It's the third style in the fifth row.

9. **Save the presentation.**

Leave the presentation open for the next exercise.

Applying a background fill

A text box, by default, has no background fill. Whatever is behind it shows through. You can apply a number of different background fills to a text box to make it opaque. You can choose solid colors, of course, from either the theme colors or the standard colors. You can also choose to apply gradients, textures, patterns, or even pictures as background fills.

REMEMBER

In this lesson, you find out about text box background fills, but this same skill carries over in other parts of PowerPoint. For example, you can apply a background fill to the entire slide, to graphic objects that have transparent backgrounds (such as some clip art images), and to pieces of a chart or a SmartArt diagram.

In this exercise, you apply a background fill to two shapes.

Files needed: `Chapter 9 Diner Formatting.pptx`, *already open from the previous exercise*

1. **On slide 4, select the Quick Lunch text box.**

2. **Click the Drawing Tools Format tab and then the Shape Fill button.**

   A palette of colors appears.

3. **Select Dark Blue, Background 2, Darker 50%.**

   It's the third color on the bottom row of the Theme Colors section. See Figure 9-9.

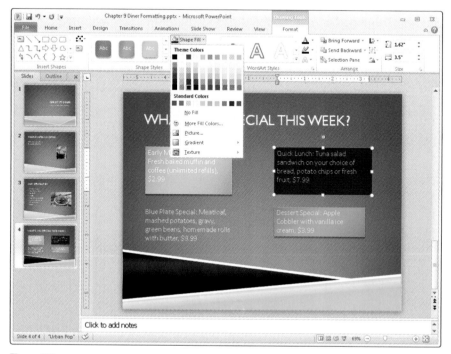

Figure 9-9

4. **Click the Blue Plate Special text box.**

5. **Click the Drawing Tools Format tab, click the Shape Fill button, and choose Gradient⇨More Gradients.**

   The Format Shape dialog box opens with the Fill controls displayed.

6. **Click the Gradient Fill button.**

7. **Open the Color button's palette and select Green, Accent 3, Darker 50% from the palette.**

   It's the 7th color in the bottom row of the Theme Colors section. See Figure 9-10.

8. **On the color slider, click the marker on the middle of the slider.**

9. **Open the Color button's palette, and click Green, Accent 3, Lighter 25%.**

   It's the 7th color in the next-to-bottom row of the Theme Colors section.

10. **Click the marker on the right end of the color slider.**

11. **Open the Color button's palette, and select Green, Accent 3, Lighter 40%.**

    It's the 7th color on the third-from-bottom row of the Theme Colors section.

12. **Click the up increment arrow on the Brightness box until it reads 45%.**

    See Figure 9-11.

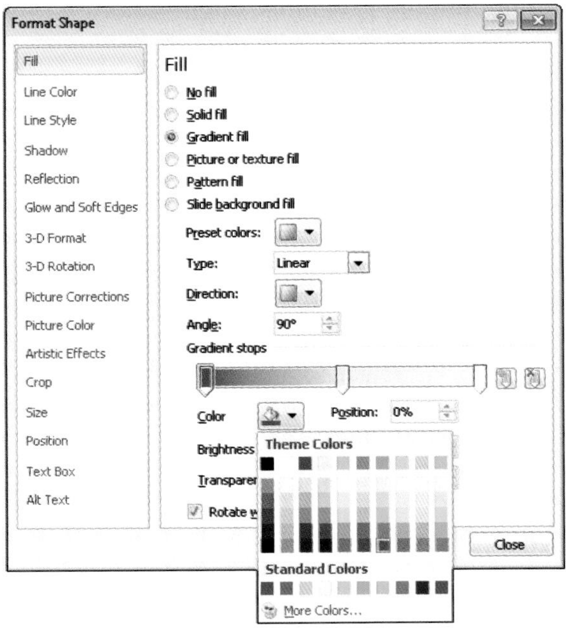

Figure 9-10

Figure 9-11

13. Click Close to close the dialog box.

14. Save the presentation.

Leave the presentation open for the next exercise.

Applying a border

By default, text boxes don't have borders, so they blend in with the slide background. You can add a border to any object, choosing a line style (solid, dashed, and so on), line color, and line weight (thickness).

In this exercise, you apply a border to two text boxes.

Files needed: `Chapter 9 Diner Formatting.pptx`, *already open from the previous exercise*

1. On slide 4, select the Quick Lunch text box.

2. **Click the Drawing Tools Format tab and then the Shape Outline button, and select the white square at the top of the palette (White, Text 1).**

   See Figure 9-12.

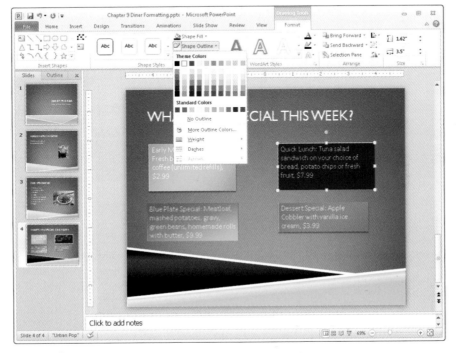

Figure 9-12

3. **Click the Drawing Tools Format tab, click the Shape Outline button, choose Weight, and choose the 2 ¼-point line.**

4. **On the slide, select the Blue Plate Special text box.**

5. **On the Drawing Tools Format tab, click the Shape Outline button and select Green, Accent 3, Darker 50%.**

   It's the 7th color in the bottom row of the Theme Colors section.

6. **Still on the Drawing Tools Format tab, click the Shape Outline button again, choose Dashes, and choose the Round Dot style (the second style on the list).**

   See Figure 9-13.

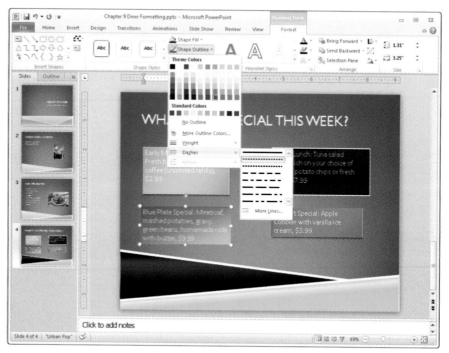

Figure 9-13

For more practice, try several other border colors, weights, and styles for the text boxes. For example, click the Shape Outline button and choose Weight⇨More Lines, click the Line Color tab, and try creating a gradient line.

7. Save the presentation.

Leave the presentation open for the next exercise.

Applying shape effects

Shape effects are enhancements like shadow, reflection, glow, and bevel that you can optionally apply to shapes (including text boxes) to dress them up. Some of the shape styles (covered earlier in the lesson) apply some of these effects, and you can also apply the effects separately.

In this exercise, you apply a border to two text boxes.

Files needed: Chapter 9 Diner Formatting.pptx, *already open from the previous exercise*

1. **On slide 4, select the Quick Lunch text box.**

2. **Click the Drawing Tools Format tab, click the Shape Effects button, and choose Bevel⇨Circle.**

   Circle is the first bevel effect under the Bevel heading. See Figure 9-14.

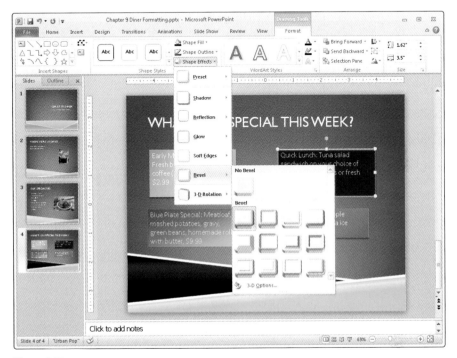

Figure 9-14

3. **Select the Blue Plate Special text box.**

4. **On the Drawing Tools Format tab, click the Shape Effects button, and choose Shadow⇨Inside Diagonal Bottom Right (the last shadow in the Inner section).**

   See Figure 9-15.

5. **In the Slide pane, select the Early Morning text box.**

6. **On the Drawing Tools Format tab, click the Shape Effects button and choose Glow⇨Teal, 8 pt glow, Accent Color 6.**

   It's the last glow in the second row of the Glow Variations section. See Figure 9-16.

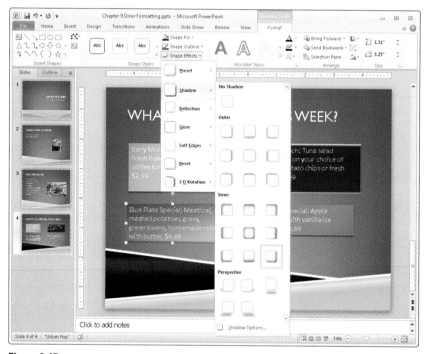

Figure 9-15

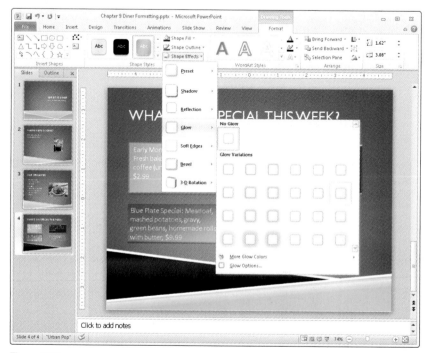

Figure 9-16

7. **Save the presentation.**

Leave the presentation open for the next exercise.

Turning text AutoFit on or off

In manually placed text boxes, a different AutoFit behavior occurs by default: The text box itself gets larger as needed to accommodate the text.

Both of those behaviors can be very useful, but you may sometimes need to change the AutoFit setting for one or more text boxes to achieve certain effects. For example, you may not want a manually placed text box to shrink if you delete some text from it, or it may be unacceptable to you for the font size used in the title of one slide to be different from that of another.

In this exercise, you change the AutoFit setting for a text box.

Files needed: `Chapter 9 Diner Formatting.pptx`, *already open from the previous exercise*

LINGO

If you type more text than will fit in that text box (which is especially common for a slide title, for example), the text automatically shrinks itself as much as is needed to allow it to fit. This feature, called **AutoFit**, is turned on by default in text placeholders. AutoFit is very useful because it prevents text from being truncated.

1. **On slide 4, select the Blue Plate Special text box.**

2. **Try to enlarge the height of the text box by dragging its bottom selection handle downward.**

   It doesn't resize.

3. **Right-click the border of the text box and click Format Shape.**

   The Format Shape dialog box opens.

4. **Click the Text Box tab along the left side of the dialog box.**

   Text box options appear.

5. **In the AutoFit section, notice the current setting: Resize Shape to Fit Text.**

   This is the reason the text box shrinks and grows depending on the text in it.

6. **Select the Do Not AutoFit option.**

   See Figure 9-17.

7. **Click Close to close the dialog box.**

8. **Drag the bottom selection handle on the text box downward to increase its height by about ¼ inch.**

Use the vertical ruler to gauge the height. Notice that now the height is resizable. See Figure 9-18.

Figure 9-17

Figure 9-18

For more practice, try typing more text into one of the slides' title boxes than will fit and watch how it shrinks in size. Then change the text box's AutoFit setting to Do Not AutoFit and see how it changes how PowerPoint handles the text. Then change the setting to Resize shape to fit text and see what happens.

9. **Save and close the presentation and exit PowerPoint.**

Summing Up

Here are the key points you learned about in this chapter:

- A theme is a design set that you apply to a presentation to change several elements at once, including background, color scheme, fonts, and the positions of placeholders in the various layouts.
- To change the theme, click the Design tab, click the More button in the Themes group, and select a theme.
- Each theme's colors and fonts can be applied separately from the theme itself.
- To apply different colors, click Design, Theme Colors.
- To apply different fonts, click Design, Theme Fonts.
- You can also format individual objects, including text boxes. Select the object and then use the Drawing Tools Format tab's commands.
- You can apply shape styles to apply presets that include background fill, border, and effects all at once. Choose from the Shape Styles gallery on the Drawing Tools Format tab.
- To format a text box's fill, click Drawing Tools Format, Shape Fill.
- To format a text box's border, click Drawing Tools Format, Shape Outline.
- To apply effects such as shadow, glow, or bevel, click Drawing Tools Format, Shape Effects.
- You can change a text box's AutoFit setting to determine what happens when there's more text than will fit in the box at its current size. To do so, right-click the text box and choose Format Shape, click Text Box, and choose an AutoFit setting in the dialog box.

Try-it-yourself lab

For more practice with the features covered in this chapter, try the following exercise on your own.

1. **Open Chapter 9 Banking.pptx and save it as** `Chapter 9 Banking Formatting.pptx`.
2. **Apply the theme of your choice.**
3. **Change to a different set of theme colors.**
4. **Change to a different set of theme fonts.**

5. On slide 7, format each of the text boxes in a different way.

6. Save the presentation and exit PowerPoint.

Know this tech talk

AutoFit: A setting that determines what happens when text overflows a text box. Either the box enlarges or shrinks to fit the text, or the text changes size, or nothing happens and the text is truncated.

Border: A line around the outside of an object.

color theme: A collection of color presets

font theme: A collection of two font presets: one for headings and one for body text.

shape styles: Formatting presets that change an object's formatting in multiple ways at once, such as applying a border, a fill, and special effects.

theme: A design set that you apply to a presentation to change several elements at once, including the background, colors, fonts, and place-holder positions.

Chapter 10

Adding Graphics and SmartArt

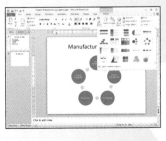

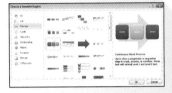

✔ Content placeholders enable you to insert clip art and photos as part of the slide's layout, so if the layout or design changes, the *graphics move as needed.*

✔ The Insert tab contains commands for manually inserting graphics, for situations where *content placeholders may not be available.*

✔ The Clip Art task pane helps you *search Microsoft's extensive collection of clips online.*

✔ By using SmartArt, you can *combine the utility of text with the attractiveness of a graphic.*

✔ With SmartArt, you can arrange text in graphical shapes so that the positioning of the shapes *adds an additional layer of meaning.*

✔ You can *save time* by converting a bulleted list to SmartArt.

✔ SmartArt can easily be converted between layouts for *different looks and meanings.*

1. What's the advantage of using placeholders to insert graphics?

Place yourself on page 305

2. How do you open the Clip Art task pane?

Open the book on page 306

3. Can PowerPoint accept `.png` and `.tif` graphics?

Ping the answer on page 310

4. What is SmartArt?

A wise explanation on page 313

5. How do you use SmartArt to create an organization chart?

Flow on to page 315

6. How do you change to a different SmartArt diagram type?

Change to page 320

7. How can you make a SmartArt diagram multicolored?

There's a rainbow of information on page 321

*F*ormatting can dramatically increase a presentation's effectiveness and impact. In PowerPoint, you can use themes to apply preset formatting to the entire presentation at once, or you can format individual elements. You can apply text formatting just as you do in other Office applications, from the Home tab, and you can apply background fills and borders to text boxes as well.

In this chapter, you learn how to apply different themes to a presentation and how to change its color and font theme settings too. You also learn how to apply a fill and a border to enhance the impact of a text box.

Inserting Graphics

You learned about inserting graphics in Word in Chapter 4, and inserting them in PowerPoint is very similar. The commands on the Insert tab in both applications include buttons for inserting a graphic from a file and also for inserting clip art.

However, PowerPoint has one big difference: placeholders. You have two ways of inserting graphics in PowerPoint: via the Insert tab (as in Word) and via the icons in a content placeholder. Depending on which method you choose, the graphic behaves differently.

The placeholder method offers several advantages. If you insert a graphic using one of the content placeholders, the graphic integrates more seamlessly with the other content on the slide, and if you change to a layout that positions that placeholder differently, or a theme that arranges the placeholders differently, the graphic moves automatically to the new position. In contrast, if you insert a graphic using the Insert tab's commands, it becomes a fixed, manually placed object on the slide, and it doesn't automatically shift when the layout shifts.

Inserting clip art

Use the following exercise to practice clip art insertion.

In this exercise, you insert clip art using a place-holder and using the Insert tab.

Files needed: `Chapter 10 Greek.pptx`

LINGO

Clip art is generic, predrawn artwork that Microsoft provides. Chapter 4 has a summary of the different types of clip art available.

1. **Open `Chapter 10 Greek.pptx` and save it as `Chapter 10 Greek Restaurant. pptx`.**

2. **In the Slides/Outline pane, click slide 2 to display it.**

3. **Select the empty content placeholder (see Figure 10-1) and then click the Clip Art icon.**

   The Clip Art task pane opens.

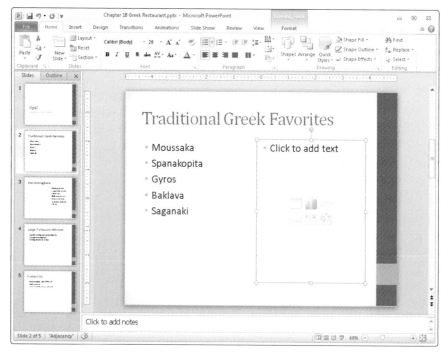

Figure 10-1

4. **In the Clip Art task pane, in the Search For text box, type** Greek.

5. **Open the Results should be drop-down list and click All Media Types. (See Figure 10-2.) Then click away from the list to close it.**

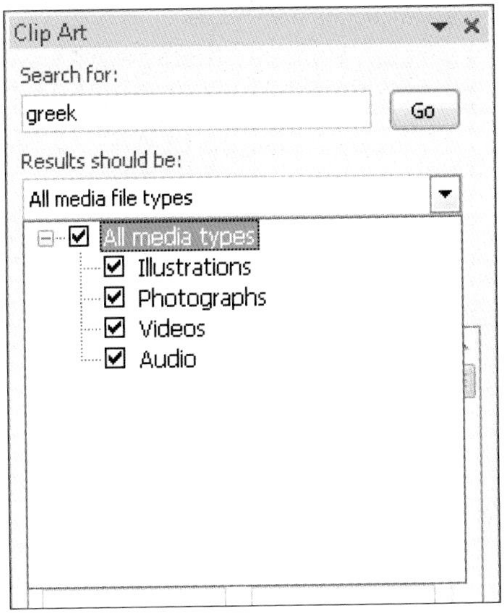

Clip Art

Search for:

| greek | Go |

Results should be:

All media file types ▾

- ☑ All media types
    - ☑ Illustrations
    - ☑ Photographs
    - ☑ Videos
    - ☑ Audio

Figure 10-2

6. **Make sure that the Include Office.com content check box is marked. Then click the Go button.**

7. **Click an image that shows Greek columns, like the one in Figure 10-3.**

   It appears in the placeholder.

8. **Click slide 5 to display it.**

   This slide has no placeholder suitable for clip art.

9. **Click the Insert tab.**

   Notice that the Clip Art button is already selected. That's because the Clip Art task pane is already open.

10. **Click the Clip Art button to toggle the task pane off; then click Clip Art again to toggle it back on.**

11. **In the Clip Art task pane, replace the text in the Search For text box with the word** phone.

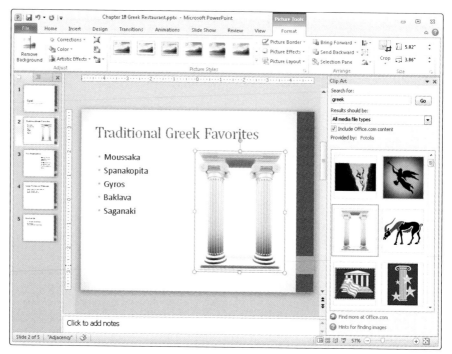

Figure 10-3

12. **Open the Results Should Be drop-down list and deselect all the check boxes except Illustrations.**

    See Figure 10-4.

13. **Click Go.**

    Drawings of phones appear.

14. **Click one of the drawings that shows a telephone.**

    It appears in the center of the slide. Figure 10-5 shows an example.

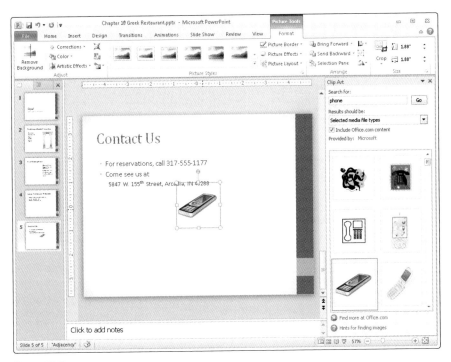

Figure 10-4

Figure 10-5

15. **Drag the picture to the upper-right corner of the slide, as shown in Figure 10-6.**

Figure 10-6

For more practice, try changing to a different theme that positions the placeholders differently (such as Aspect). Notice that the picture on slide 2 is repositioned automatically. However, notice that the picture on slide 5 stays put, regardless of the theme applied.

16. **Save the presentation.**

Keep the presentation open for the next exercise.

Inserting pictures from files

You can also insert pictures you've acquired yourself, either from someone else or from your own digital camera or scanner. These pictures are stored as separate files on your hard drive or other media. PowerPoint supports many different picture formats, including `.tif`, `.jpg`, `.gif`, `.bmp`, and `.png`.

Just like with clip art, you can insert a picture either with the Insert tab's command or with the placeholder icon.

In this exercise, you insert clip art using a placeholder and the Insert tab.

Files needed: `Chapter 10 Greek.pptx`

1. **In the Slides/Outline pane, click slide 3 to display it.**

2. **In the content placeholder, click the Insert Picture from File icon.**

See Figure 10-7.

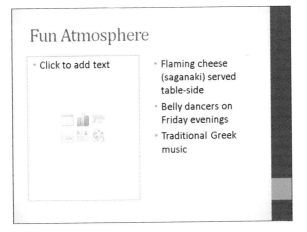

Figure 10-7

3. **In the Insert Picture dialog box, navigate to the location containing the data files for this lesson. Select flamge.jpg and click the Insert button.**

See Figure 10-8. The flaming cheese appears in the placeholder.

Figure 10-8

4. **Click slide 4 to display it.**

This slide doesn't have a placeholder for a picture.

5. **On the Insert tab, click the Picture button.**

The Insert Picture dialog box opens. It's the same dialog box as in Figure 10-8.

6. **Click `room.jpg` and click the Insert button.**

   The picture appears in the center of the slide, overlapping the text. See Figure 10-9.

Figure 10-9

7. **Drag the lower-right corner selection handle on the picture toward the center of the picture until the picture is 4 inches wide.**

   Use the ruler to gauge the size.

8. **Drag the picture below the bulleted list.**

   See Figure 10-10.

Figure 10-10

9. Save the presentation and close it.

Leave PowerPoint open for the next exercise.

Creating SmartArt

SmartArt enables you to present text in a graphical way, bridging the gap between decorative images and ordinary text. With SmartArt, a plain bulleted list can become much more appealing to read. You can also use SmartArt to present information conceptually in ways that plain text alone can't achieve.

Converting text to SmartArt

The easiest way to create SmartArt is to convert an existing bulleted list to SmartArt. That way you don't have to retype the text.

LINGO

SmartArt is a type of artwork you can create in PowerPoint or other Office programs that places text paragraphs in shapes and arranges the shapes to create additional meaning about the text. For example, an organization chart or a pyramid diagram conveys information about text by the text's position in the diagram.

In this exercise, you convert a bulleted list to a Process SmartArt diagram.

Files needed: Chapter 10 Manufacturing.pptx

1. **Open** Chapter 10 Manufacturing.pptx **and save it as** Chapter 10 Manufacturing Diagrams.pptx**.**
2. **On slide 1, click in the bulleted list to move the insertion point there; then press Ctrl+A to select all the text.**
3. **On the Home tab, click the Convert to SmartArt Graphic button.**

   A menu of SmartArt styles opens. See Figure 10-11.

TIP

You can point to a diagram type to see it previewed on the slide before you commit to a certain type by clicking it.

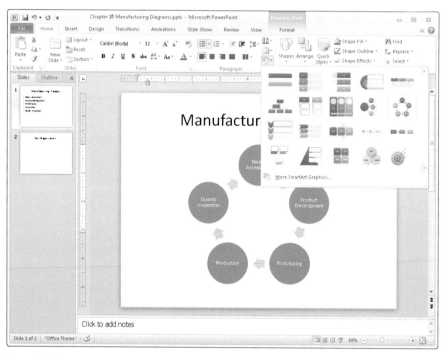

Figure 10-11

4. Click the Basic Cycle diagram.

It's applied to the bulleted list.

5. Save the presentation.

Leave the presentation open for the next exercise.

Inserting a SmartArt diagram

If the text doesn't already exist in the presentation, you may find it easier to create a SmartArt diagram from scratch and then type the text in it as you go. You can choose from several diagram types, such as Process, List, Hierarchy, and Matrix. Each is well-suited for presenting a different type of information.

In this exercise, you create a new Hierarchy SmartArt diagram.

Files needed: `Chapter 10 Manufacturing Diagrams.pptx`, *already open from the previous exercise*

1. **In the Slides/Outline pane, click slide 2 to display it.**

2. **On the Insert tab, click the SmartArt button.**

   The Choose a SmartArt Graphic dialog box opens.

TIP

If this slide had contained a content placeholder, you could have clicked the SmartArt icon in the placeholder to start this diagram. This slide didn't have a placeholder, so you're creating the diagram from the Insert tab.

3. **Click the Hierarchy category.**

4. **Click the Organization Chart sample.**

   It's the first sample in the first row. See Figure 10-12.

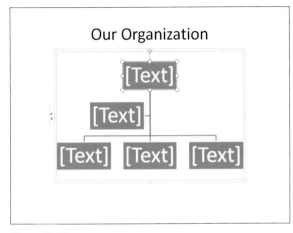

Figure 10-12

5. **Click OK.**

   A blank organization chart appears, as shown in Figure 10-13.

Figure 10-13

6. **Click in the topmost [Text] placeholder and type** Janet Green.

The text in the placeholder shrinks in size to accommodate the text, and the text placeholders in all the other boxes also changes to that same size for consistency.

7. **Click the second [Text] placeholder and press Delete to remove it from the diagram.**

The diagram should now resemble Figure 10-14.

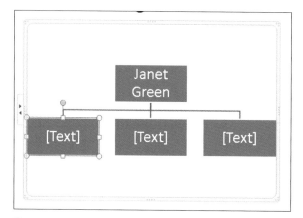

Figure 10-14

8. **Click in the leftmost of the three [Text] placeholders and type** Kim Fairfield. **Press Enter and then type** Director of Operations.

9. **Click in the middle [Text] placeholder and type** Brady Jackson. **Press Enter and then type** Director of Manufacturing.

10. **Click the rightmost [Text] placeholder and type** Eve Williams. **Press Enter and then type** Director of Personnel.

The diagram should resemble Figure 10-15 at this point.

11. **Click the Brady Jackson box to select it.**

12. **Click the SmartArt Tools Design tab and then click the Add Shape button.**

A box appears for a subordinate below Brady.

13. **In the new box, type** Ann Rayne. **Press Enter and type** Quality Assurance Manager.

14. **With the new box still selected, click the down arrow to the right of the Add Shape button, opening a menu of new shape types.**

See Figure 10-16.

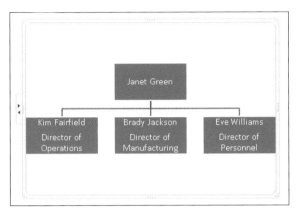

Figure 10-15

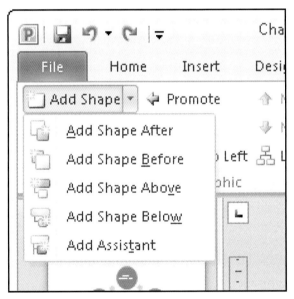

Figure 10-16

15. Click Add Shape After.

A new box appears at the same level of hierarchy as the previous one.

16. **In the new box, type** Roger Park. **Press Enter and type** Equipment Manager. **Then click away from the diagram to deselect it.**

The slide should look like Figure 10-17.

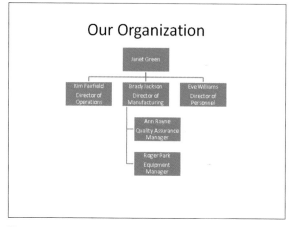

Figure 10-17

17. **Save the presentation.**

Leave the presentation open for the next exercise.

Modifying a SmartArt diagram

After creating a SmartArt diagram, you may want to modify it. Modifications can include changing the diagram type or layout, adding or removing shapes, and changing the order in which shapes appear.

In this exercise, you will modify a SmartArt diagram.

Files needed: Chapter 10 Manufacturing Diagrams.pptx, *already open from the previous exercise*

1. **In the Slides/Outline pane, click slide 1 to display it.**

2. **Click the frame of the SmartArt diagram to select the entire diagram.**

3. **Click the SmartArt Tools Design tab and then click the More button in the Layouts group.**

4. **Click More Layouts.**

   The Choose a SmartArt Graphic dialog box opens.

5. **Click the Process category.**

6. **Click the Continuous Block Process layout.**

   See Figure 10-18.

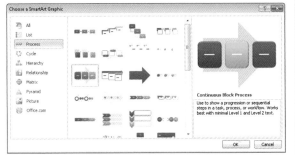

EXTRA INFO

Not all diagrams make sense when you change to a different diagram type. In this example, the text still works logically, but when you convert to a different type, be aware of the meaning of the data. For example, a pyramid or hierarchy chart wouldn't work very well for a step-by-step process.

Figure 10-18

7. **Click OK.**

   The new diagram type is applied.

8. **On the SmartArt Tools Design tab, click the Right to Left button.**

   The diagram switches direction.

9. **On the SmartArt Tools Design tab, click the Left to Right button.**

   It changes back to its original direction.

10. **Still on SmartArt Tools Design tab, click the Text Pane button if the text pane does not already appear.**

    A text pane appears to the left of the diagram. See Figure 10-19.

11. **In the text pane, change the word *Production* to *Manufacturing*.**

12. **Click the Close (X) button on the text pane to close it.**

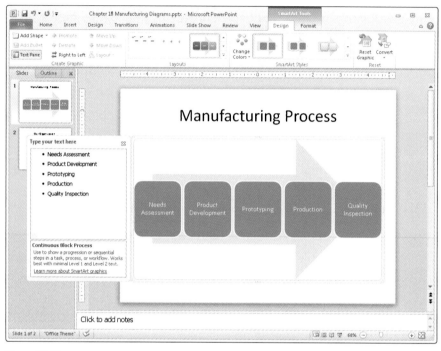

Figure 10-19

13. **On the diagram, click the Quality Inspection shape and press the Delete key to remove it.**

14. **Save the presentation.**

Leave the presentation open for the next exercise.

Formatting a SmartArt diagram

A number of methods for formatting a SmartArt diagram are available. You can apply SmartArt Styles, for example, that format the entire diagram at once using a preset format that's tied in with the document's theme colors and effects. You can also change the colors of the diagram as a whole. Finally, you can apply formatting to specific shapes within a diagram, separately from the diagram as a whole.

In this exercise, you format two SmartArt diagrams.

Files needed: `Chapter 10 Manufacturing Diagrams.pptx,` *already open from the previous exercise*

1. **In the Slides/Outline pane, click slide 1 to display it if it isn't already displayed.**

2. **Click the diagram to select it if it is not already selected.**

3. **On the SmartArt Tools Design tab, click the More button in the SmartArt Styles group, opening a gallery of choices.**

4. **In the Best Match for Document section, click the Intense Effect style.**

   See Figure 10-20.

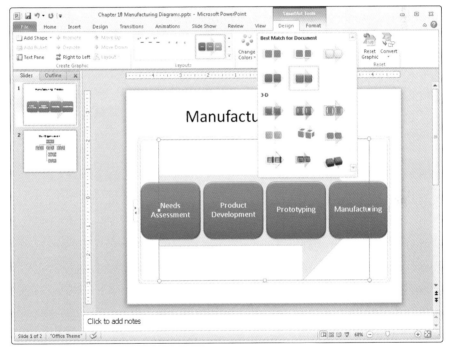

Figure 10-20

5. **Click the SmartArt Tools Design tab and then click the Change Colors button.**

   A gallery of color choices appears. See Figure 10-21.

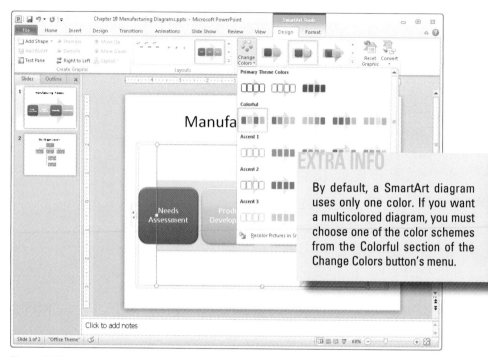

By default, a SmartArt diagram uses only one color. If you want a multicolored diagram, you must choose one of the color schemes from the Colorful section of the Change Colors button's menu.

Figure 10-21

6. **Click the Colorful – Accent Colors sample (the first one in the Colorful section).**

   The colors in the diagram change.

7. **In the Slides/Outline pane, click slide 2 to display it, and click the SmartArt diagram.**

8. **On the SmartArt Tools Design tab, click the More button in the SmartArt Styles group, opening a gallery of choices.**

9. **Click Polished (the first sample in the 3-D section of the list).**

10. **Click the SmartArt Tools Design tab, click the Change Colors button, and select the Colorful – Accent Colors sample.**

    The diagram changes to show each level of the hierarchy as a different color. See Figure 10-22.

11. **Click the Janet Green shape at the top of the diagram.**

12. **On the SmartArt Tools Format tab, click the Shape Fill button and click the black square in the top row of the Theme Colors section.**

    That shape becomes black. See Figure 10-23.

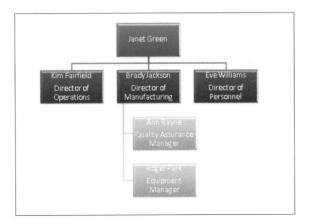

Figure 10-22

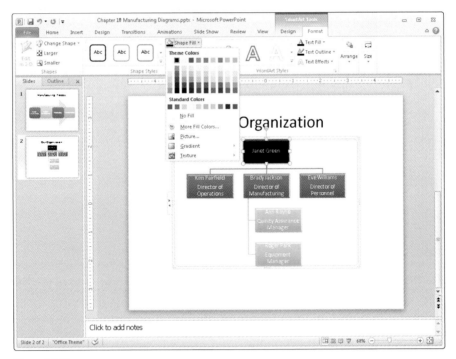

Figure 10-23

13. **Save the presentation and close it.**

14. **Close PowerPoint.**

Summing Up

Here are the key points you learned about in this chapter:

- You can insert graphics via the placeholders on a slide's layout or via the Insert tab's buttons for inserting various types of content.

- To insert clip art, open the Clip Art task pane. You can do so by clicking Insert, Clip Art or by clicking a Clip Art placeholder icon. Then search for the clip art by keyword and type.

- To insert a picture from a file, click Insert, Picture or click an Insert Picture from File icon on a content placeholder.

- SmartArt presents text in a graphical way by placing each paragraph in its own shape and arranging the shapes to create additional meaning.

- You can convert existing text to SmartArt by clicking Home, Convert to SmartArt Graphic.

- To insert a new SmartArt diagram, click Insert, SmartArt or click the Insert SmartArt icon on a content placeholder.

- The SmartArt Tools Design tab provides options for changing the diagram type, style, and colors.

- You can format individual elements of a diagram from the SmartArt Tools Format tab.

Try-it-yourself lab

For more practice with the features covered in this chapter, try the following exercise on your own.

1. **Start a new, blank presentation.**

2. **Change the first slide's layout to Title and Content.**

3. **Use the Insert SmartArt Graphic icon in the content placeholder to start a new diagram.**

4. **Use a Horizontal Hierarchy diagram to create a tournament bracket diagram for a single-elimination sports tournament.**

   Figure 10-24 shows an example, but you can use your own sports teams.

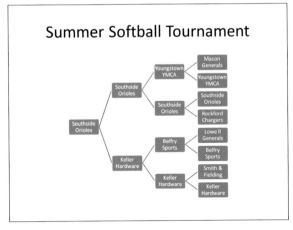

Summer Softball Tournament

Figure 10-24

5. **Apply the colors and SmartArt Style of your choice.**

6. **Save the presentation as `Chapter 10 Tournament.pptx` and exit PowerPoint.**

Know this tech talk

clip art: Generic predrawn artwork, accessed from the Clip Art task pane in Office applications.

Adding Movement and Sound to a Presentation

✔ Transitions *make the movement more interesting* from one slide to another.

✔ You can use animations *call attention to specific objects* on a slide.

✔ An entrance animation *brings an object onto the slide separately* from the rest of the slide's content.

✔ An exit animation *removes an object from a slide separately* from the rest of the slide's content.

✔ An emphasis effect *draws attention to an object* that is neither entering nor exiting.

✔ You can place a sound clip on a slide to *play back audio content* during the slide show.

✔ You can place a video clip on a slide so that the *video content is a part of the PowerPoint show.*

1. **What's the difference between a transition and an animation?**

It's clearly differentiated on page 329

2. **How do you speed up a transition effect?**

Race to the answer on page 332

3. **Can you assign sounds to transitions?**

The assignment is executed on page 334

4. **How do you apply an emphasis animation effect?**

There's an effective solution on page 338

5. **How do you reorder the animation effects on a slide?**

Order up the answer on page 340

6. **How can you copy the animation from one object to another?**

Another problem solved on page 342

7. **Can you use a Flash video clip in PowerPoint?**

Flash to the answer on page 347

*H*ave you ever heard the term "Death by PowerPoint"? It means being bored to death by a dull, long, lifeless presentation, usually with someone droning on about the slide's text-heavy content in too much detail.

To avoid causing this kind of agony for your audience, you can enliven your slides by adding movement and sound to them. You can set up different transition effects for moving from one slide to another, and you can animate the individual objects on a slide so that they enter or exit the slide or emphasize a certain point.

You can also add sound and video clips to a presentation. In earlier versions of PowerPoint, some types of video were difficult to integrate, but PowerPoint 2010 is greatly improved in this area, and you can integrate many sound and video types seamlessly into your show.

Adding Slide Transition Effects

Some of the transition effects have effect options that determine the direction of the action. For example, a Wipe transition may wipe from the left, right, top, or bottom, or from one of the corners. Other effects have no such options because they can happen only one way. If options are available, you can click the Transitions tab and choose them from the Effect Options button's menu.

LINGO

Transitions are movements from one slide to another. The default transition effect is None, which means the slide simply goes away and the next one appears. Some of the alternatives include Fade, Push, Wipe, Split, and Cut, to name only a few. You can apply transitions from the Transitions tab.

You can also set several other properties for a transition. You can assign a sound to it, for example, and you can control its duration (speed). You can choose when the transition should occur:

✔ On mouse click

✔ Automatically after a certain amount of time has passed

In the following exercises, you add transitions to slides and customize their options and properties.

Applying a transition to a slide

Each transition has default settings, so you can apply a basic transition effect with just a few clicks. You can then optionally fine-tune those settings later.

In this exercise, you apply several different transitions and then watch the presentation in Slide Show view to check them.

File needed: Chapter 11 Diner.pptx

1. **Open Chapter 11 Diner.pptx and save it as Chapter 11 Diner Movement.pptx.**
2. **In the Slides/Outline pane, click slide 1 to select it.**
3. **Click the Transitions tab.**
4. **Select the Push effect:**

    • If you see the Push effect in the Transition to This Slide group, click it.

    • Otherwise, click the More button to open a gallery of transition effects, as shown in Figure 11-1, and then click Push.

    The Push effect is selected and is previewed on the slide. Notice that a star symbol appears to the right of slide 1 now. This star indicates that a transition or an animation is associated with the slide.

5. **Click slide 2 to select it.**
6. **Select the Wipe effect:**

    • On the Transitions tab, if you see the Wipe effect in the Transition to This Slide group, click it.

    • Otherwise, click the More button to open a gallery of transition effects, and then click Wipe.

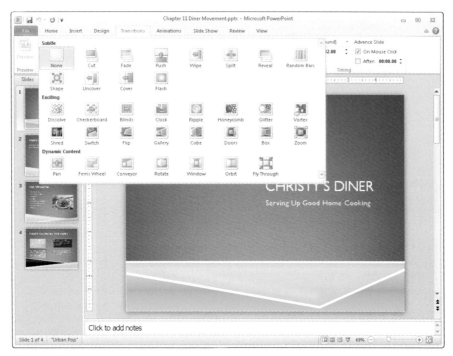

Figure 11-1

7. Click slide 3 to select it.

8. On the Transitions tab, click More and then click the Cube effect.

9. On the Slide Show tab, click the From Beginning button to watch the show and preview your transitions.

10. Click to move through the slides. When you reach the end of the slide show, click again to return to Normal view.

11. Click slide 3 to select it.

12. Click the Transitions tab and then the Apply to All button.

   The transition effect from slide 3 (Cube) is now applied to all the slides in the presentation.

Using Apply to All is much faster and easier than applying the same transition effect manually to multiple slides. If you don't want it to affect certain slides, you can remove the transition from those slides later by choosing None as the transition effect for them.

13. **Repeat Steps 9 and 10 to view the presentation and check the transitions again.**

14. **Save the presentation.**

Leave the presentation open for the next exercise.

Changing a transition's options

Different transitions have different options available. Some of the transitions are directional in nature, so you have a choice of which way the transition moves. The direction could be toward a side of the screen, or it could be clockwise or counterclockwise.

All transitions have a Duration setting, which governs how quickly they occur. The longer the duration, the slower the transition. Most transitions take only a few seconds by default.

Finally, a transition can include a sound or not. PowerPoint has a short list of preset sounds it provides for your use; you can also specify a sound file that you have stored on your hard drive if you prefer.

In this exercise, you modify the settings for slide transitions and assign a sound effect.

File needed: `Chapter 11 Diner Movement.pptx`*, already open from the previous exercise*

1. **Click slide 1 to select it.**

2. **Click the Transitions tab, click the Effect Options button, and choose From Top.**

   The transition is previewed on the slide. See Figure 11-2.

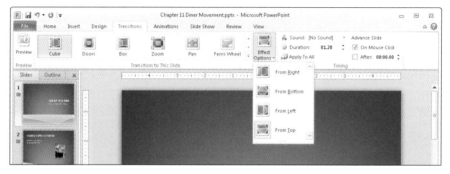

Figure 11-2

3. Click the down increment arrow on the Duration box once to change the duration to 1.00 seconds.

4. Open the Sound drop-down list and click Camera.

   See Figure 11-3.

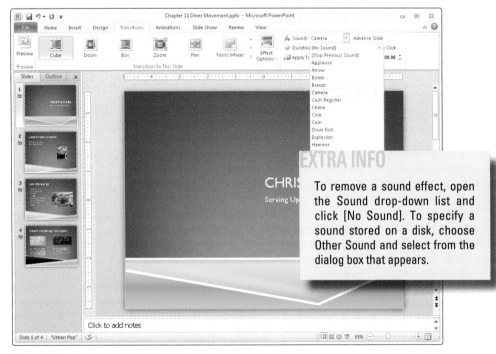

Figure 11-3

5. Click the Apply to All button.

6. Click the Slide Show tab and then the From Beginning button to watch the show and check your transitions.

7. Click to move through the slides. When you reach the end of the slide show, click again to return to Normal view.

8. Save the presentation.

Leave the presentation open for the next exercise.

Setting slides to advance manually or automatically

Slides advance on mouse click by default. That means that no matter how long you leave a slide onscreen, PowerPoint won't try to advance to the next slide until you give the signal. (That signal can be an actual mouse click, or it can be the press of a key, such as Enter, spacebar, or the right-arrow key.)

If you want certain (or all) slides to advance automatically after a certain amount of time, you can specify this advancement on the Transitions tab. You can specify an automatic transition instead of or in addition to the default On Click behavior.

In this exercise, you modify the settings for slide transitions and assign a sound effect.

File needed: `Chapter 11 Diner Movement.pptx`, *already open from the previous exercise*

1. **Click slide 1 to select it.**

2. **On the Transitions tab, in the Timing group, select the After check box.**

3. **Click the up increment arrow on the After text box until the value reads 00:05:00, as in Figure 11-4.**

Figure 11-4

4. **Click the Apply to All button.**

5. **Click the Slide Show tab and then the From Beginning button to watch the show and check your transitions.**

   Don't click; just wait for the five seconds to elapse so that the next slide will appear.

6. **When you reach the end of the slide show, click again to return to Normal view.**

7. **Save the presentation.**

Leave the presentation open for the next exercise.

Animating Objects

You can create four types of animations in PowerPoint:

✔ An **entrance animation** governs how an object appears on the slide.

✔ An **exit animation** governs how an object leaves the slide.

✔ An **emphasis animation** makes the object do something to call attention to itself when it is neither entering nor exiting; this may include changing color, moving around, or making a sound.

✔ A **motion path animation** (not covered in this lesson) moves an object on the slide following a predefined path you specify. It's kind of like setting down model railroad tracks and letting the object be the train moving on the track.

Creating an entrance animation

Use an entrance animation whenever you want certain content on a slide to appear after the slide background has already appeared (and possibly other content on the slide, too). Any objects that you don't animate will appear at the same time the slide background does; any objects you animate will appear after that, in a sequence you specify. You can modify and reorder animations after creating them from the Animation Pane.

In this exercise, you create some entrance animation effects and order them using the Animation Pane.

File needed: Chapter 11 Diner Movement.pptx, *already open from the previous exercise*

1. **Click slide 1 to select it.**

2. **Click the slide's title, *Christy's Diner*.**

3. **Click the Animations tab and then the Add Animation button. In the Entrance section, select Fly In.**

   See Figure 11-5.

4. **Click the slide's subtitle, *Serving Up Good Home Cooking*.**

5. **On the Animations tab, click the Add Animation button. In the Entrance section, select Grow & Turn.**

TIP

Notice that numbers appear next to the text boxes on slide 1, showing the order in which the animations will occur.

6. **On the Animations tab, click the Preview button to watch a preview of the animations on the slide.**

7. **Still on the Animations tab, click the Animation Pane button.**

A pane appears to the right of the slide, showing the animations on the slide. See Figure 11-6.

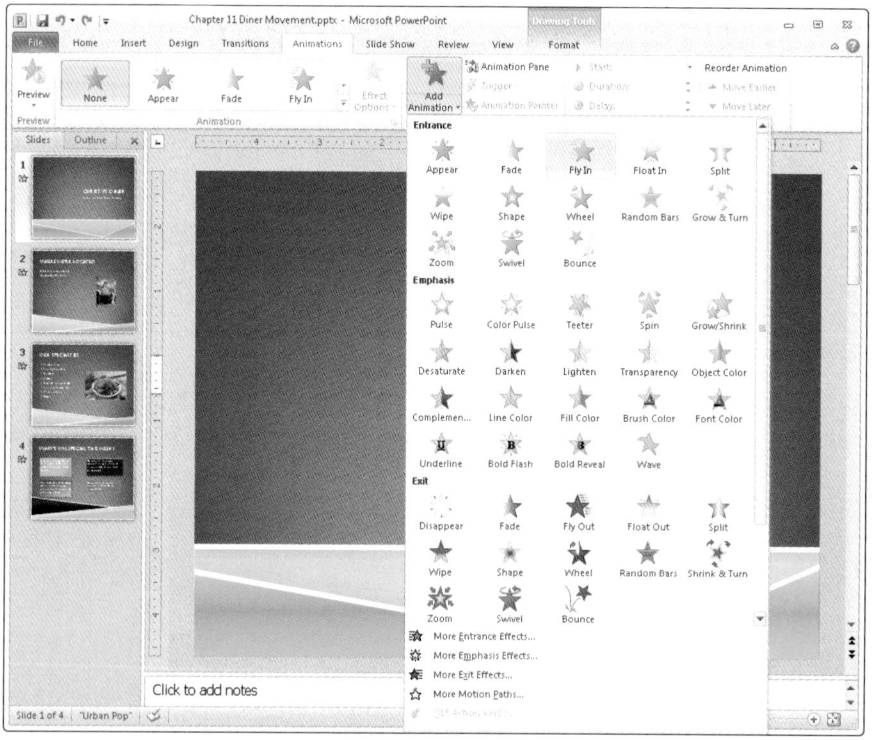

Figure 11-5

8. **In the Animation Pane, click the first animation.**

9. **Click the down-pointing Re-Order arrow at the bottom of the Animation Pane.**

The selected animation moves down to position 2, so the subtitle's animation is before the title's animation. See Figure 11-7.

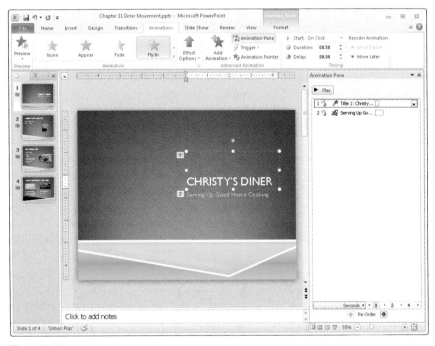

Figure 11-6

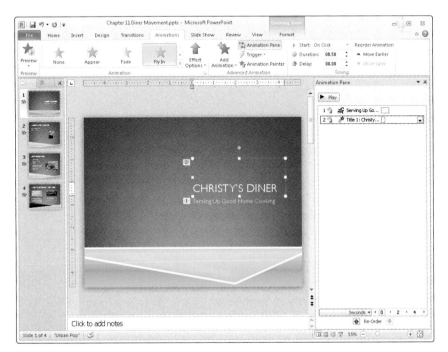

Figure 11-7

10. **On the Animations tab, click the Preview button to watch a preview of the animations on the slide.**

11. **Save the presentation.**

Leave the presentation open for the next exercise.

Creating an emphasis animation

An emphasis animation calls attention to an object on a slide when it is neither entering nor exiting. PowerPoint offers many types of emphasis animations, including shrink/grow, spin, and color change.

You can quickly copy animations from one object to another with the Animation Painter command. This is handy when several objects on a slide should be animated identically.

In this exercise, you create some emphasis animations and copy an emphasis animation to multiple objects using Format Painter.

File needed: `Chapter 11 Diner Movement.pptx,` *already open from the previous exercise*

1. **Click slide 2 to select it, and click the photo on the slide.**

2. **Click the Animations tab and then the Add Animation button. In the Emphasis section, select Grow/Shrink.**

3. **Click slide 4 to select it.**

4. **On the slide, click the Early Morning Eye Opener text box.**

5. **On the Animations tab, click the Add Animation button. In the Emphasis section, select Teeter.**

   See Figure 11-8.

6. **On the Animations tab, double-click the Animation Painter button.**

   The feature turns on and stays on.

7. **Click each of the other text boxes on the slide (except the slide title) to copy the Teeter animation to them.**

   You can click them in any order you like.

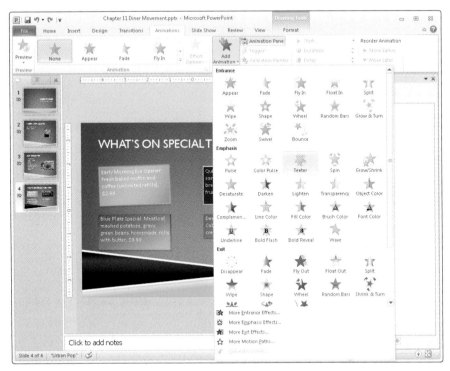

Figure 11-8

If you had single-clicked Animation Painter in Step 6, it would have stayed on for only one usage and then turned off.

8. **On the Animations tab, click the Animation Painter button to turn off the feature.**

9. **On the Animations tab, click the Preview button to preview the slide's animation sequence.**

10. **Save the presentation.**

Leave the presentation open for the next exercise.

Creating an exit animation

An exit animation causes an object to leave the slide before the next slide appears. Without an exit animation applied, an object stays onscreen until the next slide appears. Exit animations are often used in combination with entrance animations to make an object enter, stay for a specified time, and then exit.

When you animate a text box that contains multiple paragraphs, each paragraph is animated separately, but you can collapse or expand the group of animations in the Animation Pane. You can format them as a group when collapsed, or you can expand the group to format an individual paragraph's animations separately.

In this exercise, you create an exit animation.

File needed: `Chapter 11 Diner Movement.pptx`, *already open from the previous exercise*

1. **Click slide 3 to select it, and select the text box that contains the bulleted list.**

   Make sure you click the outside of the text box so that the border of the text box appears solid, rather than dashed.

2. **Click the Animations tab and then the Add Animation button. In the Exit section, click Fly Out.**

   The bulleted list is animated. Numbers appear next to each item in the bulleted list on the slide, indicating their order in the animation. A single item appears in the Animation Pane showing the entire animation sequence. See Figure 11-9.

Figure 11-9

3. **Click the Expand button below the animation in the Animation Pane to expand the list of animations in the group.**

   See Figure 11-10.

4. **On the Slide Show tab, click the From Current Slide button and click through the slide's content to see how the exit animation appears.**

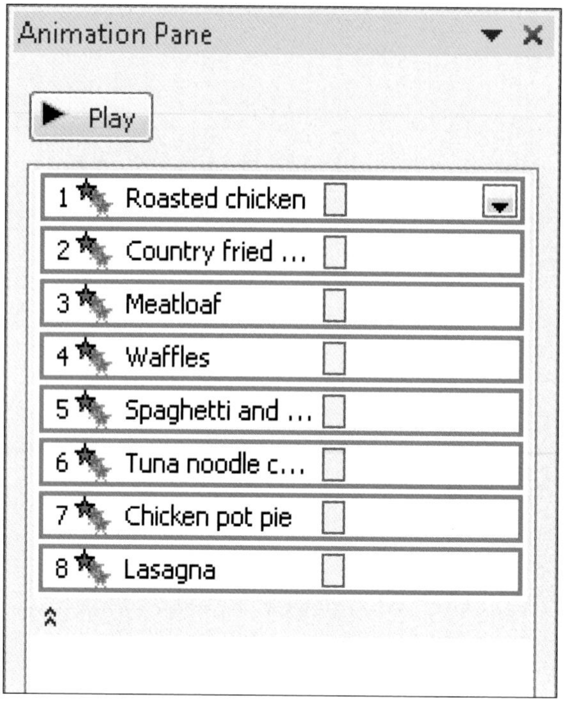

Figure 11-10

5. **Press Esc to return to Normal view.**

6. **Save the presentation.**

Leave the presentation open for the next exercise.

Changing an animation's options

Animation options include the duration, the delay, and the sound effects assigned to an animation. You can set all these from the Animations tab. You can also set animation options via a dialog box interface.

In this exercise, you modify the options for animations.

File needed: `Chapter 11 Diner Movement.pptx`, *already open from the previous exercise*

1. **Click slide 1 to select it and then click the *Christy's Diner* text box.**

2. **On the Animations tab, click the up increment arrow on the Duration text box until the Duration is set to 02.00.**

3. **Click the up increment arrow on the Delay text box until the Delay is set to 01.00.**

   See Figure 11-11.

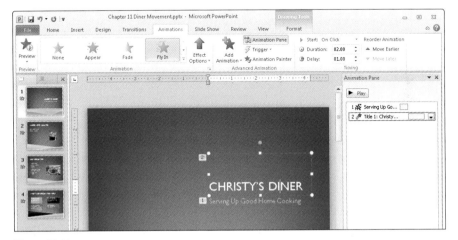

Figure 11-11

4. **Click slide 2 to select it and then click the photo to select it.**

5. **On the Animations, click the Effect Options button. In the Amount section, select Huge.**

   The animation previews on the slide. The size is too large.

6. **In the Animation Pane, right-click the animation for the photo and choose Effect Options.**

   The Grow/Shrink dialog box opens.

7. **On the Effect tab, open the Size drop-down list, and in the Custom box, type 175%.**

   See Figure 11-12.

8. **Open the Sound drop-down list and select Breeze.**

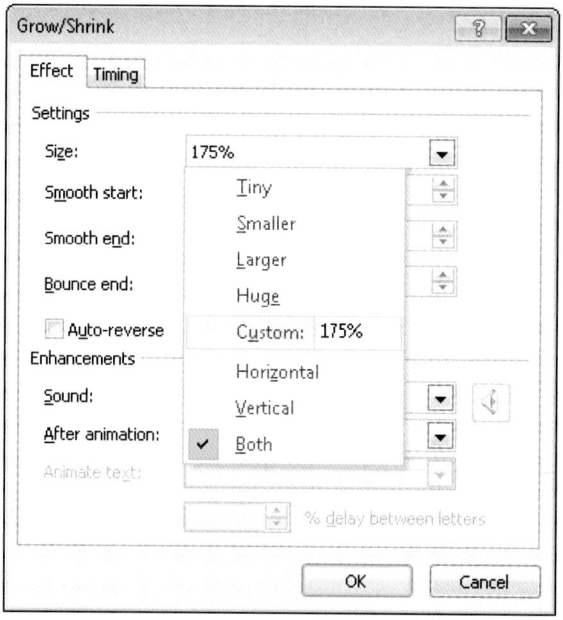

Figure 11-12

> ### 9. Click OK.
>
> The animation previews on the slide, and now the size of the growth is more appropriate.
>
> ### 10. Save the presentation and close it.
>
> *Leave PowerPoint open for the next exercise.*

Inserting Sounds and Videos

Another way to make a presentation more interesting is to include multimedia content such as sounds and video clips. You can place clips directly on a slide and set them up to play either automatically or on click.

Inserting a sound clip on a slide

When you place a sound clip (sometimes called an audio clip) on a slide, a speaker icon appears to represent it. Playback controls appear beneath the icon, so you can control the clip during the show. You can set the clip to playback on click or automatically.

TIP

You can control whether or not the playback controls appear by marking or clearing the Show Media Controls check box on the Slide Show tab.

In this exercise, you place a sound clip on a slide and control its playback.

File needed: `Chapter 11 Beethoven.pptx`

1. Open `Chapter 11 Beethoven.pptx` and save it as `Chapter 11 Beethoven Clip.pptx`.

2. Click the Insert tab and then the Audio button.

   The Insert Audio dialog box opens.

3. Navigate to the folder containing the data files for this lesson.

4. Select `Beethoven's Ninth.wma` (see Figure 11-13) and click the Insert button.

5. A speaker icon appears in the center of the slide, with playback controls beneath it.

   See Figure 11-14.

6. Click the Slide Show tab and then the From Beginning button.

   The slide appears in Slide Show view.

7. Click the Play button (triangle) in the playback controls.

   The clip begins playing.

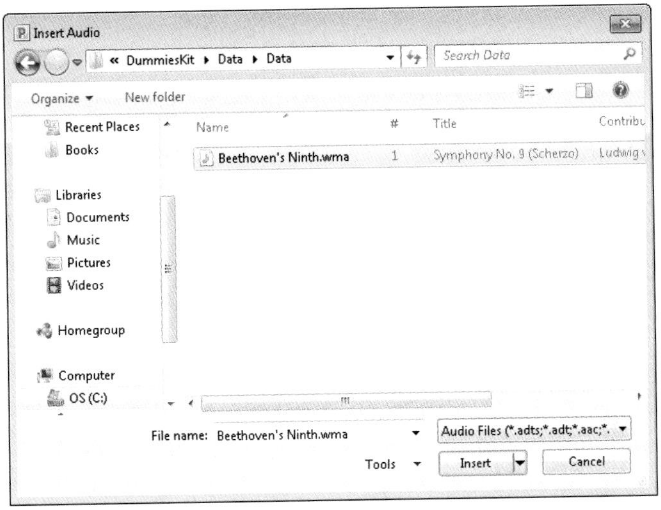

Figure 11-13

Figure 11-14

8. **Press Esc to return to Normal view.**

9. **Select the speaker icon.**

10. **Click the Audio Tools Playback tab, open the Start drop-down list, and select Automatically.**

    See Figure 11-15.

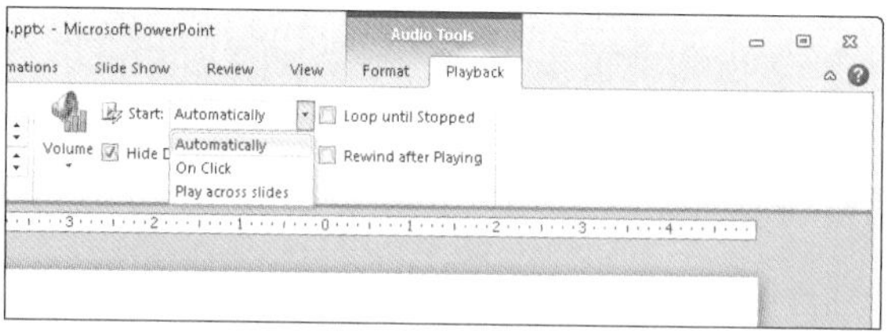

Figure 11-15

11. **Select the speaker icon, and on the Audio Tools Playback tab, select the Hide During Show check box.**

    This step hides the speaker icon in Slide Show view.

12. **Click the Slide Show tab and then the From Beginning button.**

    The slide appears in Slide Show view, and the music starts playing automatically.

13. **Press Esc to return to Normal view.**

EXTRA INFO

If this presentation contained multiple slides, this sound would stop playing when you advanced to the next slide because of the setting you chose in Step 10. If you wanted the sound to continue across multiple slides, you would instead use the Play Across Slides setting.

14. **Save the presentation and close it.**

Leave PowerPoint open for the next exercise.

Inserting a video clip on a slide

PowerPoint 2010 accepts video clips in a variety of formats, including Windows Media, Windows Video, QuickTime, MP4, and Flash. This is a giant step forward from the capabilities of earlier versions of PowerPoint! You can place a video clip on a slide either within a content placeholder or as a stand-alone item. You can also apply formatting to a video clip, such as a video style that governs the shape and appearance of the clip's frame.

 REMEMBER Using a placeholder means that the clip will be resized or shifted as needed if you change layouts or themes; inserting a clip manually makes it stay as-is regardless of the layout or theme. To insert a video clip, click the Insert tab and then the Video button.

In this exercise, you place a video clip on a slide using a content placeholder and apply a video style to it.

File needed: `Chapter 11 Run.pptx`

1. **Open `Chapter 11 Run.pptx` and save it as `Chapter 11 Run Video.pptx`.**

2. **On the content placeholder, click the Insert Media Clip icon.**

   See Figure 11-16. The Insert Video dialog box opens.

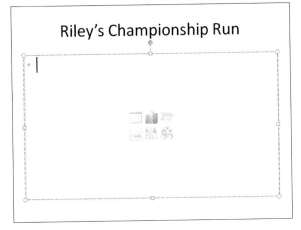

Figure 11-16

3. **Navigate to the folder containing the data files for this lesson and click `AgilityRun.wmv`.**

See Figure 11-17.

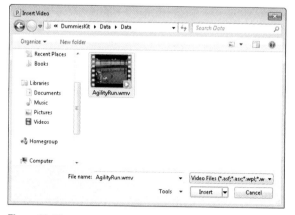

Figure 11-17

4. **Click the Insert button.**

The clip is inserted on the slide.

5. **On the Video Tools Format tab, click the More button to open the Video Styles gallery.**

See Figure 11-18.

6. **In the Subtle section, click Center Shadow Rectangle (the second style).**

7. **Click the Video Tools Format tab, click the Video Shape button, and click a rounded rectangle.**

The video clip's frame changes shape.

8. **On the Video Tools Playback tab, click Volume and then Low.**

This clip has a lot of background noise, and the sound is not integral to the meaning of the clip.

9. **Click the Slide Show tab and then the From Beginning button to open the slide in Slide Show view.**

10. **Click the Play button (the triangle) under the video clip to play it.**

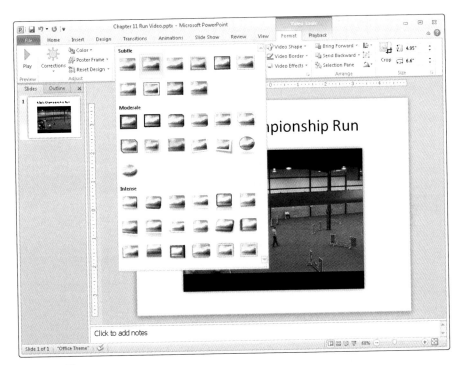

Figure 11-18

When you are done watching the video clip, press Esc to return to Normal view.

11. Save and close the presentation and exit PowerPoint.

 *Summing Up*

Here are the key points you learned about in this chapter:

- ✔ Transitions are movements from one slide to another. You can set up transitions on the Transitions tab.

- ✔ To control the speed of a transition, set its duration. To automatically allow a transition to occur without a mouse click, set the After value to a number of seconds.

- ✔ By clicking Transitions and then Effect Options, you can specify a direction or other options for a transition effect.

- ✔ Animations make individual objects move. You can create entrance, emphasis, exit, and motion path animations.

- ✔ An entrance animation controls how and when an object enters the slide. If an object isn't animated, it enters at the same time as the slide's background.

- ✔ An emphasis animation calls attention to an object that is neither entering nor exiting. A motion path animation does the same thing, but by moving along a prescribed path.

- ✔ An exit animation controls how and when an object exits the slide. If an object has no exit animation, it exits when you transition to the next slide.

- ✔ Using the Animation Pane, you can sequence and fine-tune multiple animations on a slide.

- ✔ Using the Animation Painter, you can copy animation effects between objects.

- ✔ To insert a sound clip on a slide, click Insert, Audio.

- ✔ To insert a video clip, use the Insert Media Clip content placeholder icon or click Insert, Video.

- ✔ After inserting a video clip, you can use the Video Tools Format tab's commands to control the appearance of the video clip frame. Use the Video Tools Playback tab's commands to control the clip's playback.

Try-it-yourself lab

For more practice with the features covered in this chapter, try the following exercise on your own.

1. Open `Chapter 11 Greek.pptx` and save it as `Chapter 11 Greek Animation.pptx`.

2. Apply a different transition to each slide.

3. Apply animation effects to at least three objects on three different slides.

Optional extra challenge:

1. Go to `www.youtube.com` and find a video of something pertaining to a Greek restaurant.

2. Below the video clip, click the Embed button to get the Embed code and then copy that code to the Windows Clipboard (Ctrl+C).

3. In PowerPoint, display one of the slides in the presentation, and then click the Insert tab and choose Video⇨Video from Web to embed the code for the video you found into the presentation.

Know this tech talk

animation: The movement of an individual object on a slide.

emphasis animation: An animation that occurs when an object is neither entering nor exiting the slide.

entrance animation: An animation that occurs as an object is entering the slide.

exit animation: An animation that occurs as an object is leaving the slide.

motion path animation: An animation that moves the object along a pre-defined path.

transition: A movement from one slide to another.

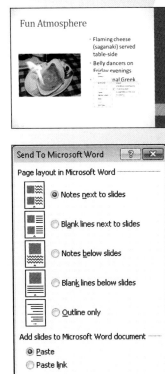

✔ Slide Show view enables you to *display a presentation full-screen* on a computer monitor or projector.

✔ Keyboard shortcuts make it easy to *move between slides* and temporarily black out (or white out) the screen.

✔ Right-clicking in Slide Show view opens a menu from which you can *jump to any slide*.

✔ The Pen tool enables you to *annotate slides with your own markup*.

✔ The Print command in PowerPoint enables you to *print handouts in various arrangements*.

✔ Exporting handouts to Word provides *additional formatting flexibility*.

1. **How do you go back to the previous slide in Slide Show view?**

View the answer on page... 335

2. **How do you turn the screen white during a presentation?**

Clear up the situation on page... 358

3. **How can you change the pen color when annotating a slide?**

Color yourself informed on page.. 359

4. **How do you customize the layout of a handout?**

Handy solutions abound on page.. 362

5. **How do you export handouts to Word?**

It's an important result on page... 365

PowerPoint 2010 gives you various methods for delivering your presentation: You can deliver a presentation live in a meeting room, broadcast it on the Internet, package it on a writeable CD, or send it out via e-mail, just to name a few.

This chapter focuses on the most popular delivery method: delivering a live show to an audience in person. You learn how to display a PowerPoint presentation onscreen, including how to move between slides and how to annotate slides with the Pen tools. You also learn how to print handouts, either in PowerPoint or in Microsoft Word.

For information about some of the other delivery methods, such as creating a CD or broadcasting and presentation, visit the Help system in PowerPoint, or check out my book *The PowerPoint 2010 Bible,* also published by John Wiley & Sons, Inc.

Displaying a Slide Show Onscreen

To give an onscreen show, use Slide Show view. It displays each slide full-screen, one at a time. For larger audiences, you may want to hook up a projector to your computer so the audience can see the slides more easily. (In Windows 7, the Windows key + P shortcut easily connects a notebook PC to a projector.)

In the following sections, you learn how to move around in a presentation, how to annotate slides, and how to save or discard the annotations afterward.

Moving between slides

To move from one slide to the next or to trigger the next on-click animation on a slide, click the left mouse button. That's all you need to know at the most basic level. You can also get much fancier than that about moving around. You can use shortcut keys to move to specific locations, and you can right-click and use the shortcut menu that appears to move around.

Right-click and choose Help in Slide Show view to get a list of the short-cut keys available.

You can also use the buttons in the lower-left corner of the screen in Slide Show view. They're very faint at first, but if you move the mouse pointer over one, it become solid. Click a button to open a menu or click the right- or left-arrow buttons there to move forward and back in the presentation.

In this exercise, you display a presentation onscreen and move around in it using various methods.

Files needed: `Chapter 12 Opa.pptx`

1. **Open `Chapter 12 Opa.pptx` and save it as `Chapter 12 Santorinis.pptx`.**

2. **On the Slide Show tab, click the From Beginning button.**

   Slide 1 appears in Slide Show view.

3. **Click to move to slide 2.**

4. **Press the spacebar to move to slide 3.**

5. **Press the right-arrow key to move to slide 4.**

6. **Press the Enter key to move to slide 5.**

You've just seen four different ways of advancing to the next slide.

7. **Press the Backspace key to move to slide 4.**

8. **Press the left-arrow key to move to slide 3.**

Now you know two different ways of moving backward in a presentation.

9. **Right-click, choose Go to Slide, and then click slide 1. (Opa!)**

   See Figure 12-1. Slide 1 appears.

Using this method, you can jump to any slide you want, at any time.

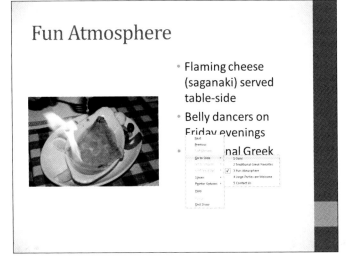

Fun Atmosphere

* Flaming cheese (saganaki) served table-side
* Belly dancers on Friday evenings

Figure 12-1

10. **Move the mouse pointer to the lower-left corner of the screen and run the mouse pointer over the icons there.**

    Notice that as the mouse pointer touches an icon, it becomes fully colored. Figure 12-2 shows all of the four icons in full color, but on your screen only one can show up in color at a time.

Figure 12-2

11. **Click the Menu button.**

    The menu that appears is very similar to the one that you saw when right-clicking in Step 9. See Figure 12-3.

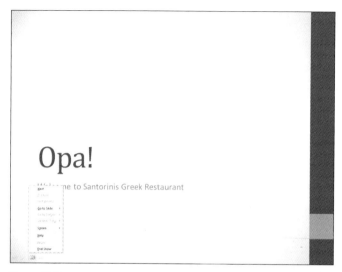

Figure 12-3

12. **Click the Next Slide button.**

    Slide 2 appears. This is yet another way to advance to the next slide.

13. **Right-click the slide and choose Screen⇨Black Screen.**

    The screen turns black. You may use this to temporarily blank out the screen so you can have a discussion, for example. See Figure 12-4.

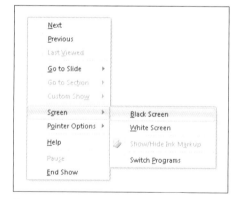

Figure 12-4

14. **Right-click the slide and choose Screen⇨White screen.**

    This step does the same thing except it's white instead of black.

15. **Press Esc.**

    The presentation goes back to Slide Show view.

16. **Press B.**

    This is a keyboard shortcut for the Screen⇨Black Screen command.

17. **Press Esc.**

    Slide Show view closes, and you are returned to Normal view.

Leave the presentation open for the next exercise.

Annotating slides with the pen tools

Two pen types are available:

- ✔ **The Pen tool** draws a solid, thin line.

- ✔ **The Highlighter** draws wide, semi-transparent highlighting.

When you leave Slide Show view after using one of the pen tools, a dialog box pops up asking whether you want to keep your ink annotations. If you choose to keep them, they appear on the slides as ink annotation objects, which are very much like line drawings that you might create by going to the Insert tab and clicking the Shapes button.

As you're giving a presentation, you may want to make some notes on the slides, such as circling a word, underlining a phrase, or highlighting a key concept. The Pen tools enable you to do all those things. Making these changes is called **annotating.**

In this exercise, you display a presentation onscreen and move around in it using various methods.

Files needed: Chapter 12 Santorinis.pptx, *already open from the previous exercise*

1. **On the Slide Show tab, click the From Beginning button to open slide 1 in Slide Show view.**

2. **In the lower-left corner of the screen, click the Pen icon, opening the Pen menu.**

3. **Choose Pen.**

    See Figure 12-5. The mouse pointer changes to a colored dot.

4. **Drag on the slide to underline the word *Opa!*.**

    It's underlined in red (the default pen color).

5. **Press Esc to cancel the pen and return to the arrow pointer.**

Arrow

Pen

Highlighter

Ink Color ▸

Eraser

Erase All Ink on Slide

Arrow Options ▸

Figure 12-5

For more practice, right-click and choose Pointer Options⇨Ink Color and then select a different color to use for the pen's ink.

6. **Click the left mouse button to advance to slide 2.**

7. **Right-click anywhere on the slide and choose Pointer Options⇨ Highlighter.**

   This is an alternative way of accessing the Pen tools. See Figure 12-6.

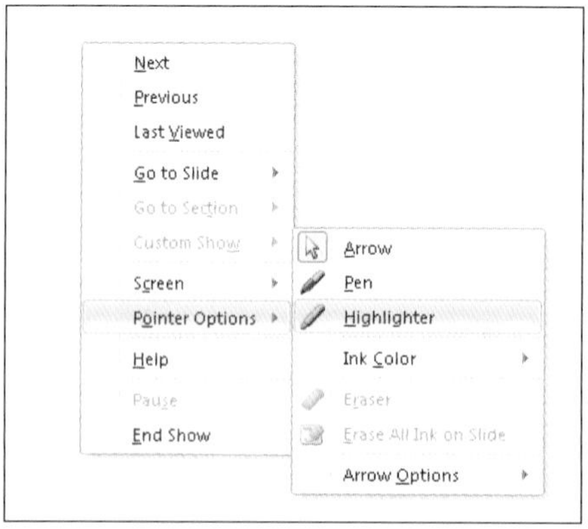

Next

Previous

Last Viewed

Go to Slide ▸

Go to Section ▸

Custom Show ▸   Arrow

Screen ▸   Pen

Pointer Options ▸   Highlighter

Help   Ink Color ▸

Pause   Eraser

End Show   Erase All Ink on Slide

                      Arrow Options ▸

Figure 12-6

8. **Drag the mouse pointer across Saganaki, highlighting it with the default highlighter color (yellow).**

9. **Right-click anywhere on the slide and choose Pointer Options⇨Arrow.**

This is an alternative way of cancelling the pen.

10. **Click repeatedly until you get to the end of the presentation.**

   A box appears, asking whether you want to save annotations. See Figure 12-7.

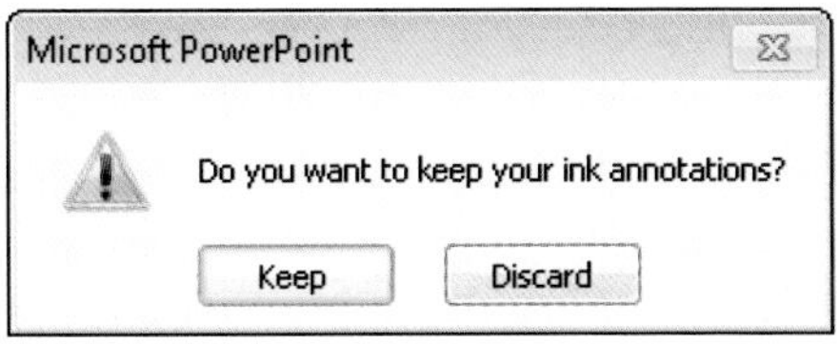

Figure 12-7

11. **Click the Keep button.**

   The presentation appears in Normal view with the ink annotations on the slides.

12. **On slide 1, click the red underline to select it. Then press Delete.**

13. **Switch to slide 3 and select the yellow highlight annotation there.**

14. **Drag the yellow highlight annotation up so that it's over Baklava.**

   See Figure 12-8.

Traditional Greek Favorites

- Moussaka
- Spanakopita
- Gyros
- Baklava
- Saganaki

Figure 12-8

15. **Save the presentation.**

Leave the presentation open for the next exercise.

Creating Handouts

When you print in PowerPoint, you have a choice of the type of printout you want. (Technically you can use any of these printout types as handouts, although the Handouts type is obviously custom-made for that purpose.) Here are the choices available:

- ✔ **Full Page Slides:** A full-page copy of one slide per sheet.

- ✔ **Notes Pages:** One slide per page, but with the slide occupying only the top half of the page. The bottom half is devoted to any speaker notes you typed into PowerPoint.

- ✔ **Outline View:** A text-only version of the presentation, structured as an outline, with the slide titles as the top-level outline items.

- ✔ **Handouts:** Multiple slides per page (two to nine, depending on your choice of settings), suitable for giving to the audience to take home.

TIP

Different numbers of slides per page have different layouts. For example, if you choose three slides per page, the layout has lines next to each slide so the audience can take notes.

You can print the handouts directly from PowerPoint, or you can export them to Word for further formatting.

Printing handouts

When you print handouts from PowerPoint, the Handout Master's settings determine the details of how the handouts appear. You may want to customize the Handout Master before you print. The Handout Master settings apply only when you're printing the Handouts layouts, not when printing full-page slides, notes pages, or outline view.

In this exercise, you customize the Handout Master and then print handouts from PowerPoint.

Files needed: Chapter 12 Santorinis.pptx, *already open from the previous exercise*

1. **On the View tab, click the Handout Master button.**

   The Handout Master opens. It's a blank layout.

2. **On the Handout Master tab, click the Slides Per Page button and choose 3 Slides.**

   The layout changes to show placeholders for only three slides per page. See Figure 12-9.

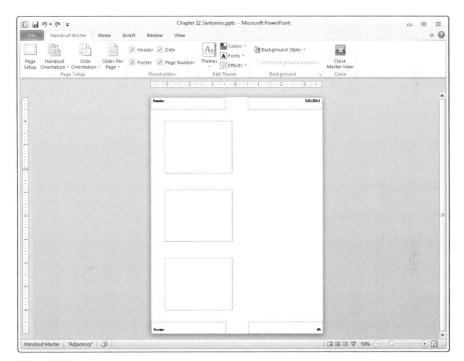

Figure 12-9

3. **Deselect the Date check box on the Handout Master tab.**

   The placeholder for the date disappears from the layout.

4. **Still on the Handout Master tab, click the Handout Orientation button and choose Landscape.**

   The layout changes to show the three slides side-by-side. See Figure 12-10.

5. **Click the Close Master View button.**

6. **Choose File⇨Print.**

7. **Click the Full Page Slides button, opening a menu, and choose 3 Slides.**

   The Print Preview shows the first handouts page with the layout you customized earlier. See Figure 12-11.

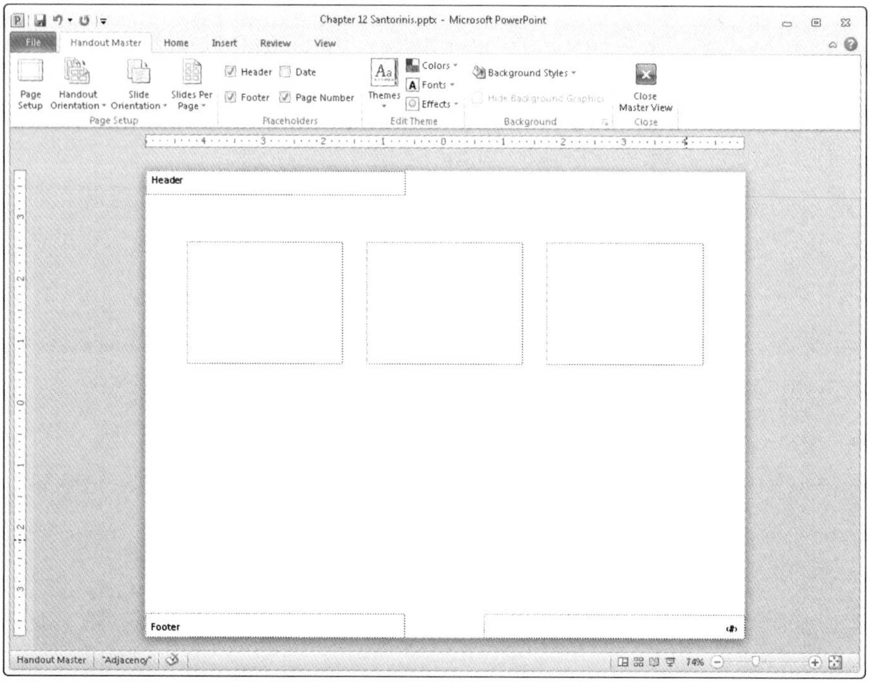

Figure 12-10

8. **Click the Print button.**

   The handouts print on your default printer.

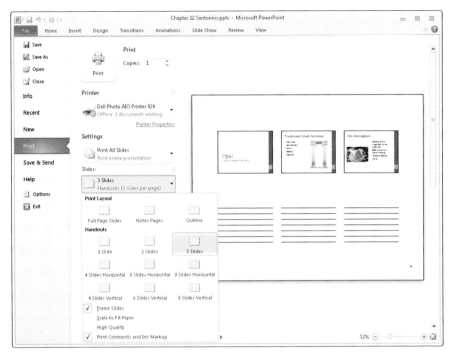

Figure 12-11

Leave the presentation open for the next exercise.

Exporting handouts to Word

For more control over handouts, you can export them to Word. When they're in Word, you can make modifications that are not possible in PowerPoint, such as changing the sizes of the slide graphics or adjusting the page margins.

In this exercise, you export handouts to Word and customize them there.

Files needed: `Chapter 12 Santorinis.pptx`, *already open from the previous exercise*

1. **Choose File⇨Save & Send⇨Create Handouts⇨Create Handouts.**

   See Figure 12-12.

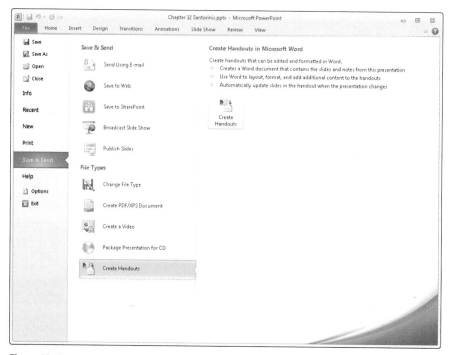

Figure 12-12

The Send to Microsoft Word dialog box opens.

2. Click Blank lines next to slides.

See Figure 12-13.

3. Click OK.

A new Word document opens containing the slides. The slides are placed in a three-column table:

The first column contains the slide numbers, the second column contains the graphics, and the third column contains lines for writing notes. See Figure 12-14.

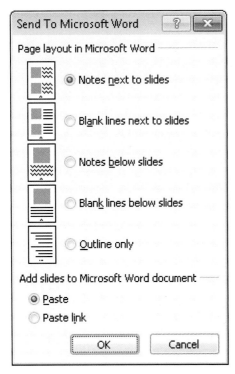

Figure 12-13

4. **Point the mouse pointer at the top of the rightmost column so that the mouse pointer turns into a black arrow pointing downward. Click.**

   The entire column is selected. See Figure 12-15.

5. **On the Home tab, choose Line & Paragraph Spacing⇨1.15.**

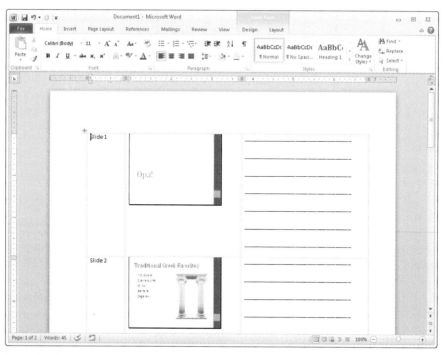

Figure 12-14

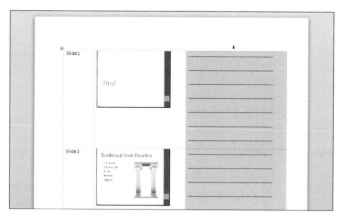

Figure 12-15

See Figure 12-16. The spacing of the blank lines in the rightmost column tightens up somewhat.

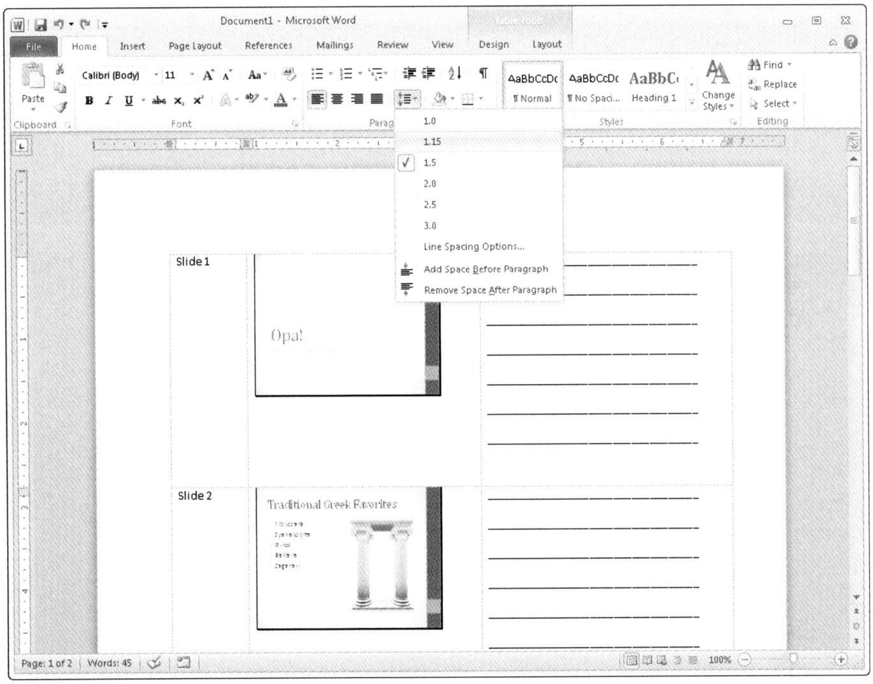

Figure 12-16

6. In Word, choose File⇨Print.

7. Click the Print button to print one copy of the handouts with the default settings.

8. Save the document in Word as `Chapter 12 Handouts.docx`.

9. Exit Word.

10. Return to PowerPoint.

Save the presentation and exit PowerPoint.

Summing Up

Here are the key points you learned about in this chapter:

- ✔ To enter Slide Show view, use the From Beginning or From Current Slide button on the Slide Show tab.

- ✔ To move to the next slide, you can press Enter, press the spacebar, press the right-arrow key, or click the Next Slide button in the lower-left corner of the slide.

- ✔ To move to the previous slide, you can press Backspace, press the left arrow key, or click the Previous Slide button in the lower-left corner of the slide.

- ✔ To jump to a certain slide, you can right-click, point to Go to Slide, and click the desired slide.

- ✔ To black the screen, press B. To white the screen, press W. To cancel either one, press Esc.

- ✔ To annotate a slide, right-click, point to Point Options, choose Pen or Highlighter, and then drag on the slide.

- ✔ To print handouts, choose File➪Print. Select a number of handouts per page and then click Print.

- ✔ To export handouts to Word for further editing, choose File➪Save & Send➪Create Handouts➪Create Handouts.

Try-it-yourself lab

For more practice with the features covered in this chapter, try the following exercise on your own.

1. Open **Chapter 12 Airline.pptx** and save it as **Chapter 12 Airline Final.pptx**.

2. **Watch the entire presentation in Slide Show view.**

3. **Export handout to Word using the Notes Next to Slides layout.**

4. **Make any changes you like in Word to make the handouts more readable and attractive.**

5. **Print one copy of the Word document on the default printer.**

6. Save the Word document as `Chapter 12 Airline Final.docx`.

7. Exit Word.

8. Return to PowerPoint, save the presentation, and exit PowerPoint.

Know this tech talk

annotate: To mark up a slide with the Pen or Highlighter tool in Slide Show view.

handouts: Hardcopy printouts designed for distribution to an audience.

Index

Symbols & Numerics

$, in absolute referencing, 155, 170, 172
=, in Excel formulas and functions, 170
! (Excel syntax), 150
(parentheses), in Excel formulas/
    functions, 146, 162–163, 164, 170
1/72 of an inch (a point), 98
.bmp, graphics file format, 24
.doc, file extension, 39
.docm, file extension, 38
.docx, file extension, 37–38
.dotm, file extension, 53
.dotx, file extension, 53
.gif, graphics file format, 24
.jpeg, graphics file format, 24
.png, graphics file format, 24
.ppt, file extension, 39
.pptm, file extension, 38
.pptx, file extension, 37–38
.pst, file extension, 37–38
.rtf, file extension, 84–85
.tif, graphics file format, 24
.vcf, vCard format, 234
.xls, file extension, 39
.xlsm, file extension, 38
.xlsx, file extension, 37–38

A

ABS function, 166
absolute referencing, Excel formulas,
    155–156, 172
active cell, worksheet, 118, 123, 125, 141

addition, math function. *See* Excel
    formulas; Excel functions
After (paragraph spacing), 98
alignment, text (Left, Right, Center,
    Justify), 92–94
amortization, loan, 163–166
animations, slide presentation
  about using, 327–329
  copying and creating emphasis, 338–339
  creating an entrance, 335–338
  creating an exit, 340–342
  setting options, 342–344
  "star" indicator, 252
  "tech talk" glossary, 351
  try-it-yourself lab, 351
  types defined, 335
annotating slides, Pen tools, 359–361, 371
application
  compared to program, 5
  defined, 49
arguments, Excel function
  about using, 157, 172
  basic functions without, 161
  financial functions, 163–164
  one-argument functions, 162
arrow keys
  application consistency, 5
  Excel worksheets, 120–121
  moving the insertion point, 64–65
aspect ratio, slide, 280
assumptions about you and this book, 3
attachments. *See also* email programs
  about transfering data, 82
  described, 88, 218
  receiving, 195–197
  sending, 201–203

attributes, 70, 88. *See also* text
   formatting
audio clips. *See* sound clips
AutoCorrect, 97
AutoFill, 129–132
AutoFit, text box, 299–300, 301, 302
automatic operations. *See* animations;
   defaults; preset features; transitions
automatic slide advance, 334
AutoRecover, 47–48
auto-size, text boxes, 276
AVERAGE function, 162, 170, 172

• *B* •

background fill
   applying, 301
   text box, 291–294
Backspace, deleting text, 64–65
Backstage View, defined, 49. *See also*
   File menu
backup drafts, 47–48
backward compatibility
   file formats, 39–41
   templates, 56
Before (paragraph spacing), 98
bevel effects, 296–299
BMP graphics format, 24
borders, 111, 302
borders, text box, 294–296
Brochures and Booklets, templates,
   54–56
Bullets and Numbered lists
   basic lessons learned, 110
   changing bullet characters, 103–106
   changing numbering style, 106–109
   creating, 102–103
   described, 102, 111
   hanging indents, 95
   list animation, 340–342
Business Card (vCard attachment),
   234–235

• *C* •

calculations, math. *See* Excel formulas;
   Excel functions
Calendar. *See* Outlook Calendar
category, defined, 246
CD, overview of lessons, 1–2
CD/DVD, writeable
   transferring data files, 81
cell address, worksheet, 118, 141
cell content, worksheet
   Clear, Cut, Delete defined, 127
   copying and moving data, 132–133
   editing choices, 127–128
   formatting, 149
   text and numbers, 125–127
   using AutoFill, 129–132
cell cursor. *See also* insertion point
   defined, 49, 118
   described, 141
   keyboard shortcuts, 120–121
cells, worksheet. *See also* multi-cell
   range
   absolute referencing, 155–156, 172
   active cell, 118, 123, 125
   Cut and Paste, 132–133
   defined, 116, 141
   Delete compared to Clear, 135
   inserting and deleting, 135–137
   moving the cursor to, 120–121
   referencing another worksheet, 150–152
   referencing cells in a formula, 148–149
   relative referencing, 152–155, 173
Center, text alignment, 92–94
character formatting, 67, 88
clip art images
   background fill, applying, 292
   basic lessons learned, 324
   defined, 325
   inserting, 306–310
Clipboard
   copy and paste, 265
   copying and moving data, 132–133, 140

cut and paste, 127
using the Clipboard, 265
clockwise/counterclockwise rotation,
    slide transition, 330
closing Office applications, 7–11
color change, animation, 338–339
colors. *See also* theme colors
    SmartArt, 321–323
    text box borders, 294–296
    text font, 67–70
    using Pen tools, 360–361
columns, worksheet. *See* Excel
    worksheets
compatibility checker
    file formats, 39–41
    templates, 56
contacts, 246. *See also* Outlook Contacts
content placeholder, graphics, 303–305,
    324. *See also* placeholder; text boxes
contiguous cells, worksheet, 122, 141
conventions used in book, 3
converter utilities, 86
copy and paste
    animations, 338–339
    Excel worksheets, 132–133, 140
    slides, duplicating, 265–266
    using the Clipboard, 265
COUNT function, 162, 170, 172
COUNTA function, 162, 170, 172
COUNTBLANK function, 162, 170, 172
custom colors, 285–288
Cut, slide transition, 329
cut and paste
    Excel worksheets, 132–133, 140
    using the Clipboard, 127

D

data files
    defined, 49
    opening/closing, 5

defaults. *See also* preset features
    AutoFit feature, 299
    blank document, 54
    Contacts list, 228–229
    e-mail, 51, 82–83, 192–194
    file format, 38
    Normal template settings, 54
    Normal view, PowerPoint, 249–250
    PowerPoint themes, 283
    slide presentation, 334
    task reminder Sounds, 242
    transition effects, 330
    try-it-yourself lab, 351
    user Documents folder, 41–42
definitions. *See* "tech talk" glossaries
Deleted Items, Outlook Mail, 203–207
Delete/deleting
    compared to Clear, 135
    defined, 127
    editing text, 64–65
    e-mail messages, 213–214
    in Excel worksheets, 134–137
    Outlook contacts, 229–231
    Outlook Tasks, 243–244
    slides from presentations, 266–268
    text and objects from slides, 278
delimited, defined, 111
depreciation, calculating, 163–166
dialog boxes, application consistency, 5
dictionary file, adding words to, 79
division, math function. *See* Excel
    formulas; Excel functions
.doc, file extension, 39
.docm, file extension, 38
.docx, file extension, 37–38
documents. *See also* Word documents
    changing onscreen views, 31–37
    creating a blank data file, 19–21
    defined, 20, 49
    error checking, 79–81
    inserting graphics, 24–27
    moving around in, 27–31

documents *(continued)*
  save/open, 37–48
  typing text into, 21–23
Documents folder, save/open files, 41–45
$ (absolute referencing), 155, 170, 172
.dotm, file extension, 53
.dotx, file extension, 53
downloads/downloading
  document templates, 54–56
  XPS Viewer, 197
Draft view, View tab, 36
drag/drag and drop
  creating/moving text/objects, 270–275
  Excel cells and content, 121–124,
    129–133, 140, 154
  files into folders, 203, 206
  folders, 179
  mouse method, 132
  pictures into documents, 24–25
  resizing objects, 110, 275
  selecting text, 65

E

editing. *See* text editing
Editing group, Home tab, Ribbon bar,
    using, 15–17
effects, 71, 88. *See also* text formatting
eLearning, assumptions, 3
electronic lessons, overview of
    topics, 1–2
e-mail account, 183, 218
e-mail programs. *See also* Outlook Mail
  changing mail server settings, 185–188
  mail server types, 183–184
  Outlook compatibility, 188
  sharing Word documents, 51
  text messaging services, 187
  transferring data files, 81–83
  web-based accounts, 82, 183
emphasis animation
  creating, 338–339
  defined, 335

encrypted connections, 184, 188
entrance animation
  creating, 335–338
  defined, 335
= (in Excel formulas and functions), 170
error checking. *See* Grammar check;
    Spell Check
Eudora (email program), 82
Excel 2010
  AutoRecover, 47–48
  basic functions summary, 48–49, 140
  data file formats, 37
  error checking, 79
  graphics file formats, 24
  opening and closing, 9–10, 116–118
  try-it-yourself lab, 49
  using the keyboard and mouse, 28–31
  using the scroll bars, 27, 29
Excel formulas
  about using, 143–144, 172
  basic lessons learned, 170
  compared to functions, 156–157
  compared to regular text, 145
  creating, 145–148
  moving and copying, 152–156
  referencing another worksheet, 150–152
  referencing cells on a worksheet,
    148–149
  "tech talk" glossary, 172–173
Excel functions
  arguments, required and optional, 157
  basic lessons learned, 170
  compared to formulas, 156–157
  creating/inserting, 159–161
  defined, 172
  "tech talk" glossary, 172–173
  try-it-yourself lab, 170–172
Excel functions, keywords
  ABS function, 166
  AVERAGE function, 162, 170, 172
  COUNT function, 162, 170, 172
  COUNTA function, 162, 170, 172
  COUNTBLANK function, 162, 170, 172
  FV function, 163, 170, 172
  IPMT function, 172

MAX function, 162, 170, 172
MIN function, 162, 170, 172
NOW function, 161
NPER function, 164, 166–168, 170, 172
PMT function, 163, 164–166, 170, 172
PPMT function, 171, 172
PV function, 163, 168–169, 170, 173
RATE function, 164, 170, 173
ROUNDUP function, 167
SUM function, 157–159, 162
TODAY function, 161
Excel workbooks
  creating, 17–19
  defined, 20, 50, 141
  inserting graphics, 24–25
  inserting text, 21–23
  referencing another worksheet, 150–152
  worksheets, changing, 137–139
Excel worksheets
  about features of, 113–114
  adding, deleting, renaming, 137–139
  basic components, 118
  cell content, creating, 125–127
  cell content, editing, 127–128
  cell content, formatting, 149
  cell content, using AutoFill, 129–132
  cell cursor, moving, 120–121
  cells and ranges, insert/delete, 135–137
  copying and moving data, 132–133
  defined, 141
  formula bar, 125
  keyboard shortcuts, cell cursor, 120–121
  keyboard shortcuts, range, 122–125
  ranges, selecting, 121–125
  referencing cells in a formula, 148–149
  rows and columns, insert/delete, 134–135
  tabs, 137–139, 141
  "tech talk" glossary, 141
  try-it-yourself lab, 141
  Zoom controls, 119
! (in Excel syntax), 150
exit animation
  creating, 340–342
  defined, 335

exponentiation, math function, 146
exporting to Word, 365–369
extensions. See file extensions

● F ●

Fade, slide transition, 329
Favorites list, Outlook, 179, 211–213, 218
File As, contact setting, 219, 228–229,
    233, 245, 246
file extensions
  data files, 37–38
  default formats, 38
  defined, 49
  graphics, 24
  macro-enabled formats, 38
file formats
  changing, 83–85
  converter utilities, 86
file management
  data files, 37–38
  graphics files, 24
File menu, File tab, Ribbon bar
  application consistency, 5, 177
  opening and closing, 17–19
File tab
  Excel, 115–116
  opening Backstage View, 19, 117
  opening File menu, 17
  Outlook, 177
  PowerPoint, 249
files, CD, overview of lessons, 1–2
fill handle, 113, 129–132
financial functions. See Excel functions
first-line indent, 94–97, 111
flag/flagging
  defined, 218
  e-mail messages, 214–215
  task list, 241
Flash, video format, 347
folders
  defined, 49
  e-mail, message-handling rules, 207–211

folders *(continued)*
  Outlook, 179
  Outlook Mail, 203–207
  save/open files, 41–45
font (typeface)
  changing bullet characters, 103–106
  changing numbered lists, 106–109
  described, 88
  PowerPoint presentations, 288–291
  size and color, 67–70
Font dialog box
  applying attributes and effects, 70–73
  choosing size and color, 67–70
  working with themes, 73–76
Font group, Home tab, Ribbon bar, 13–14
font theme, 288–291
  basic lessons learned, 301
  defined, 302
  try-it-yourself lab, 301
formatting. *See* text formatting
formula bar, worksheet, 125
formulas and functions. *See* Excel
    formulas; Excel functions
Full Screen Reading view, View tab, 37
FV function, 163, 170, 172

G

GIF graphics format, 24
glossary. *See* "tech talk" glossaries
glow effects, 296–299
Gmail (web-based e-mail), 82, 183
gradients, as background fill, 291–292
Grammar check
  about using, 51
  using, 79–81
graphics. *See also* animations; Slides;
    transitions
  background fill, applying, 292
  basic lessons learned, 324
  as bullet characters, 103–106
  clip art images, 306–310
  file extensions, 24

pictures from file, 24, 310–313
practice exercise, 24–27
SmartArt, converting text to, 313–314
SmartArt, editing, 318–320
SmartArt, formatting, 320–323
SmartArt, inserting, 314–318
"tech talk" glossary, 324–325
try-it-yourself lab, 324–325
gridlines, 111

H

Handouts, PowerPoint presentation
  available choices, 362
  basic lessons learned, 370
  defined, 371
  exporting to Word, 365–369
  printing, 362–365
hanging indent, 94–97, 111
Header & Footer group, Insert tab,
    Ribbon bar, using, 13
hidden files, 47–48
Highlighter (Pen tool), 359–361
Home tab on the Ribbon bar
  about using, 13–14
  Font dialog box, 72–73
  Italic button, 72
  Text Effects button, 71–72
horizontal alignment, 92–94, 111
horizontal ruler, 277
Hotmail (web-based e-mail), 82, 183
HTTP web-based e-mail, 82, 183
HyperText Transfer Protocol (HTTP),
    183, 218

I

icons, used in this book, 3–4
IMAP (Internet Mail Access Protocol),
    183, 218
Inbox, Outlook Mail, 203–207
Incoming mail server, 188

incoming/outgoing ports, 191
indentation, paragraph, 94–97, 112
Insert Function, 159–161, 170
Insert tab on the Ribbon bar
  about using, 12
  inserting graphics into documents, 24–27
insertion point. *See also* cell cursor
  defined, 24, 50
  first-line indents, 97
  moving around documents, 27–28
  text boxes, 273
  text editing, 64–65, 88
  typing into placeholders, 268–270
integrated learning, online, 1
interest rate, loan, 163–166
Internet. *See also* Microsoft Office
      Online; websites
  integrated learning classes, 1
  web-based email programs, 82
Internet Mail Access Protocol (IMAP),
      183, 218
Internet Service Provider (ISP)
  incoming/outgoing ports, 191
  mail server types, 183, 218
  troubleshooting e-mail setup, 188–191
IPMT function, 172
Italic button, 72–73
italics, conventions used in book, 3

J

JPEG graphics format, 24
Junk Mail
  configuring the filter, 214–215
  e-mail folder, 203–207
  filter described, 218
Justify, text alignment, 92–94, 112

K

keyboard shortcuts
  application consistency, 5
  connecting a PC to a projector, 355

Excel worksheets, 120–121
  moving the insertion point, 28
  paragraph formatting, 92
  selecting text blocks, 66
  Slide Show view, 355–356
  text attributes, 70
  worksheets, range selection, 122–125

L

Landscape, page orientation, 59–61, 88
leading. *See* vertical spacing
Left, text alignment, 92–94
length of loan, calculating, 166–169
line spacing, 98–101
Links group, Insert tab, Ribbon
      bar, 12–13
loan payments, calculating, 163–166
"lock down," cell references, 155
lost files, recovering, 47–48

M

macro-enabled file format, 38
macros, defined, 38
Mail. *See* Outlook Mail
manual operations. *See* defaults; preset
      features
manual slide advance, 334
margins. *See* page margins
math functions and formulas. *See* Excel
      formulas; Excel functions
MAX function, 162, 170, 172
message-handling rules, 207–211
Microsoft Excel. *See Excel entries*
Microsoft Mobile, 187
Microsoft Office Online
  PowerPoint templates, 257–259
  PowerPoint themes, 283
Microsoft Office suite
  about features of, 5–6
  application consistency, 48–49, 177, 249

Microsoft Office suite *(continued)*
  applications, opening and closing, 7–11
  creating documents, 19–20
  defined, 50
  File menu, 17–19
  Ribbon bar, 11–17
Microsoft Outlook. *See* Outlook 2010
Microsoft PowerPoint. *See*
    PowerPoint 2010
Microsoft Windows Updates, 214
Microsoft Word. *See* Word 2010; Word
    documents
Microsoft XPS Document Writer, 86
MIN function, 162, 170, 172
Mirrored margin, 58
mixed references, Excel formula, 155
monthly payments, calculating, 163–166
motion path animation, 335
mouse, using the
  copying and moving data, 132–133
  navigating documents, 28–31
  Slide Show view, 357–358
MP4, video format, 347
multi-cell range, worksheet
  compared to "active cell," 123
  copying and moving data, 132–133
  defined, 121
multiplication, math function. *See* Excel
    formulas; Excel functions

N

Name box, worksheet, 118, 141
noncontiguous cells, worksheet, 122
Normal template, 53–54
Normal view, PowerPoint, 34,
    249–250, 280
notes. *See* Outlook Notes
Notes pane, PowerPoint, 34, 250, 254,
    279, 362
NOW function, 161, 170, 172

NPER function, 164, 166–168, 170, 172
number of payments, 163–168
Numbered list, 112. *See also* Bullets and
    Numbered lists

O

Office 97-2003
  changing file formats, 83–85
  file formats, 39
  template compatibility, 56
Office 2007
  changing file formats, 83–85
  file compatibility, 79–81
Office 2010 applications
  about features of, 5–6
  application consistency, 48–49, 177
  compatibility checker, 39–41
  file extensions, 37
  opening and closing, 7–11
Office.com (website)
  template downloads, 51
  Word tutorials, 86
1/72 of an inch (a point), 98
one-argument functions, 162
online course, 1–2
onscreen views. *See also* Slide Show view
  about changing, 31–32
  application consistency, 5
  zooming in/out, 32–33
opening applications, 7–11
opening documents
  about finding and, 41–45
  Open dialog box, 5
  practice exercise, 46
  recovering lost work, 47–48
orientation. *See* page orientation
Outbox, Outlook Mail, 203–207
Outgoing mail server (SMTP), 189–191
Outlook 2010
  about using, 175–177
  basic lessons learned, 217

data file formats, 37
email programs, 82
error checking, 79
opening and viewing, 178–182
"tech talk", 3, 49–50, 88, 111, 141,
    172–173, 246
try-it-yourself lab, 3, 49, 87–88, 111, 141,
    170–172, 246
Outlook 2010 Account Settings
  changing mail server settings, 185–186
  creating an e-mail account, 183–185
  creating another e-mail account, 187
  troubleshooting e-mail setup, 188–191
Outlook Calendar, opening/viewing,
    180–181
Outlook Contacts
  about using, 219–221
  contacts, adding/editing, 221–224
  contacts, deleting/restoring, 229–231
  contacts, displaying/navigating, 224–228
  contacts, sorting/storage, 228–229
  e-mail, attaching Contacts to, 234–235
  e-mail, sending to contacts, 232–233
  opening and viewing, 181–182
Outlook Express (email program), 82
Outlook Mail. *See also* e-mail programs
  attachments, Contact records, 234–235
  attachments, receiving, 195–197
  attachments, sending, 201–203
  basic lessons learned, 217
  compatibility, web-based providers, 82,
    183, 188
  e-mail, deleting, 213–214
  e-mail, flagging, 214–215
  e-mail, reading, 194–195
  e-mail, replying to/composing, 197–201
  e-mail, sending/receiving, 192–194
  e-mail, using Contacts, 231–234
  Favorites list, 179, 211–213
  managing Folders, 203–207
  Notes and other objects, 246
  opening and viewing, 179–180
  Reading pane, 179–180
  storing messages, 206–207
"tech talk" glossary, 218
try-it-yourself labs, 217–218
using the To-Do List with, 236
Outlook Notes
  basic lessons learned, 245
  defined, 246
  opening and viewing, 177, 182
Outlook Tasks
  about using, 219–221
  basic lessons learned, 245
  completed tasks, 240
  creating a task, 237–238
  deleting tasks, 243–244
  opening and viewing, 182, 235–236
  setting a reminder, 241–243
  "tech talk" glossary, 246
  try-it-yourself lab, 246
  updating a task, 239–241

● *P* ●

Page Layout tab, 58–59
page margins
  defined, 57, 88
  horizontal alignment, 92–94
  vertical alignment, 98–101
  Word documents, 57–59
page orientation
  defined, 88
  Outlook Mail, 180
  Word documents, 59–61
page size, 59–61
paragraph, selecting and editing, 65–66
paragraph alignment buttons, 14
paragraph formatting. *See also* text
    formatting
  about features of, 89–90
  basic lessons learned, 110
  described, 91, 112
  horizontal alignment, 92–94
  indentations, 94–97
  text boxes, 271
  try-it-yourself lab, 111
  vertical spacing, 98–101

Paragraph group, Home tab, Ribbon bar, 14–15
parentheses ( )
  basic arguments, 162–163
  basic lessons learned, 170
  financial functions, 164
  math formulas, 146
patterns, as background fill, 291–292
payments, calculating, 163–168
Pen tools, annotating slides, 359–361
Picture bullets, 104–106
pictures
  as background fill, 291–292
  from file, 24, 310–313, 324
placeholder. *See also* content
    placeholder; text boxes
  adding text, 268–270
  Excel functions, 157
  formatting, 290–300
  function arguments, 157, 172
  moving and resizing, 273–277
  PowerPoint slides, 247, 251, 260
  SmartArt, 315–316
  templates, 62–63
  themes, 283
  video clips, 347, 350
PMT function, 163, 164–166, 170, 172
PNG graphics format, 24
point (1/72 of an inch)
  defined, 112
  font size, 67, 88
  vertical spacing, 98
POP3 (Post Office Protocol 3), 183, 218
Portrait, page orientation, 59–61, 88
ports, incoming/outgoing, 191
PowerPoint 2010. *See also* Slides
  about using, 247–249
  AutoRecover, 47–48
  basic lessons learned, 48–49
  copying compared to duplicating, 265
  creating a presentation, 19–21
  data file formats, 37
  error checking, 79

exporting to Word, 365–369
graphics file formats, 24
Help system, 355
inserting pictures, 24–27
Notes/Notes Page, 34, 250, 254, 279, 362
onscreen Slide Show, 353–355
onscreen views, 31–32, 34–35
opening and closing, 9–10
opening and viewing, 249–250
typing text into presentations, 21–23
The PowerPoint 2010 Bible (Wiley), 355
PowerPoint presentations, creating
  available views, 253–254
  basic lessons learned, 279, 301
  deleting slides, 266–268
  deleting text/objects, 278
  onscreen Slide Show, 355–359
  opening and navigating, 250–253
  presentations, new, 255–257
  presentations, templates, 257–259
  slides, duplicating, 265–266
  slides, from Slides/Outline pane, 261–265
  slides, new, 259–260
  "tech talk" glossary, 280
  text placeholders, 268–270
  textboxes, 270–272
  try-it-yourself lab, 280
  using Pen tools, 359–361
PowerPoint presentations, formatting
  about, 281–283
  AutoFit text, 299–300
  background fill, applying, 291–294
  borders, applying, 294–296
  changing themes, 283–285
  color theme, 285–288
  font theme, 288–291
  Shape Styles, applying, 290–291
  special shape effects, applying, 296–299
PowerPoint presentations, graphics
    and SmartArt. *See also* content
    placeholder
  about using, 303–305
  basic lessons learned, 324
  clip art, inserting, 306–310

pictures from file, inserting, 310–313
"tech talk" glossary, 325
try-it-yourself lab, 324–325
PowerPoint presentations, handouts
available choices, 362
basic lessons learned, 370
exporting to Word, 365–369
printing, 362–365
PowerPoint presentations, special
effects
about using, 327–329
basic lessons learned, 350
manual/automatic slide advance, 334
"tech talk" glossary, 351
try-it-yourself lab, 351
using animations, 335–344
using sound clips, 344–347
using transitions, 329–333
using video clips, 347–349
PPMT function, 171–172
.ppt, file extension, 39
.pptm, file extension, 38
.pptx, file extension, 37–38
practice exercises. *See also* try-it-
yourself labs
applications, open/close, 8–17
AutoRecover, 47–48
bullets and numbered lists, 102–109
documents, creating, 19–21
documents, creating from templates,
54–57
documents, inserting graphics, 24–27
documents, open/save, 39–47
documents, printing, 85–86
documents, themes, 73–76
documents, typing text into, 21–23
error checking, 79–81
Excel, opening and viewing, 116–119
Excel formulas, financial functions,
163–169
Excel formulas, math functions, 156–163
Excel formulas, writing, 145–156
Excel workbooks, 137–139

Excel worksheets, 120–137
File menu, 17–19
keyboard and mouse, 28–31
margins, page size and orientation,
57–61
Outlook 2010, open/view, 178–182
Outlook Contacts, add/manage, 221–231
Outlook Contacts, e-mailing, 231–235
Outlook Mail, attachments, 195–197,
201–203
Outlook Mail, compose/send e-mail,
197–201
Outlook Mail, incoming e-mail, 203–216
Outlook Mail, send/receive e-mail,
192–195
Outlook Mail, setting up an account,
183–191
Outlook Tasks, 236–244
paragraph formatting, 94–101
text editing, 62–66
text formatting, 67–79
transfering data files, 82–85
zooming in/out, 32–33, 119
present value, loan, 168–169
presentation, defined, 20, 50, 249,
280. *See also* PowerPoint
presentations; slide
preset features. *See also* defaults
AutoFill, 129–132
color theme, 281, 285–286
font theme, 281, 288–290
line spacing, 98–101
page margins, 57–58
Shape Styles, 290–291
SmartArt, 320
style sets, 76–78
"tech talk" glossary, 302
text fonts, 91
transition sounds, 332–333
WordArt, 71
Print, Word documents, 85–86
Print Layout view, View tab, 35
printer selection, 85
program, compared to application, 5

.pst, file extension, 37–38
Push, slide transition, 329, 330
PV function, 163, 168–169, 170, 173

• *Q* •

Quick Access Toobar
  about using, 14–15
  Excel 2010, 115–116
Quick Style gallery, 112
QuickTime, video format, 347

• *R* •

range, worksheet
  defined, 121, 141
  Excel functions, inserting, 159–161
  Excel functions, use of, 157
  inserting and deleting, 135–137
  keyboard shortcuts, 122–125
  written name format, 122
RATE function, 164, 170, 173
records. *See* contacts
recovering lost work, 47–48
reflection effects, 296–299
relative referencing, Excel formulas,
  152–155, 173
reminder, Tasks, 246. *See also* Outlook
  Tasks
Ribbon bar
  about using Tabs, 11–17
  application consistency, 5, 119
  Excel 2010, 115–116
  Outlook, 177
  PowerPoint, 259–260
Rich Text Format (.rtf file), 84–85
Right, text alignment, 92–94
ROUNDUP function, 167
rows, worksheet. *See* Excel worksheets
RSS Feeds (Really Simple Syndication),
  203–204

rule, message-handling, 218
ruler, PowerPoint, 277
Rules Wizard, message-handling, 207–211

• *S* •

Sample Templates
  changing content view, 34–35
  stored on your hard drive, 56–57
Save/Save As
  application consistency, 5
  saving for the first time, 38
saving documents
  about data file formats, 37–38
  creating content, 38–39
  file locations, 41–45
  folders, 41–45
  practice exercise, 39–41
  recovering lost work, 47–48
ScreenTips, using, 12
scroll bars
  application consistency, 5
  defined, 50
  Excel, 115–116
  moving around documents, 27–28
  PowerPoint, 250–251
scroll box, defined, 50
sections, PowerPoint, 258
Secure Password Authentication (SPA),
  189–190
selection handle
  basic lessons learned, 279
  described, 275, 280
  moving boxes and frames, 273
  resizing boxes and frames, 275
self-assessment questions, 2
Send to OneNote 2010, 86
Sent Items, Outlook Mail, 203–207
shadow effects, 296–299
shape effects, text box, 296–299, 301
Shape Styles, text box, 290–291, 301, 302
Sheets. *See* Excel worksheets

shortcuts. *See* keyboard shortcuts; macros

shrink/grow, animation, 338–339, 344

skill-building exercises, 2

slide, defined, 249, 280

slide layout, 268, 280

Slide pane, 250–252

slide projector, 355

Slide Show view
  about using, 353–355
  annotating slides, 359–361
  available views, 253–254
  basic lessons learned, 370
  creating handouts, 362–365
  keyboard shortcuts, 355–356
  moving between slides, 355–359
  "tech talk" glossary, 371
  try-it-yourself lab, 370–371

Slide Sort view
  changing content view, 34–35
  rearranging presentations, 253–254

Slides. See also graphics; *PowerPoint entries*
  animations, inserting, 335–344
  AutoFit feature, 299–300
  basic lessons learned, 279, 301
  clip art, inserting, 306–310
  creating new, 259–260
  creating with Slides/Outline pane, 261–265
  deleting, 266–268
  pictures, inserting, 310–313
  SmartArt, inserting, 313–318
  text, typing into placeholders, 268–270
  text, typing into text boxes, 270–272
  text and objects, deleting, 278
  text and objects, moving, 273–275
  text and objects, resizing, 275–277
  try-it-yourself lab, 301–302

Slides, special effects
  about using, 327–329
  basic lessons learned, 350
  manual/automatic slide advance, 334
  "tech talk" glossary, 351
  try-it-yourself lab, 351
  using animations, 335–344
  using sound clips, 344–347
  using transitions, 329–333
  using video clips, 347–349

Slides/Outline pane, PowerPoint
  copying compared to duplicating, 265
  creating new slides, 261–265
  described, 250
  duplicating slides, 265–266
  opening and navigating, 251–252
  section groupings, 258

SmartArt
  about using, 313
  basic lessons learned, 324
  creating, new, 314–318
  creating, text conversion, 313–314
  editing, 318–320
  formatting, 320–323
  try-it-yourself lab, 324–325

SMTP (Outgoing mail server), 189–191

software, program compared to application, 5

sound clips, slide presentation
  about using, 327–329, 344
  inserting, 344–347

Sounds
  animation options, 342–343
  setting a task reminder, 242
  transition preset, 332–333

special effects. *See* SmartArt; WordArt

Spell Check
  about the feature, 51
  using, 79–81

spin, animation, 338–339

Split, slide transition, 329

spreadsheet, 141. *See also cell/cells entries*; *Excel entries*

standard colors, 67–70, 88, 287–288

Start menu
  application consistency, 48
  opening/closing applications, 7–11, 117

starting value, loan, 168–169
status bar
  Excel, 115–116
  Microsoft Office, 11
  Outlook, 177
  PowerPoint, 249, 253
study aids, icons, 4
style/style sets
  applying, 76–79
  defined, 88, 112
  Quick Style gallery, 112
subfolders, 44
subtraction, math function. *See* Excel
  formulas; Excel functions
suite. *See* Microsoft Office suite
SUM function, 157–159, 162, 170, 173
Symbols, as bullets, 103–105
syntax, Excell function
  argument sequence, 157
  financial functions, 164

• T •

Table, defined, 112
Tabs on the Ribbon bar, using, 11–17
tasks, 236, 246. *See also* Outlook Tasks
"tech talk" glossaries
  about using, 3
  clip art images, 325
  Excel formulas and functions, 172–173
  Excel worksheets, 141
  Office applications, 49–50
  Outlook Mail, 218
  paragraph formatting, 111
  PowerPoint, 280
  Slide Show, 371
  transitions and animation, slide, 351
  Word documents, 88
technical details, finding, 2
templates
  defined, 53, 88, 257, 280
  free online downloads, 51, 54–56
  Normal template defaults, 53–54

PowerPoint presentations, 256, 257–259
  stored on your hard drive, 56–57
  text placeholders, 62–63
temporary hidden files, 47–48
text alignment (Left, Right, Center,
  Justify), 92–94
text attributes and effects, formatting,
  70–73
text blocks, selecting and editing, 65–66
text boxes. *See also* placeholder
  about creating, 21–21
  animations, 335–344
  AutoFit feature, 299–300
  auto-size, 276
  background fill, applying, 291–294
  basic lessons learned, 279, 301
  borders, applying, 294–296
  clip art, inserting, 306–310
  formatting, 281–283
  pictures, inserting, 310–313
  Shape Styles, applying, 290–291
  SmartArt, inserting, 313–318
  special shape effects, applying, 296–299
  try-it-yourself lab, 280, 301–302
  typing into fixed placeholders, 268–270
  typing into manually created, 270–272
  Word document templates, 56
text editing
  AutoFit feature, 299–300
  creating and deleting, 64–65
  selecting blocks/paragraphs, 65–66
  template text placeholders, 62–63
Text Effects button, 71
text font. *See* font (typeface)
text formatting. *See also* paragraph
  formatting
  attributes and effects, 70–73
  basic features of, 51
  character formatting, 67
  font, size and color, 67–70
  style sets, 76–79
  working with themes, 73–76
text messages, 234–235

text messaging services, 187
text placeholder. *See* placeholder;
   text boxes
text wrap, 92, 271, 272, 277
textures, as background fill, 291–292
theme colors. *See also* colors
  about working with, 73–76
  basic lessons learned, 301
  defined, 88, 302
  Excel worksheet tabs, 137–139
  Notes and other objects, 246
  PowerPoint presentations, 257, 285–288
  text, 67–70
  try-it-yourself lab, 301
Themes
  defined, 73, 88, 280, 302
  PowerPoint presentation, 256–259,
     283–285
  selecting, 74–76
TIF graphics format, 24
Time, setting a task reminder, 242–243
TODAY function, 161, 170, 173
To-Do List, 236, 246. *See also* Outlook
   Tasks
transitions, slide presentation
  about using, 327–329
  creating/inserting, 330–332
  described, 329–330
  editing, 332–333
  manual/automatic slide advance, 334
  "star" indicator, 252
  "tech talk" glossary, 351
  try-it-yourself lab, 351
troubleshooting tips
  about finding, 2
  e-mail account setup, 188–191
try-it-yourself labs. *See also* practice
   exercises
  about using, 3
  Excel functions, 170–172
  Excel worksheets, 49, 141
  Outlook Mail, 217–218
  Outlook Tasks, 246

paragraph formatting, 111
PowerPoint, 280
Slide Show, 370–371
SmartArt, 324–325
transitions and animation, slide, 351
Word documents, 87–88
typeface. *See* font

U

Undo button, 14–15
USB drives, transferring files, 81
users, Documents folder, 41–42
utilities converter, 86

V

vCard format (.vcf), 234
vertical ruler, 277
vertical spacing (leading), 98–101, 112
video clips, slide presentation
  about using, 327–329, 344
  inserting, 347–349
  try-it-yourself lab, 351
View tab on the Ribbon bar
  application consistency, 119
  changing content view, 35–37
viruses, 195

W

web-based email programs. *See* e-mail
   programs
websites
  conventions used in book, 3
  finding common paper sizes, 60
  Microsoft Office Online, 257–259, 283
  Office 2010 online course, 2
  Office template downloads, 51
  Word tutorials, 86
Windows 7
  keyboard shortcuts, 355
  save/open files, 41–42

Windows 7 eLearning Kit For Dummies (Wiley), 2
Windows Mail, 82
Windows Media, video format, 347
Windows Updates, 214
Windows Vista, save/open files, 41–42
Windows XP, 82
Wipe, slide transition, 329, 330
Word 2010
  AutoRecover, 47–48
  basic lessons learned, 48–49
  data file formats, 37, 83–85
  error checking, 79
  graphics file formats, 24
  onscreen views, 31–37
  saving documents, 39–41
  using the keyboard and mouse, 28–31
  using the scroll bar, 27–28
  utilities, 86
  window resizing, 15–16
  zooming in/out, 32–33
Word documents. *See also* Bullets and Numbered lists; documents; paragraph formatting
  about features of, 51–52
  basic lessons learned, 86–87
  changing file formats, 83–85
  converter utilities, 86
  creating a blank document, 53–54
  creating from a template, 54–57
  creating text, 21–23
  editing text, 62–66
  error checking, 79–81
  formatting text, 67–79

inserting graphics, 24–25
page margins, 57–58
page size and orientation, 59–61
printing, 85–86
saving PowerPoint presentations, 365–369
transferring files by email, 81–83
try-it-yourself lab, 87
Word tutorials, 86
WordArt, 70–73
WordPerfect, 85
workbook/worksheet. *See cell/cells entries; Excel entries*
writeable CD/DVD, transferring files, 81

X

.xls, file extension, 39
.xlsm, file extension, 38
.xlsx, file extension, 37–38
XPS Viewer, 197

Y

Yahoo! Mail (web-based e-mail), 82, 183

Z

Zoom controls
  application consistency, 5
  Excel, 115–116, 119
  Outlook Contacts, 182
  zooming in/out, 32–33

End-User License Agreement

READ THIS. You should carefully read these terms and conditions before opening the software packet(s) included with this book "Book". This is a license agreement "Agreement" between you and John Wiley & Sons, Inc., "WILEY". By opening the accompanying software packet(s), you acknowledge that you have read and accept the following terms and conditions. If you do not agree and do not want to be bound by such terms and conditions, promptly return the Book and the unopened software packet(s) to the place you obtained them for a full refund.

1. **License Grant.** WILEY grants to you (either an individual or entity) a nonexclusive license to use one copy of the enclosed software program(s) (collectively, the "Software") solely for your own personal or business purposes on a single computer (whether a standard computer or a workstation component of a multi-user network). The Software is in use on a computer when it is loaded into temporary memory (RAM) or installed into permanent memory (hard disk, CD-ROM, or other storage device). WILEY reserves all rights not expressly granted herein.

2. **Ownership.** WILEY is the owner of all right, title, and interest, including copyright, in and to the compilation of the Software recorded on the physical packet included with this Book "Software Media". Copyright to the individual programs recorded on the Software Media is owned by the author or other authorized copyright owner of each program. Ownership of the Software and all proprietary rights relating thereto remain with WILEY and its licensers.

3. **Restrictions on Use and Transfer.**

    (a) You may only (i) make one copy of the Software for backup or archival purposes, or (ii) transfer the Software to a single hard disk, provided that you keep the original for backup or archival purposes. You may not (i) rent or lease the Software, (ii) copy or reproduce the Software through a LAN or other network system or through any computer subscriber system or bulletin-board system, or (iii) modify, adapt, or create derivative works based on the Software.

    (b) You may not reverse engineer, decompile, or disassemble the Software. You may transfer the Software and user documentation on a permanent basis, provided that the transferee agrees to accept the terms and conditions of this Agreement and you retain no copies. If the Software is an update or has been updated, any transfer must include the most recent update and all prior versions.

4. **Restrictions on Use of Individual Programs.** You must follow the individual requirements and restrictions detailed for each individual program in the "About the CD" appendix of this Book or on the Software Media. These limitations are also contained in the individual license agreements recorded on the Software Media. These limitations may include a requirement that after using the program for a specified period of time, the user must pay a registration fee or discontinue use. By opening the Software packet(s), you agree to abide by the licenses and restrictions for these individual programs that are detailed in the "About the CD" appendix and/or on the Software Media. None of the material on this Software Media or listed in this Book may ever be redistributed, in original or modified form, for commercial purposes.

5. **Limited Warranty.**

    (a) WILEY warrants that the Software Media is free from defects in materials and workmanship under normal use for a period of sixty (60) days from the date of purchase of this Book. If WILEY receives notification within the warranty period of defects in materials or workmanship, WILEY will replace the defective Software Media.

(b) WILEY AND THE AUTHOR(S) OF THE BOOK DISCLAIM ALL OTHER WARRANTIES, EXPRESS OR IMPLIED, INCLUDING WITHOUT LIMITATION IMPLIED WARRANTIES OF MERCHANTABILITY AND FITNESS FOR A PARTICULAR PURPOSE, WITH RESPECT TO THE SOFTWARE, THE PROGRAMS, THE SOURCE CODE CONTAINED THEREIN, AND/OR THE TECHNIQUES DESCRIBED IN THIS BOOK. WILEY DOES NOT WARRANT THAT THE FUNCTIONS CONTAINED IN THE SOFTWARE WILL MEET YOUR REQUIREMENTS OR THAT THE OPERATION OF THE SOFTWARE WILL BE ERROR FREE.

(c) This limited warranty gives you specific legal rights, and you may have other rights that vary from jurisdiction to jurisdiction.

6. **Remedies.**

   (a) WILEY's entire liability and your exclusive remedy for defects in materials and workmanship shall be limited to replacement of the Software Media, which may be returned to WILEY with a copy of your receipt at the following address: Software Media Fulfillment Department, Attn.: *Office 2010 eLearning Kit For Dummies*, John Wiley & Sons, Inc., 10475 Crosspoint Blvd., Indianapolis, IN 46256, or call 1-800-762-2974. Please allow four to six weeks for delivery. This Limited Warranty is void if failure of the Software Media has resulted from accident, abuse, or misapplication. Any replacement Software Media will be warranted for the remainder of the original warranty period or thirty (30) days, whichever is longer.

   (b) In no event shall WILEY or the author be liable for any damages whatsoever (including without limitation damages for loss of business profits, business interruption, loss of business information, or any other pecuniary loss) arising from the use of or inability to use the Book or the Software, even if WILEY has been advised of the possibility of such damages.

   (c) Because some jurisdictions do not allow the exclusion or limitation of liability for consequential or incidental damages, the above limitation or exclusion may not apply to you.

7. **U.S. Government Restricted Rights.** Use, duplication, or disclosure of the Software for or on behalf of the United States of America, its agencies and/or instrumentalities "U.S. Government" is subject to restrictions as stated in paragraph (c)(1)(ii) of the Rights in Technical Data and Computer Software clause of DFARS 252.227-7013, or subparagraphs (c) (1) and (2) of the Commercial Computer Software - Restricted Rights clause at FAR 52.227-19, and in similar clauses in the NASA FAR supplement, as applicable.

8. **General.** This Agreement constitutes the entire understanding of the parties and revokes and supersedes all prior agreements, oral or written, between them and may not be modified or amended except in a writing signed by both parties hereto that specifically refers to this Agreement. This Agreement shall take precedence over any other documents that may be in conflict herewith. If any one or more provisions contained in this Agreement are held by any court or tribunal to be invalid, illegal, or otherwise unenforceable, each and every other provision shall remain in full force and effect.

About the CD

This README file contains information to help you get started using Dummies eLearning. This course requires no installation.

System Requirements

Dummies eLearning will provide all required functionality on the following Microsoft operating systems:

- ✔ Microsoft Windows 7
- ✔ Windows Vista
- ✔ Windows XP
- ✔ Windows 2000
- ✔ Windows 2003 Server

The following browsers will be supported under Windows:

- ✔ Microsoft Internet Explorer 6.0 or higher
- ✔ Mozilla Firefox 2.x or higher

To run a QS3 CD-ROM, the system should have the following additional hardware/software minimums:

- ✔ Adobe Flash Player 8
- ✔ A Pentium III, 500 MHz processor
- ✔ 256 MB of RAM
- ✔ A CD-ROM or DVD-ROM drive

A negligible amount of disk space must be available for tracking data. Less than 1 MB will typically be used.

For the sake of performance with any multimedia system, it is always good to have a certain percentage of free space available on the drive.

Launch Instructions

Setup Instructions for Windows Machines:

1. **Put CD in CD drive.**

2. **Double-click on the My Computer icon to view the contents of the My Computer window.**

3. **Double-click on the CD-ROM drive icon to view the contents of the Dummies eLearning CD.**

4. **Double-click on the start.bat file to start the Dummies eLearning CBT.**

   Your computer may warn you about active content. Click Yes to continue starting the CD. The CD may create new tabs in your browser. Click the tab to see the content.

The browser offers the option of using the lessons from the CD or from the web site:

✔ To use the web version, click that option and follow the instructions. The web version may require a registration code from the book.

✔ To use the CD, click that option and follow the instructions. Agree to the EULA and install Flash Player, if prompted. Allow disk space usage by clicking the allow button, if prompted.

Operation

After you enter your user name, the eLearning course displays a list of topics. Select any topic from the list by clicking its Launch button. When the topic opens, it plays an introductory animation. To watch more animations on the topic, click the Next button (the arrow pointing right) at the bottom of the screen to play the next animation.

If you want to switch to another lesson or another topic, use the list on the left side of the topic window to open a lesson and select a topic.

Some topics have a hands-on activity section that lets you perform a task on your own. To see the activity from start to finish, click Show Me Full Demo. If you want to try the tasks for yourself, click Guide Me Through to see the animation in sections and repeat it yourself. If you're ready to solo, click Let Me Try to work through all the steps yourself without coaching. (If you need a helping hand to finish, just click Hint at the bottom of the window, then click Show Me Clue in the dialog box.) When you perform the activity, be sure to position the cursor directly over the subject you want to click; your computer may not respond the first time you click. To end the activity, click the X at the bottom of the Milestone box.

Some topics have an active tab for resources on the right side of the window. By default, Windows opens this content in a new window. If you have another compressed file manager installed, such as WinZip, your system may behave differently.

Troubleshooting

What do I do if the page does not load?

It is possible that you have a security setting enabled that is not allowing the needed Flash file to run. Please check to be sure that pop up blockers are off, ActiveX content is enabled, and the correct version of Shockwave and Flash are on the system you are using.

Please contact your system administrator or technical support group for assistance.

What do I do if the Add User window appears when the course loads and there are no names in the Learner Name list, but I have previously created a user account?

Software The course stores your information on the machine on which you create your account, so. first make sure that you are using the eLearning For Dummies course on the same machine on which you created your Learner account. If you are using the course on a network and use a different machine than the one on which you created your account, the software will not be able to access your Learner record.

If you are on the machine on which you created your account, close the course browser window. Depending on the configuration of your machine, sometimes a course will load before accessing the user data.

If this still does not work, contact your network administrator for more assistance.

What do I do if I click on a Launch button but nothing happens?

This may occur on machines that have AOL installed. If you are using the course from a CD-ROM and you are an AOL subscriber, follow the following steps:

1. **Exit the course.**

2. **Log on to AOL.**

3. **Restart the course.**

What do I do if the Shockwave installer on the ROM says that I have a more recent version of the plugin, but the software still says that I need to install version 8.5 or higher?

Download the latest version of the Shockwave plugin directly from Adobe's website:

```
http://www.adobe.com/downloads/
```

If prompted to install Flash Player to view the CD's content, you can download the latest version from the same URL.

ple & Macs

ad For Dummies
8-0-470-58027-1

hone For Dummies,
h Edition
8-0-470-87870-5

acBook For Dummies, 3rd
dition
8-0-470-76918-8

ac OS X Snow Leopard For
ummies
8-0-470-43543-4

usiness

ookkeeping For Dummies
8-0-7645-9848-7

b Interviews
or Dummies,
d Edition
8-0-470-17748-8

esumes For Dummies,
h Edition
8-0-470-08037-5

tarting an
nline Business
or Dummies,
h Edition
8-0-470-60210-2

ock Investing
or Dummies,
d Edition
8-0-470-40114-9

uccessful
me Management
or Dummies
8-0-470-29034-7

Computer Hardware

BlackBerry
For Dummies,
4th Edition
978-0-470-60700-8

Computers For Seniors
For Dummies,
2nd Edition
978-0-470-53483-0

PCs For Dummies, Windows
7 Edition
978-0-470-46542-4

Laptops For Dummies,
4th Edition
978-0-470-57829-2

Cooking & Entertaining

Cooking Basics
For Dummies,
3rd Edition
978-0-7645-7206-7

Wine For Dummies,
4th Edition
978-0-470-04579-4

Diet & Nutrition

Dieting For Dummies,
2nd Edition
978-0-7645-4149-0

Nutrition For Dummies,
4th Edition
978-0-471-79868-2

Weight Training
For Dummies,
3rd Edition
978-0-471-76845-6

Digital Photography

Digital SLR Cameras &
Photography For Dummies,
3rd Edition
978-0-470-46606-3

Photoshop Elements 8
For Dummies
978-0-470-52967-6

Gardening

Gardening Basics
For Dummies
978-0-470-03749-2

Organic Gardening
For Dummies,
2nd Edition
978-0-470-43067-5

Green/Sustainable

Raising Chickens
For Dummies
978-0-470-46544-8

Green Cleaning
For Dummies
978-0-470-39106-8

Health

Diabetes For Dummies,
3rd Edition
978-0-470-27086-8

Food Allergies
For Dummies
978-0-470-09584-3

Living Gluten-Free
For Dummies,
2nd Edition
978-0-470-58589-4

Hobbies/General

Chess For Dummies,
2nd Edition
978-0-7645-8404-6

Drawing
Cartoons & Comics
For Dummies
978-0-470-42683-8

Knitting For Dummies,
2nd Edition
978-0-470-28747-7

Organizing
For Dummies
978-0-7645-5300-4

Su Doku For Dummies
978-0-470-01892-7

Home Improvement

Home Maintenance
For Dummies,
2nd Edition
978-0-470-43063-7

Home Theater
For Dummies,
3rd Edition
978-0-470-41189-6

Living the
Country Lifestyle
All-in-One
For Dummies
978-0-470-43061-3

Solar Power Your Home
For Dummies,
2nd Edition
978-0-470-59678-4

Internet

Blogging For Dummies,
3rd Edition
978-0-470-61996-4

eBay For Dummies,
6th Edition
978-0-470-49741-8

Facebook For Dummies, 3rd
Edition
978-0-470-87804-0

Web Marketing
For Dummies,
2nd Edition
978-0-470-37181-7

WordPress
For Dummies,
3rd Edition
978-0-470-59274-8

Language & Foreign Language

French For Dummies
978-0-7645-5193-2

Italian Phrases
For Dummies
978-0-7645-7203-6

Spanish For Dummies,
2nd Edition
978-0-470-87855-2

Spanish For Dummies,
Audio Set
978-0-470-09585-0

Math & Science

Algebra I For Dummies,
2nd Edition
978-0-470-55964-2

Biology For Dummies,
2nd Edition
978-0-470-59875-7

Calculus For Dummies
978-0-7645-2498-1

Chemistry For Dummies
978-0-7645-5430-8

Microsoft Office

Excel 2010 For Dummies
978-0-470-48953-6

Office 2010 All-in-One
For Dummies
978-0-470-49748-7

Office 2010 For Dummies,
Book + DVD Bundle
978-0-470-62698-6

Word 2010 For Dummies
978-0-470-48772-3

Music

Guitar For Dummies,
2nd Edition
978-0-7645-9904-0

iPod & iTunes
For Dummies,
8th Edition
978-0-470-87871-2

Piano Exercises
For Dummies
978-0-470-38765-8

Parenting & Education

Parenting For Dummies,
2nd Edition
978-0-7645-5418-6

Type 1 Diabetes
For Dummies
978-0-470-17811-9

Pets

Cats For Dummies,
2nd Edition
978-0-7645-5275-5

Dog Training For Dummies,
3rd Edition
978-0-470-60029-0

Puppies For Dummies,
2nd Edition
978-0-470-03717-1

Religion & Inspiration

The Bible For Dummies
978-0-7645-5296-0

Catholicism For Dummies
978-0-7645-5391-2

Women in the Bible
For Dummies
978-0-7645-8475-6

Self-Help & Relationship

Anger Management
For Dummies
978-0-470-03715-7

Overcoming Anxiety
For Dummies,
2nd Edition
978-0-470-57441-6

Sports

Baseball
For Dummies,
3rd Edition
978-0-7645-7537-2

Basketball
For Dummies,
2nd Edition
978-0-7645-5248-9

Golf For Dummies,
3rd Edition
978-0-471-76871-5

Web Development

Web Design
All-in-One
For Dummies
978-0-470-41796-6

Web Sites
Do-It-Yourself
For Dummies,
2nd Edition
978-0-470-56520-9

Windows 7

Windows 7
For Dummies
978-0-470-49743-2

Windows 7
For Dummies,
Book + DVD Bundle
978-0-470-52398-8

Windows 7 All-in-One
For Dummies
978-0-470-48763-1